P9-EAY-096

Foreword

Students with language learning disabilities (LLD) attend every school. Generally speaking, the school environment, and particularly the secondary school environment, is one in which it is difficult for them to thrive. But thrive they can.

To teach LLD students effectively requires a solid understanding of the way in which they think and why they behave as they do. Curriculum needs to enhance their capacity to learn, and it must be planned to allow LLD students the years they require to consolidate essential skills and to mature. Support programs, for either individuals or small groups, should aim to develop skills that are necessary for students to achieve the goals of the mainstream curriculum. All of this requires knowledge; collaboration between parents, teaching staff, speech pathologists and other professionals involved with the students; a well-designed curriculum; and flexible school structures.

How can this be done? In *Working together: linking skills and curriculum for adolescents with a language learning disability*, the authors provide invaluable information to answer this frequently asked question. The reader has the assurance of knowing that the information provided is based on years of experience of working effectively with LLD students over the period of their school lives, and developing approaches to schooling that work.

In Section 1, the authors have distilled the relevant theory of memory, language and the emotional development of adolescents to provide readers with a context in which to place students and their particular learning difficulties. This section also provides considerable detail relating to the importance of developing oral and particularly written language, and its critical role in successful learning: a goal in itself and a tool for more sophisticated learning. One of the strengths of this section and of the book generally is that the difficulties commonly experienced by LLD students, and the problems these cause, are explained in the context of the students' overall learning behaviours. This section is rich with practical advice, giving direction to teachers in ways to approach the curriculum. The great obstacles to progress—anxiety and consequent avoidance—are given significant attention, for these are hurdles which cause students to fall before reaching their potential.

The teaching units in Section 2 serve as models for designing curriculum and explicitly identify strategies that are necessary for teaching LLD students. These units are tried and proven, having been designed for mainstream classes where students have diverse abilities, and include those with LLD who have been able to participate and learn effectively. Activities likely to trigger anxiety are highlighted, as are key strategies for developing language skills and monitoring comprehension and learning. This section provides direction to specialist teachers designing support programs by indicating the additional skills and content to be targeted if the LLD student is to effectively participate in class.

Students with LLD can have productive and successful school lives. It requires understanding of the students' needs, well-planned curriculum and flexible school structures. When education professionals of different disciplines collaborate, drawing on their specific areas of expertise to develop curriculum and strategies, the outcomes are beneficial for all students.

It is a pleasure to commend *Working together: linking skills and curriculum for adolescents with a language learning disability*, and to compliment the authors, Mandy Brent and Chris Millgate-Smith, who show such commitment to educating students.

Florence Gough
Consultant speech pathologist
July 2008

Contents

Authors' acknowledgments

Chris Millgate-Smith would like to acknowledge the following people, who all contributed in some way to the text:

- Florence Gough, not only for her editing skills but for her inspiring work with students in the classroom
- Di Growchowska, who designed the science unit (Chapter 12)
- Rosalie Hiah, for her advice on the maths unit (Chapter 10)
- the history department at Southwood Boys Grammar School, upon whose work the history unit (Chapter 8) is based
- colleagues and students at Tintern Schools, Melbourne.

Not least, she is indebted to her family—Mike, Josh and Isabella Smith—for their unwavering support and encouragement.

Mandy Brent would like to acknowledge the care and support of her husband Russ Houghton and the encouragement of her parents and children.

She would like to thank Jarrad Lum, Jenny Zerafa, the editor Florence Gough, and the speech pathologists at Extra Ed—Liz Fitzpatrick, Karen Lewis, Karen Walter and Rebecca Brown—simply the best.

And then, finally, there was the unexpected arrival of breast cancer, which delayed the completion of this book and brought an insight into writing the chapters on anxiety and memory which was not there before.

At last I am wearing the gold chain earrings
Music is coming back into my life
Silent tears are running down my face
The coral, turquoise and pearl earrings tumble
From my hands
And I fall forward
Over the line
Into the light
Finished.

Source acknowledgments

The authors and publisher wish to thank the following for permission to reproduce copyright material.

Chapter 3

Carnegie Corporation, for material (p. 30), from G Biancarosa & CE Snow 2006, *Reading next—a vision for action and research in middle and high school literacy: a report to Carnegie Corporation of New York*, 2nd edn, Alliance for Excellent Education, Washington DC. Copyright © reprinted with permission from Carnegie Corporation of New York. For a full report, go to: www.carnegie.org/literacy

Chapter 4

John Langrehr, for question checklists (p. 47) from J Langrehr 1993, *Better questions, better thinking*, Longman, Melbourne.

Chapter 5

Pan Macmillan, for the extract (p. 67) by John Marsden from J Marsden 1995, *The third day, the frost*, Pan Macmillan, Sydney. Reprinted by permission of Pan Macmillan Australia Pty Ltd. Copyright © JLM Pty Ltd 1995.

Chapter 6

Florence Gough, for the interview (pp. 78–80) with Dan and his parents.

Chapter 7

Elsevier, for Figure 7.1 (p. 87). This figure was adapted from Figure 1.3 published in AD Baddeley 2006, 'Working memory', in SJ Pickering (ed.), *Working memory and education*, Elsevier, London. Copyright © Elsevier, London (2006).

Chapter 9

ABC, for extract (pp. 131–33) from *Catalyst* program 'Hair regrowth', by Dr Paul Willis. First published by ABC Online, 25 May 2006. Reproduced by permission of the Australian Broadcasting Corporation and ABC Online. © 2006 ABC. All rights reserved.

ACP Magazines, for editorial (p. 126) 'School is a Double Edge Sword', published in *Dolly*, September 2006. Reprinted with permission from acpysyndication.com.

Matthew Brent, for the photograph on p. 134.

Appendices

Rebecca Brown, for Appendix 5 (pp. 233–4), 'Writing PowerPoint presentations: harder than it looks!'

Robin Brown, for Appendix 5 (p. 235), 'Hyperlinking in PowerPoint'.

Every effort has been made to acknowledge and contact copyright owners. However, should any infringement have occurred, ACER tenders its apology and invites copyright owners to contact ACER.

SECTION 1

Skill development for curriculum access

CHAPTER 1

Setting out the basics

Following on from the success of *One in eleven* (Brent, Gough & Robinson 2001), this companion book aims to look further at how to effectively teach students with a language learning disability (LLD) by combining knowledge derived from two important areas: curriculum development, and cognitive and strategy instruction. There is a great deal of information available regarding what is involved in learning. Memory, comprehension and vocabulary are crucial, as are significant behavioural factors including motivation and anxiety. In this book, this knowledge is integrated into a well-planned curriculum that focuses on skills and engages the student. The aim is to mesh both areas of knowledge in the regular classroom in a practical way to improve comprehension and the completion of work.

In this approach, comprehension of the curriculum is central, and the assumption is that teachers and support staff will discuss how they will teach and work together so that individual students achieve a solid understanding. There is a strong focus on improving the language and literacy outcomes for students with a language learning disability. This is based on the opinion, gained from practical experience, that it is possible to significantly improve the literacy of LLD students, which in turn leads them into a more satisfying life with greater work opportunities.

Who are students with a language learning disability?

A proportion of the population of students with normal intelligence find language learning difficult—whether it is understanding and using spoken language, or learning to read, write and spell. The language we are talking about here is not the social language used with friends over a coffee or to discuss the football, but the language needed to learn to organise, analyse and question information and the world around us. Language learning difficulties occur despite the fact that the students are capable in many other areas of learning and life. It is largely a result of the way the brain organises, sequences and stores language, and its sounds, word and sentence meanings. Some students cannot remember and understand instructions as well as others. Some students do not know the meaning of as many words as others and struggle to put their ideas on paper. This group provides a challenge to our traditional methods of teaching, in terms of content and traditional classroom structures. The Introduction and Chapter 1 of *One in eleven* describes these students and their difficulties in more detail.

2

The importance of literacy instruction in the secondary curriculum

While specific language disability is seen as a different disorder to dyslexia (that is, unexpected difficulty learning to read, write and spell given normal IQ), both often coexist in students with LLD (Catts et al. 2005). Decoding and comprehension are both affected in LLD students, because both require competence in all levels of language. Shaywitz (1996) has suggested a two-level model of language that links together various language components. Some language components are seen to be fundamental to other more complex, higher level skills and form the *lower language module*. If there are difficulties at this lower level, then the skills in the *upper language module* may be undermined and so problems will be seen in all levels of language. For some students, the lower language module may function adequately but difficulties may exist within the upper language module. See figure 1.1.

Figure 1.1 Language model

Upper language module
- discourse—connected sentences
- syntax—grammatical structures
- semantics—vocabulary and word knowledge

Lower language module
- phonology—processes the distinctive sounds that make up language. Before words can be stored in memory or retrieved from memory they must be broken down into their phonemic units by the phonological module.

(Adapted from Shaywitz 1996)

It is the lower module that impacts on decoding and word retrieval, and the upper module that impacts on comprehension. Most students with LLD have difficulties in both modules.

In primary school, reading, writing and spelling are initially dependent on good oral language. By the secondary years, the progress toward more mature oral language becomes very dependent on reading and written language. Language and literacy skills are critical and intertwined. Students with language learning disabilities are placed at a double disadvantage if their literacy skills are weak, as they do not have access to the most efficient method of supporting a weak memory—reading and writing. Their oral language skills stall without the support of literacy to extend them. Written language remains limited and the higher level language skills of planning, editing, reorganising information, and developing and sustaining logical argument do not develop well. Those students who cannot read well enough to access the curriculum form a significant number of the students who have behavioural problems and who are regularly absent from school.

How to increase literacy instruction for at-risk students in the secondary setting: a curriculum model

This text focuses on a curriculum model that has a strong strategy instruction framework and that largely embeds literacy instruction in the curriculum. However, it is often the case that this curriculum-based instruction for many LLD students may also need to coexist with 3–4 hours per week of individual or very small group literacy instruction.

This approach also makes the following assumptions about the learning environment.

- There is a team approach involving the classroom teacher and other professionals such as special education staff and speech pathologists. Good interpersonal and team skills are critical, along with excellent organisation.

- The curriculum is written and available at least one term in advance, and is preferably available online.

- A long-term program of instruction should be available to develop the language and literacy skills of LLD students. A six-month intensive program is insufficient for carrying out the recommendations in this text. No matter how good the teaching or the program, it takes years of instruction to develop language and literacy skills in LLD students.

- A range of service delivery options is provided. To cater for individual differences and emotional development in adolescence, suitable instruction may occur in the regular classroom, in small groups and/or individually.

- Direct instruction in decoding, fluency and comprehension is provided in individual and/or small group classes.

- The curriculum is flexible, and offers less rather than more content to allow more time for skill development.

- There is an individual student case-management approach.

- Regular professional development on key areas is available to staff.

- An extremely high level of school-based coordination is needed. To integrate the curriculum and deal with parents and the many professionals involved with LLD students, the teacher must be an excellent coordinator. Good organisational and interpersonal skills, and an appropriate time allocation to do the job are essential conditions.

Separate schools to teach literacy for LLD students

Some intervention models support an intensive language–literacy program where students attend a specialised school until their skill level is sufficient for them to be reintegrated back into their regular school. Criticisms of these separate school options have been well documented and include stigmatisation, social difficulties re-entering regular school and concerns about lack of a challenging curriculum in such settings. Cost is also a consideration, as the majority of these schools are fee-paying. However, some of the newer models for this approach provide a more targeted teaching program which should not be dismissed out of hand, especially if teaching literacy to at-risk LLD students in individual secondary schools or districts is not given a high priority. This type of model is not, however, the focus of this text.

The structure of this book

Section 1: Skill development for curriculum access

By secondary school, weak skill development prevents many students from participating fully in the curriculum. This section covers direct instruction for students in the areas of:

- understanding motivation and anxiety
- memory and thinking
- reading (both decoding words and understanding what they read)
- vocabulary
- writing
- self-awareness and empathy.

Section 2: Skills and strategies embedded in the curriculum

This section incorporates the critical language and literacy skill development needed by students with LLD into six units that cover the major disciplines: English, maths, science and history. The units include a diverse range of texts and provide detailed instructions for the teacher and support staff on how to teach the language of the unit regardless of the discipline. They are all based on age-appropriate curriculum for a mixed-ability class and can be used as a base model for schools to develop their own cross-curriculum units. LLD students are expected to participate in all areas of curriculum.

Each unit carefully sequences the introduction of tasks to maximise comprehension and skill development. Adequate time is allowed for connecting new material to previous learning, and for recall and reflection, and the units are carefully structured to limit excessive content. Teaching points where stress may significantly impact on learning (and especially on comprehension) are highlighted. Feedback to clarify and reduce anxiety is also discussed and examples provided. Within each unit are different teaching strategies and variety to maintain attention.

Section 3: Backing up the curriculum

This section discusses and gives practical ideas about how to monitor the comprehension of students in the classroom. It also discusses school organisation, curriculum and literacy needs, and the importance of adults in maximising the learning of LLD students.

CHAPTER 2

Reducing anxiety and increasing motivation

Students with LLD can suffer from debilitating anxiety. This may be readily recognisable or may display itself in behaviours that are not immediately identified as anxiety-based. Anxious students may present as offhand and uninterested in their schoolwork, or they may avoid their difficulties and attempt to control their anxiety by not starting tasks, not completing them or not handing them in. Students can go to astounding lengths in these types of behaviours, which can lead to extraordinary frustration for teachers.

If anxiety related to a student's LLD has not been recognised and addressed appropriately before the senior secondary years, there can be an explosion of inappropriate and angry behaviour that relates directly to the anxiety, to the students' false ideas about themselves, to the learning strategies they put in place and to their understanding of what a secondary school curriculum demands. It is important to be able to recognise the presence of anxiety (which may or may not be evident initially) as distinct from the LLD, and to understand that the anxiety may be blocking the student's ability to achieve progress with the LLD. Not surprisingly, those students who understand and control their anxiety are able to learn better than those who cannot. This chapter will look at the role of curriculum and classroom planning in managing anxiety.

> In Year 7, Maryanne always said that work was easy and that she knew it all—she didn't need any help. Despite this, her teachers found it impossible to convince her to show them any of the work she had completed. In class, she managed to avoid showing them anything that she was currently working on. At first, teachers felt that she was acutely self-conscious and tended to respect her need for some distance. They noted that she spent most of her time on aspects of tasks that did not involve written language. Where reading and diagrams were needed, she spent time on these, but at the end of the class she packed up quickly and was gone.
>
> When teachers asked to see her work, she usually had some pressing reason why she could not stay to show them, and when they arranged later times to see her, she forgot to come. When she was asked to bring >>

>> work that she said she had completed, it was always left at home, in her locker or handed in to another teacher. Getting to the bottom of all these excuses always revealed that she had not been able to start work that involved any form of written language—her very major weakness. The consequence of a 0 grade was totally ineffective in dealing with her anxiety and improving her learning. This only came about when the avoidance was systematically addressed.

Adolescents with language learning disabilities are often overwhelmed by anxiety because of long-term experiences with failure at school. They often visualise themselves failing before they even begin the task. Their anxiety does not always show in the cultural stereotypes of shaking and trembling, but more often in avoidance and explosive outbursts. For some students, the anxiety can be largely internal but becomes more overt as the demands of the curriculum increase. Students who may appear to cope well in early secondary school years may well show this anxiety at home and at school in the senior secondary years.

How anxiety shows in a student

An anxious student:

- tires easily
- is restless and irritable
- tends to perfectionism, pessimism and overcautious behaviour
- tends to panic or overreact
- has moderate sleeping difficulties
- has difficulty with concentration (e.g. mind going blank)
- has volcanic outbursts, often followed by contrition
- demonstrates denial.

(Adapted from McGrath and Edwards 2000)

In addition, a student suffering anxiety:

- fails to hand in work—although it may have been completed
- struggles to ask questions (a combination of both anxiety and language disorder)
- is often absent from school.

For information on identifying the 'avoiders', the 'exploders' and the 'internally anxious' LLD students, see the lists at the end of this chapter.

Curriculum structures and anxiety

Certain curriculum structures often lead inadvertently to increased anxiety in LLD students.

- *Crowding of the curriculum.* If LLD students are given too much material that is presented too rapidly, without time for a thorough introduction of the topic, they will find it difficult to work through the topic in depth or to link it effectively with previously learned material. This results in an escalating difficulty with comprehension, and fails to provide students with the opportunity to address their failure to understand. It directly prevents the consolidation of skills, increases anxiety, and convinces the student that they cannot do the work.

- *Lack of opportunity for repetition and monitoring.* Without the opportunity for repetition and the capable completion of key skills over several years, LLD students' anxiety about learning will only increase.

LLD and anxiety: getting the skills and believing you have them

B Break down tasks into small, achievable steps.

M Monitor the comprehension and completion of each step.

C Complete.

R Repeat.

R Repeat.

R Repeat.

- *Group work without monitoring of individual comprehension and skill development.* While group work is less likely to trigger anxiety (Jensen & Dabney 2000), this can be a two-edged sword. If a student is inclined to be allocated or tends to take roles in group work which play to their strengths but do not develop critical language skills, the student's skill development may be affected. An individual's comprehension must be checked, and skill development individually monitored, at all times—even when the individuals are part of a group.

Sue was waiting to get written feedback on her essay from her teacher before starting the next written assignment. She was very pleased with the work she had handed in because she thought it was her best work, and wanted to use the teacher's comments to help improve her skills. While waiting, she did not start the next written task and did not meet the deadline to hand it in. She was very angry when she was asked where her second piece of work was, and, when her first written piece was returned, she was even more distressed to find that she had not understood the task and did not get the mark she expected. A lot of anxiety comes from misunderstanding, and from a mismatch between the expectations and beliefs of a student and those of the teacher. Often, teachers are unaware of this.

- *Verbal instruction to the whole class as a group.* Whole-class instruction means that the teacher is not able to adequately judge whether or not students comprehend key material. There need to be opportunities to reinstruct either individually or in small groups (with an upper limit of four students) to build up comprehension skills and to work through anxiety when learning. Clear written instructions also need to be provided to compensate for language and memory difficulties.

> Laura, a Year 10 student, was completing a unit on film review genre within a group. The teacher had a review from the newspaper as a model that included the star rating of the reviewer. Laura was enjoying the activity in her small group and was highly motivated, as she regularly went to the movies with friends. However, in a session to check her comprehension of class material, it emerged that she did not understand the star rating and thought four stars was a bad review as it was 'out of 10'. Testing showed that Laura had a normal IQ, but had weak comprehension and very high anxiety. In her individual sessions it emerged constantly that information was not well understood or connected. While group work lowered her anxiety, it did not always improve her comprehension.

- *The need to make choices from too many alternatives.* Within the curriculum, offering choices is viewed as a positive feature but some caution is needed because offering a wide range of choices is a trigger for anxiety in many people (*Catalyst* 2006). For LLD students, providing choice can be positive, but the choices should be limited, and teachers should check that a student has made an appropriate decision and started work.

- *The presentation of tasks with insufficient scaffolding.* Scaffolding guides students through the sequence of small steps involved in mastering and completing a task. Without adequate scaffolding, students are overwhelmed rather than extended, and do not develop their full cognitive potential or skill set. It is not uncommon to find LLD students who are not expected to complete written tasks even to the paragraph level, or to complete oral language tasks even in front of one person. With scaffolding and appropriate expectations, however, LLD students will progress. Very few LLD students should be exempt from completing core oral and written language tasks, especially if they are given tailored expectations, and can access specialised software and individual instruction as needed.

- *Lack of detailed cross-discipline vocabulary instruction.* LLD students have difficulty with comprehension of multiple word meanings. This becomes most obvious with vocabulary used across different subject areas (for example, 'gorge' in geography and 'gorge' in eating). Unless there is direct instruction to teach word meanings, these students have difficulty understanding and retaining the meanings of abstract words, and struggle with the huge volume of subject-specific vocabulary they are expected to know.

- *Limited opportunity for direct instruction in key areas of difficulty.* Skills such as decoding, fluency and word analysis require instruction for a sustained period of time. Without this, these skills will not develop to the level students require to handle the written material presented by teachers. To be able to decode and comprehend newspaper articles and literature requires continued instruction throughout the secondary years. Stopping this process too soon results in failure to comprehend, anxiety and associated disengagement from the curriculum.

Fred worked for a long time on his decoding skills and they gradually improved to an age-appropriate level. Retesting showed that decoding had significantly improved but that he still needed to improve his comprehension and fluency. He was so excited. It had been a hard road and he often felt discouraged, but his persistence had paid off and now he had a result. The first thing he wanted to do was to tell his father and celebrate with the family. Experience shows that it is only when students are really discouraged and disengaged that they do not want to improve or to please their parents.

Teachers need to be alert to the behaviours that reflect anxiety and consciously monitor them. Such anxiety behaviour indicators (called 'flashpoints' in this book) might be that students do not begin tasks or do not check their comprehension, or that teachers find themselves failing a student for work that is not submitted. If teachers do not follow up students who consistently fail to complete work because of anxiety, then the faulty strategy of avoidance is reinforced and there is no meaningful consequence that confronts the anxiety if the work is not handed in.

Anxiety flashpoints

Common anxiety flashpoints are:

- the beginning of the school year and any change of teacher
- poor comprehension at the beginning of verbal/written introduction to a new topic
- starting tasks (it is important to check that everyone has started the task; if not, check comprehension and increase brainstorming time)
- large assignments which are not chunked into manageable sections
- lack of a timeline included in the project (in this case, students can rapidly fall behind peers, anxiety and negative self-talk increase, and anger or avoidance is displayed)
- fear of public humiliation (when a teacher asks for responses, students become concerned that they might be put on the spot)
- getting work back
- constraints of the syllabus with external examinations
- student expectations are not met
- senior years and exam situations (students may find the anxiety so hard to deal with that they leave an exam in panic).

The impact of an overcrowded curriculum on anxiety

The fear of failure and associated avoidance behaviours of LLD students are compounded by a busy curriculum and the teacher's focus on getting through an ever-expanding amount of work. This limits the time and attention that can be given to LLD students. If both the student and the school fail to identify anxiety as a core behaviour, misunderstanding and mismanagement of the student can occur.

The failure to identify the impact that anxiety has on learning and to understand the longstanding nature of LLD means that many students develop, and continue to hold, faulty beliefs about learning in general, and their learning in particular. For example, a student may think that an English essay can be written without reading the novel, or that, despite what the teacher requires, 'nobody else edits their work'. These can be very hard beliefs to shift, especially in adolescence, but can, in some part, be counteracted when students complete tasks by systematically working through smaller steps. Small steps and work completion are very important in reducing anxiety.

Lack of repetition in an overcrowded curriculum hinders the consolidation of skills and prevents students from overcoming anxiety associated with learning. Even with clear instructions and practice, anxiety about work will arise and LLD students, like many people with anxiety, can 'have the skill but doubt they have it' (Wilson 2007). The best strategy is to structure the curriculum to support LLD students through their learning despite their anxiety.

LLD students have difficulty understanding that a particular set of skills they are learning can apply across different areas, for example, that the essay plan and paragraph skills they are learning in English can be used in history and hospitality. Beliefs, for example, that reading has nothing to do with being a motor mechanic, or that preparing an oral presentation is irrelevant to working as a carpenter limit the learning of skills necessary for adult life, including taking down information over the phone, reading technical manuals and explaining things clearly to customers.

How student anxiety shows in the classroom

An anxious student:

- begins a task and seems to tire very quickly
- cannot settle to a task and stay on track
- goes back and forwards to the lockers, etc.
- complains that their seat is uncomfortable and they need to move or sit on the floor
- does not want to sit near a particular person or the window
- starts the same material over and over again
- focuses on the appearance of work—its presentation, getting out the right pencils, etc.—rather than its content
- tends to look away rather than look at the speaker or listen to the task
- may mask anxiety by smugness, irritability, flippancy and a 'don't care' attitude
- forgets under exam conditions
- forgets even simple instructions.

Curriculum strategies to deal with anxiety

The following strategies can be used to improve learning for all students, as well as those with LLD. The curriculum modules in Section 2 of this text incorporate many of these, while the notes to teachers and support staff in Section 2 aim to highlight the anxiety flashpoints listed above.

- *Preteaching.* Anxiety has a marked impact on comprehension. Preteaching in small groups can assist with both the language learning disability and the anxiety as students have the opportunity to slowly connect new information to existing information before the teacher introduces new ideas to the class. This maximises students' chances of understanding and remembering the material (Brent, Gough & Robinson 2001).

- *Brainstorming, categorisation and organisation of ideas.* Brainstorming to generate ideas, followed by categorising and organising these ideas, forms the basis for the next stage of the work: sequenced presentation of material.

- *Assignments divided into manageable chunks.* This way, students are not overwhelmed and do not feel that the task is beyond them.

- *Tasks that incorporate thinking about and recalling material presented in class.* This 'thinking time' provides the opportunity to monitor recall and comprehension, for example, key words with definitions.

- *Timelines for each stage.* Check that these timelines are met. Immediate follow-up is necessary if a timeline is not adhered to. This can pre-empt avoidance behaviour and the panic that often results as the deadline approaches. Despite good planning by teaching staff, some LLD students regularly experience panic when they fail to adjust their timelines to meet the needs of the task. This can be part of normal adolescent development, but is compounded in some cases by temperament and the inflexibility that can be part of the learning of LLD students.

- *Organisational strategies.* Helpful strategies include noting assignments, along with dates for work to be completed, in the school planner or record book.

- *Reinstruction, either individually or in very small, targeted groups.* Reinstruction and monitoring comprehension is necessary, as whole-class instruction is not sufficient. This keeps the student moving through the curriculum and minimises anxiety.

- *Close interaction between parents, teachers and support staff.* This is advisable so that anxiety related to curriculum tasks can be followed up and addressed immediately to break the avoidance cycle.

- *Comprehension and completion check points.* Monitoring ongoing learning within assignments and class tasks means that issues that arise can be addressed in a timely way. This keeps students feeling involved and coping.

- *Opportunities to monitor planning and prioritising.* Students should not spend inordinate amounts of time on aspects of tasks not warranting it. For example, students may spend a lot of time downloading materials without moving on to the categorising and writing aspects of a task.
- *Completing as much as possible within school time.*
- *Setting core tasks plus extension tasks.*
- *Reassuring students that their perceived weaknesses will not be exposed publicly.* Tasks such as reading aloud may cause students great anxiety.
- *Curriculum modification so that work is within the student's capacity.* As students master steps, gradually reduce modification as far as possible. Modification is about scaffolding and simplifying the language in tasks to make them more accessible and do-able for students. Modification should never reinforce avoidance (Brent, Gough & Robinson 2001).
- *Adequate time for completion of homework.* Homework should never be due the next day, or introduce new concepts.
- *Homework instructions that are written and available online.* Students and family members need to be able to check and hopefully deal with any comprehension difficulties immediately.

Reporting back

Students with LLD need clear assessment criteria and precise feedback to allow success to be identified and built on. However, the problem is that they rarely read the teachers' comments, even those that are well set out on criterion-referenced assessment sheets. A way around this is to develop a system to look in detail at teachers' comments in class. A simple chart, such as the following, can be used to keep records across the curriculum and form the basis for discussion. It is important that a follow-up task is set for the students to practise any areas identified as needing improvement.

What I did well	What I can improve on next time

Dividing comments under these headings helps identify areas of strength and weakness. They can also be used by teachers and support staff to focus their intervention, and to assist LLD students to improve their skills and develop questions to ask the teacher. Receiving and understanding the teacher's feedback is significant for increasing self-motivation and keeping students involved in learning. Conferencing with the teacher is very effective for LLD students.

> Ashley was very surprised to find that the TEEL paragraph structure she had learned about in English could also be used when answering questions about what she had learnt in hospitality when her recipe failed. Her marks, along with her anxiety levels, improved when she used a four-sentence answer, giving an example and describing what she would do next time.

Grading students is never easy, and teacher comments like 'good effort' are often translated by the student to mean 'tried but didn't make it' or 'not a good job'. It may be sufficient to just write 'good'. Examples of helpful comments can be found in Chapter 14.

> *Maximise learner feedback. Because feedback reduces uncertainty ... it increases coping abilities while lowering the pituitary–adrenal stress responses.*
>
> (Jensen 1998, p. 33)
>
> LLD students need:
>
> - clearly written, specific feedback that includes positives
> - individual conferencing about their work with teachers and support staff to lower anxiety
> - practice in giving and receiving appropriate feedback from peers, using a structured format designed by peers and teacher at first
> - mixed-age group work, where students learn to give and receive feedback to those older and younger than themselves
> - an understanding of criteria-referenced assessment and how to use it to develop their own learning and improve their performance
> - records of their personal best to measure their own progress—the impact of these records is enhanced if the teacher identifies specific areas of improvement and helps students develop their next goal.

Management of students with LLD and anxiety

Teamwork

The management of students with LLD and associated anxiety needs a team approach to address appropriate curriculum, learning support, and changing the thinking and beliefs students have about learning. This change occurs partly through good collaborative relationships between members of school staff who have an agreed approach to the learning needs presented by the student. This team may include subject and special education teachers, speech pathologists, counsellors, psychologists and parents. A curriculum-based approach that pays particular attention to language development—vocabulary, grammar, comprehension, and the structure of oral and written work—is best. Such an approach also considers the memory difficulties identified in LLD students, and allows for recall, repetition and chunking of information (examples can be found in Section 2). The result is improvement in language and literacy, the development of skills in the core curriculum, and the management of anxiety. To achieve all this is difficult without a range of staff who have allocated time, and a range of service delivery options: in classrooms, small groups and individualised instruction.

Changing thinking

Building success through chunking, and by working in small steps toward skill development, provides a challenge to the catastrophic thinking typical of LLD students. It helps to present skill acquisition as something that takes time and follows a logical order. An apprenticeship model (where it is clear that students are learners and not expected to know everything) may have advantages for the way LLD students think about learning.

> The working hypothesis for many anxious language learning disabled students is:
>
> *Learning is hard, I may be shamed. I need to be on my guard and flee, attack or avoid if I feel uncertain as it is a threat to my psychological wellbeing.*
>
> (Adapted from McGrath & Edwards 2000, p. 56)

However, even with a clearly written curriculum and good support, LLD students may persist with their beliefs that every new learning experience has the potential to be catastrophic. This black-and-white thinking and overgeneralising of one bad event into a lifetime of failure may need to be addressed in individual counselling sessions with a psychologist. Here, students can work in more detail on success imagery and cognitive distortions, role-play situations such as asking teachers questions about their work, and deal with more personal issues.

Less severe anxiety associated with learning can also be dealt with through programs carried out at school: see Martin (2007), discussed later in this chapter. More severe anxiety needs the specialised input and intervention of psychiatrists, psychologists or counsellors to identify the anxiety type and appropriate treatment paradigms, and to advise school staff.

Classroom organisation

When presenting to a large group, it is difficult for a teacher to check on individual student comprehension. Chapter 14 makes specific recommendations in this area, including using the '10–2 Stop and Summarise' technique of Rowe (1986). Poor comprehension causes confusion for LLD students and also precipitates anger and anxiety.

At the beginning of a task, as often as possible divide students into small groups of no more than four to check comprehension of tasks. Reinstruct as necessary. Provide additional scaffolding or opening sentences to get students started.

Chronic non-starters generally have comprehension difficulties either with the language in the task, or with the purpose and audience, and may need more small-group and individualised instruction.

Individual curriculum-based sessions

Speech pathologists or special educators often carry out curriculum-based sessions with a focus on skill development, particularly in the areas of comprehension, vocabulary and decoding. Many students arrive at these sessions in a state of anxiety. They often feel the work is impossible and that there is nothing that can be done—it is all hopeless, and, even more debilitatingly, *they* are hopeless. They generally blame everyone else, believing that the fates have conspired against them, and that success or failure is out of their hands. Left in this state, they procrastinate, which increases their anxiety and achieves little. Often, they are stuck somewhere among the anxiety flashpoints.

The point of difficulty needs to be quickly identified and the student moved through it. While it is important to acknowledge feelings, the focus of these sessions needs to be on a curriculum-based outcome and the completion of a task. To achieve this, the following strategies may help.

- Acknowledge the student's feelings and reframe them, but do not spend too much time in this area. Grounding students in real tasks can be most effective in reducing anxiety (Stober & Borkovec 2002), so move quickly to small skill steps and concrete curriculum-based activities.

- Use phrases such as, 'It is normal to feel uncomfortable about ...', 'Would you talk to your friend this way?' and 'How would you talk to them?'

- Distinguish quickly between what can be changed and what cannot. Students cannot change the teacher, the senior curriculum or the fact there is a test next week, but they can set up a study guide and complete a series of questions.

- Have the student select the area of the curriculum they need to work on if possible. This assists with learning to prioritise and taking responsibility for their learning. It is important to confront areas of difficulty and not to work on anything that students can do independently themselves.

- Be aware that many LLD students avoid what they feel they cannot do.

- Make sure that all skill areas are developed by using scaffolding and small steps. This reduces perceptions of risk and fear of failure.

- Remain focused on the task. Redirect the student's thinking to the end goal and encourage persistence.

- Deal with anxiety by identifying the step the students cannot do and reinstructing them. This way, they can complete the task, especially if they have individual sessions. If comprehension is the problem, rephrase the questions. If it is writing topic sentences, for example, brainstorm and give lead-in sentences such as,

'In this paragraph I want to say that ...' Follow this with oral language questioning, then modelling and writing.

- Keep a calm, modulated voice, gradually bringing the student back to the task in hand. It is best to quickly and calmly focus on the task rather than on the student's anxiety. Trying to bolster a student by making positive statements about them without showing them exactly what to do does not empower an LLD student and can increase anxiety.

- Rephrase the language of an anxious student from 'It's impossible' into more calming statements: 'I can do this if I add in more steps' or 'I can do the first bit'.

- Stay positive.

- Use Pipher's strategy to have adolescents think of 'time travel'. If it is a bad day, focus them on the past 'and remember happy times or times when problems were far worse', or focus on the future and remind them that they are 'on course towards long-term goals and that certain experiences will not last for ever' (Pipher 1996, p. 258). For some students, the focus may be a future career after school; for others, it is enough to focus on the relief and satisfaction of the completion of a task, the development of a skill, the weekend off or a good night's sleep once they have finished. Celebrate small gains. Persistence is about moving forward—even if it is 'inching' to the finish line.

- Keep LLD students realistic about what learning involves. For example, it takes time to learn to write. Tell them, 'You may need between 2 and 8 practices over 3–4 years to master each writing genre. That's normal'.

- Provide a setting that allows LLD students quiet and uninterrupted thinking time to integrate ideas at a higher level.

- Prevent LLD students from constantly comparing their learning to that of their peers.

- Focus on the task and their personal best to monitor progress.

Direct school-based instruction to increase motivation and decrease anxiety

Research by Martin (2007) found that direct teacher instruction can improve motivation. Martin has developed teacher notes and student workbooks that discuss behaviours such as persistence, anxiety, failure avoidance and self-control. Completion of his program has led to a marked improvement in student motivation. When interviewed for *The Education Age* (Milburn 2006, p. 3), Martin said, 'You need to address their self-belief, their persistence, their anxiety, learning the value of school ... all of these key dimensions are the things that come together to motivate a child'. Students with LLD already need access to this direct instruction as part of their secondary instruction.

Martin sees anxiety as a major impediment to motivation, and defines motivation as 'the energy and drive to try hard, study effectively, improve and work to [the student's] potential' (Martin 2003, p. 5). He says that to motivate students, we need to look at what they think as well as what they do.

Jensen (2005) suggests that, in the school environment, 'very high levels of stress over time are damaging and can impair cognition' (p. 74) and 'for students to be able to think well, they absolutely must be able to manage their emotional states' (p. 121). Awareness of emotions can be developed through interaction in ritual, drama, movement and celebration, as well as writing about feelings, identifying emotions and understanding the 'direct links between how they feel and how they think' (p. 121).

Summary

Anxiety in LLD students contributes significantly to learning difficulties. Detailed curriculum planning, developing students' understanding of themselves as learners, and direct instruction in motivation all play a part in improving learning outcomes for LLD students.

Connections to Section 2 and 3

- Chapter 9: Steps 1, 11
- Chapter 8: Steps 1, 6
- Chapter 14

The avoiders

Look for students who:

- are pleasant until confronted, when they may become very angry or explosive
- are good at distracting
- often do things that please teachers and distract from completing the work, such as present beautiful work and headings, rule straight lines, be helpful and cooperative
- lie to protect themselves—the lying gets people off their back
- make claims such as 'I've done it', 'I've handed it in', 'It's at home' and 'I did it but I've lost it'.

What to do:

- Check the curriculum, locate areas of learning difficulty (either individually or in a small group) and ensure the student completes the task.
- Involve subject teachers and parents.
- Handle issues privately to avoid embarrassment.
- Follow up the student's progress using diligence and kindly persistence.

The exploders

Look for students who:

- immediately refuse to complete a task
- exhibit behaviour that is irrational and verbally abusive
- show aggressive body language.

What to do:

- Remove them from the situation until they calm down.
- Check the curriculum, locate areas of learning difficulty (either individually or in a small group) and ensure the student completes the task.
- Check for any precipitating event, such as a misunderstanding with teacher, humiliation, etc.
- Involve subject teachers and parents.
- Handle issues privately to avoid embarrassment.
- Follow up the student's progress using diligence and kindly persistence.

The internally anxious

Look for students who:

- are cooperative and want to do the right thing
- 'fall apart' under pressure
- display out-of-character behaviour
- become angry and frustrated if they feel work is too difficult
- focus anger on the teacher
- show a big difference between behaviour at home and at school
- often mask the extent of anxiety at school
- are more emotionally volatile at home and 'dump' on parents, particularly their mothers
- struggle to maintain self-esteem.

What to do:

- A few positives can quickly lower anxiety.
- Clear feedback and assistance for students to take the next step forward are critical.
- Role play alternative ways of dealing with situations that precipitate anxiety.

CHAPTER 3

Enhancing decoding and reading fluency

While most LLD students have difficulty in all key reading skills, some LLD students may have difficulty with comprehension only. The key reading areas are:

- *Decoding.* This is the knowledge of the relationship between sounds and symbols and the ability to decipher words.

- *Fluency.* Fluency is measured by accuracy, rate (usually measured in words per minute, or WPM), and expression.

- *Vocabulary development and reading comprehension.* See Chapter 4 for more detailed discussion.

Decoding, fluency and comprehension problems are directly related to the language disorder

LLD students' difficulties with reading are directly related to their language disorder (see Chapter 1). In the brain, language can be conceptualised as a hierarchy of modules. At the lower level of the hierarchy is the *phonological* (or *sound sequencing*) module 'which is dedicated to processing the distinctive sound elements of language' (Shaywitz 2003, p. 41). It is weakness in this area that results in the decoding difficulties we see in LLD students. As a result of these problems with processing and analysing sound, LLD students store words inaccurately in the brain and so have trouble when they come to say, read or write them accurately. Resulting word retrieval problems can be seen not only with literacy tasks but in general conversation as well. The explosion of new subject-specific vocabulary at secondary level places particular pressure on the weak phonological system.

From the phonological module, we move up the language hierarchy in the brain to the *upper language module*, which includes semantics, syntax and discourse. Semantics gives meaning to spoken and written language, syntax involves putting words together to make sentences (vocabulary and grammar) and discourse involves using these language skills appropriately in extended spoken and written language. Students with problems in areas of the upper language module experience difficulties understanding and using vocabulary and grammar, and in constructing sentences in oral and written language.

Finally, the executive processing aspect of brain functioning tests, checks, plans and evaluates performance. While executive processing is not part of the language hierarchy itself, it is an intrinsic part of the effective functioning and coordination of language. In adolescence, executive processes are still developing but most LLD students will have more difficulty in organising, planning and monitoring their learning than do their peers.

Most LLD students have difficulties in all parts of the language system. A subgroup of students is able to decode well but has limited understanding of what they are reading. LLD students' decoding, fluency and comprehension skills are particularly vulnerable to fatigue and pressure.

Continuing to teach decoding and fluency at secondary school

It is important to continue to teach decoding and reading fluency at secondary school for several reasons.

- Many LLD students have not received long-term systematic instruction. They can continue to make significant improvements with appropriate intervention.

- Those who have received good long-term instruction will still need support. This is needed if students are to successfully make the jump to more complex material and decode unfamiliar words found in a range of texts and newspaper articles at the secondary level.

- LLD students need to decode accurately. Often LLD students are not decoding all the sounds in a word and have gaps in their understanding of how sound/ symbol relationships work. This is especially so for multisyllabic words, but sequencing difficulties are also evident in single-syllable words where students may insert sounds. For example, they may read 'carp' as 'crap', 'tandem' as 'tamden', 'certainly' as 'certrainly', 'exclaimed' as 'explained'. While these are only minor decoding errors, they have a significant impact on comprehension. Words with vowels represented by more than one letter (such as 'awkward' and 'recruitment'), and vowel spellings that have multiple sound choices ('thought' and 'sweater') also cause problems, as does syllable division between vowels in words like 'di-al' and 'de-ni-al'. Until other alternatives become available, students can hear the pronunciation of words (albeit in an American accent) by going to the Merriam-Webster Online Dictionary (2008) at <www.m-w.com>.

- LLD students often substitute words when reading text. However, because of their underlying difficulties with grammar, the word substitutions are not necessarily grammatically similar to the text and this adds to their comprehension difficulties. For example, a student may read 'flooding' (a verb) instead of 'floodlight' (a noun) and 'patient' instead of 'impatiently'.

Good decoding and fluency are essential for comprehension of text, which is the important end goal of reading. Being able to read the written language that is all around them at secondary school is a critical step for LLD students in coping with the curriculum and using the Internet. It is also extremely significant in post-school success and in obtaining employment. Reading and writing are the quickest, most socially acceptable and most useful methods of supporting the weaker auditory short-term memory and associated working memory difficulties which so often impact on the learning of LLD students.

Giving LLD students the time they need (often years) to master decoding and fluency

Instruction in decoding and fluency is most effective, and generally well tolerated, if the instruction relates directly to the curriculum or to learning goals LLD students have set themselves. It is also important to take into account individual differences in temperament and rate of learning when deciding on the type of program or whether there should be individual or small-group sessions. This instruction may need to continue well into young adulthood, depending on how far students want to proceed in their education and the level of reading their courses entail. No program, no matter how good, will work if the LLD adolescent is unmotivated or hostile. Nor will it be effective if the student is still developing the skills of insight, and the ability to hold a goal in mind and take a path to the goal that may be different from the path of their peers.

It is possible to teach most LLD students to decode to a basic level (for example, decoding simple news items in the newspaper or on the Internet) if they receive systematic instruction from an early age. Unfortunately, if they arrive at secondary school without good basic decoding skills in place, it is much more difficult to do—but it is still possible.

Callie had a very severe phonological disorder combined with coordination and visuospatial difficulties. She was fortunate to receive explicit instruction throughout her primary school years and by secondary school could read most texts. Her spelling, however, remained very poor, and she was not an independent user of the keyboard or spellchecker as it was impossible for her to get her spelling attempts close enough for the computer to recognise.

In secondary school, it was decided to try once more, and complete an intensive program focusing on the syllable level for spelling, with the goal of improving accuracy of the first two syllables so the correct word could be selected by the spellchecker. After several months, having improved enough, she was prepared to try an intensive typing program again with the support of an aide, after having had no success in Years 5 and 6. This time she was successful and achieved her goal of being able to use the keyboard to type her essays. While her spontaneous spelling of many words remains inaccurate (for example, 'perswaid' for 'persuade'), Callie can independently make most changes herself.

Using computer programs to maintain motivation and support the development of decoding and fluency

LLD students with very weak decoding and fluency can be well supported by the use of voice-activated and screen-reading software. As well as keeping motivation high and enabling students to complete work to a higher standard, these programs often increase LLD students' decoding, fluency and comprehension because they provide greater exposure to text. Sometimes, after a period of time using voice-activated software, there are improvements in reading and spelling—especially if, concurrently, students are receiving decoding instruction.

When these improvements occur, it is worth teaching keyboarding skills through carefully structured programs to further increase students' literacy skills and independence. Keyboard instruction for students who have improved their spelling accuracy to at least the first two syllables of a word leads to further improvement with reading and spelling, as the correct word usually comes up as one of the options on the spellchecker and students become increasingly more accurate in selecting the correct word. Even at Year 9 (which can seem late), some students are ready for additional work on spelling and keyboard skills, despite having been unsuccessful in the past. It is very important to work with older students who, without intensive support, are prone to develop depression and disengage from the curriculum.

> Language assessment using the TOAL-3 (Test of Adolescent and Adult Language) found Tom had a severe receptive and expressive language disorder, with his best score in the sub-test *listening grammar*. He had made very little progress in literacy despite additional assistance for his literacy difficulties at primary school. He felt he would never read. By secondary school he had become very depressed and withdrawn, and teachers found it hard to assess him as he clearly understood a lot but was not able to produce much independently. He was trained to use a computer program with voice-recognition software, and reinstructed in sound–symbol correspondence and simple spelling. After nine months of intervention, his spelling scores improved by 14 months. He moved from reading material at a 6.5–7.5-year age level to confident reading at an 8.5–9.5-year level, and became increasingly fluent with material at the 10–11-year level.

Assessment strategies for developing curriculum materials and intervention programs

Whole-school standardised assessment

A general assessment of decoding, spelling and reading comprehension should be done prior to beginning secondary school so that those students at risk can be identified. Teachers then know the reading level of their students and can recommend appropriate reading materials (including web sites) and adapt some handouts to an appropriate reading level. It is helpful to have reading assessments that tease out the different components of reading—decoding, fluency and comprehension—and to have spelling tests which provide normed comparisons.

Such tests enable teachers and support staff to look at underlying phonological awareness and weaknesses in sound–symbol correspondence, especially in the areas of vowels, blends, syllable count and the phonograms more common in multisyllabic words. Intervention can thus be appropriately targeted. The traditional group test in which a student has to silently read a paragraph and then answer questions is one form of assessment, but it does not provide all the information needed for subsequent instruction.

Additional assessment and interview

Prior to beginning an appropriate intervention, students who have been identified as having difficulty decoding should receive additional testing in decoding and fluency, either individually or in a small group. As these students will have a scatter of skills, it is important to use non-words for decoding assessment. Examples of non-words are 'ug', 'sug', 'skug', 'skult' and 'skeen'. The use of non-words checks if students are actually decoding using sound and symbol, or if they have learned words as a whole or in context. If the latter is the case, when they come to words they do not know, they will not have effective word attack skills.

Some LLD students can read simple texts but have minimal decoding skills. This becomes very obvious at the secondary level when they encounter unfamiliar words of two or more syllables. Analysis of their spelling errors to compare with their decoding errors helps focus the intervention. For example, a student who spells words of three or more syllables as two-syllable words often does not read these words accurately (e.g. 'incredulous'). Students who do not use multisyllabic words in their writing often cannot decode them, especially when prefixes and suffixes are added (e.g. 'discontinuous' or 'disposition').

Information about phonological awareness, rapid automatic naming and working memory completes the picture and indicates the likely impact of these on the pace of learning. A rapid automatic naming test (where students are required to name familiar visual stimuli as quickly as they can) is part of many commonly used tests of language. It is included in the CELF-4 (a popular and comprehensive language assessment tool used by speech pathologists) because it has been found to be a predictor of language, learning and reading disorders, and provides both a speed and error count. Students with significant working memory problems will progress a lot more slowly than peers without these difficulties.

> Will was not coping with the curriculum in Year 9 and was becoming a distraction in class. It was noticed that he could not decode many of the handouts. His comprehension of class work was also poor. Surprisingly, his initial assessment showed that his decoding on this test seemed to be adequate. When the assessment used non-words, however, the extent of his decoding problems became very evident. He had learned to rely on his visual memory to read words. His spelling level was significantly below that of his peers and he had severe discrimination difficulties with vowels and blends.

Setting a base fluency measurement

Additional assessment should include setting a base fluency measurement using norms (Hasbrouck & Tindal 2005). By secondary school, 150 WPM is an average reading fluency rate. Students reading at a lower rate are likely to find reading to be a slow and tedious task, and there will be an impact on comprehension even after taking into account different rates associated with text complexity. When text decoding and fluency rate are adequate, students and teachers are freed up to concentrate on comprehension.

Using a range of texts to check decoding and fluency

While formal assessment gives a good idea of an LLD student's decoding and comprehension skills, the test materials are often well below the level of decoding and comprehension required to read a range of texts, such as newspaper articles, web sites, and classic novels like *Wind in the willows* and *Lord of the flies*. Stand-alone paragraphs used in tests do not stretch a LLD student's comprehension and analytical ability to connect to prior information, or to understand the broader social issues that form part of many class discussions and opinion pieces, and more sophisticated language.

In texts that place greater demands on comprehension, any decoding errors will further confuse an already difficult task. Even those students who perform within the average range for their grade level (but at the lower end) on some tests of decoding will struggle with the level and quantity of reading expected of them at school. They need the opportunity for additional instruction on decoding and fluency especially at the multisyllabic level, keeping in mind that the purpose of this instruction is to make decoding accurate so that students can concentrate on comprehension.

Using a sequence of steps to check sound and decoding skills

Ideally, by the time LLD adolescents arrive at secondary school they should have received systematic and long-term instruction in decoding at primary school. However, many do not receive this instruction, or only receive it for a short period of time, and so do not consolidate their skills—especially in the very important areas of blends and multiple vowel spellings. Most phonological awareness tests have materials and norms which are well below secondary school level but which can be used for a quick overview of skills and weaknesses. Paul (2006) has a set of complex phonological production tasks more suited to the secondary level. Often it is not necessary to take secondary school students back to phonological awareness training, as the same results can be achieved by a detailed phonics program that systematically addresses decoding.

Table 3.1 Sequence for checking sound and decoding skills

Sound and decoding skills	Comments
Single-letter vowels In particular, note any confusion between a/u and e/i.	Look for discrimination of a/u and e/i .This needs to be done first with auditory training (not worksheets that students work on alone). Check reading and spelling of these sounds using non-words, e.g. 'ug' and 'ag'.
Consonants In particular, check those consonants that have more than one sound—'c', 'g', 's'—and more unfamiliar consonants, such as 'qu' and 'y'.	Even students who have all these sounds correct may need reinstruction when they move to blends and multisyllabic words. Difficulty with generalisation (taking an earlier learnt skill and applying it to new situations) is often part of a language disorder.
Blends Some LLD students appear to read blends in real words but have difficulty with single, short vowels with blends in nonsense words, indicating this decoding skill is not consistently established for reading and spelling. Spelling may show vowels not always stable and blends omitted.	This is a very significant area of instruction and for many students the sound boundaries between consonants are not clearly discriminated, e.g. a 'sl' blend sounds like a distortion of 's'. The student then omits the blend or a part of it. A considerable amount of work in discrimination, reading and spelling needs to be done with blends in both initial and final position, first using single-letter vowels, for example, 'slip' and 'lamp'. For very weak students it is also important to include words with the blend in both positions, e.g. 'stand'. Instruction in this area can take 12–18 months for very weak students.
Long and short vowels e.g. from 'cap' to 'cape'	At this point, many students struggle to maintain stable vowel sounds, and the introduction of blends further complicates this, e.g. grape.
Multiple phonograms e.g. 'ee', 'au', 'aw', 'ar', 'oa', 'ur' 'ow', 'ou', 'oo', 'ew', 'ui', 'ey', 'igh'	Many LLD students do not receive direct instruction in this area. They may do many worksheets following the visual pattern, but without significant sound work matching the letters to the sounds, they are unable to use the patterns effectively in reading and spelling.
Suffixes and syllables This is a significant area of difficulty. It requires direct instruction, especially once blends are well established.	Blends and vowels need to be stable in the sequence outlined above before real success in this area is possible. Often LLD students show a complete collapse in sequencing sounds in spelling and word attack in reading.

> *Why didn't they just tell me?*
>
> (Words from a student with a severe decoding difficulty, in a session with a speech pathologist as he learnt the decoding system of English. Why indeed?)

Table 3.1, on page 27, provides a sequence and some comments on areas of difficulty encountered by LLD students. Sound work needs to be incorporated into each level—pen and paper worksheets without auditory training do not teach phonological awareness. Phonological awareness training needs listening, and the human voice or very natural-sounding computer voice as its primary means of instruction. It is also important at each level to check for recognition (reading) and recall (spelling). Recall in spontaneous spelling gives a window into the student's sound system and areas that require further instruction. The most common areas for further instruction are outlined below.

Decoding training should be accompanied by fluency training and a spelling program which complements the decoding skills being taught. Good spelling programs include more detailed teaching of phonology, but students who have significant difficulties in these areas will need additional specialist input from support staff. It is worth reiterating the importance of monitoring progress in decoding and fluency while at the same time checking comprehension, which is equally critical and affected by slow decoding and the language disorder (see Chapter 4).

Building on good basic decoding skills

LLD students who arrive at secondary school with decoding skills relatively intact may still struggle with decoding the texts presented to them across various subjects. In particular, newspaper articles, novels (especially classics), subject-specific texts, handouts and web sites all present decoding challenges. Systematic instruction is needed to lift their decoding to the secondary level, especially for more complex, unfamiliar words. Fluency training for more demanding texts is also well worth the effort. A good practical measure of adequate independent decoding skills at the secondary level is the ability to decode opinion pieces from tabloid newspapers. Comprehending them is an additional area that requires explicit instruction by classroom teachers (see Chapter 4 and Section 2).

For LLD students, decoding is strengthened by systematic teaching of the structure of written language (see Chapter 5), which empowers them to write longer pieces of work. Longer written pieces, especially if handwritten or not spellchecked by the computer, give a window through spelling into any remaining phonological limitations or patterns that need to be taught or revised.

Sometimes decoding is not taught at secondary school because it is considered that students will find it boring. However, boredom and negative behaviour are generally not a problem if the specific decoding patterns and fluency to be targeted are taken from key passages that students need to read in class and then use for oral discussion or as part of written work.

Initially, LLD students with decoding problems may be unaware of the extent of their comprehension difficulties. If they improve their ability to decode classroom materials, then the significant language comprehension problems become more apparent. In this case, behaviour problems to cover confusion and anxiety are likely to emerge as the complexity of the curriculum increases.

Improving very weak decoding skills

Alarm bells should ring when LLD adolescents start secondary school with inadequate decoding, comprehension and written language. These students will not be independent students in the secondary setting, and are most at risk of serious behaviour problems, ranging from depression to acting out. Some of the angriest students in the secondary setting have unacknowledged language-based literacy problems, and often, unfortunately, have not received the long-term interventions and modifications they need. *One in eleven* (Brent, Gough & Robinson 2001) offers suggestions for modifying the curriculum to assist these students.

In tandem with teaching specific decoding instruction, it is important to increase LLD students' comprehension with a curriculum designed to allow engagement and participation. This will increase LLD students' independence and self-esteem, and provide a sense of hope and belonging. Extensive modification of the curriculum (see *One in eleven*), voice-activated software for writing (such as Dragon NaturallySpeaking, <http://www.nuance.com/naturallyspeaking>), and individual attention and training to expand their oral language and allow them to convert it into written form on the computer need to be quickly put in place (see Chapter 5).

Teachers and support staff need to be acutely aware of the impact of anxiety and shame, especially on those students who are prone to explosive outbursts (see Chapter 2). Purpose and personal relevance are also critical in the curriculum work for these students. With appropriate supports in place, teachers should expect completion of important core work and use the student progress record (see Chapter 14) for giving and receiving feedback in a structured manner. This takes some of the personalisation away from discussions about students' work. Computers also enable students to look at their work more critically and separate out feelings of inadequacy. Changes can be made easily on the computer.

It is a major effort for schools and staff to put the technology, curriculum and support staff in place for individual students. Once these are in place, it is possible to look at literacy programs that are available for secondary students to improve decoding, fluency and comprehension. There are many programs that provide the basic decoding principles and it is a matter of selecting the program that best matches the student and the context. No program will work well if the student is not motivated and, despite economies of scale, many angry and embarrassed adolescents do not adapt well, at least initially, to group instruction, even in small groups. In the experience of this writer, there are sometimes gender differences:

while some girls find a group supportive, many adolescents (both boys and girls, but particularly boys) do not want to attend a group until a certain level of competency is established.

Programs do not claim, nor are they able, to quickly enable LLD students with severe decoding difficulties to read all the class texts, web sites and handouts they receive at the secondary level. However, decoding will continue to improve if students are motivated and the work complements what they need in class, and especially if combined with written language work (see Chapter 5).

Selecting commercial reading programs

- Reading materials that match scripted programs are not often of high interest to LLD students at the secondary level but are very useful for establishing fluency. Significant time is then needed to find and prepare suitable curriculum-based materials.

- Students with diagnosed psychiatric problems often react badly to scripted programs, possibly because their borderline capacity to cope means they need more emotional engagement from adults working with them. A structured yet unscripted program is often better for these students.

- The '15 elements of effective adolescent literacy programs' (Biancarosa & Snow 2006) provides guidelines for evaluating literacy programs, thereby helping in the selection of the most appropriate program for an individual or small group.

Key elements in programs designed to improve adolescent literacy achievement in middle and high schools

Instructional improvements

1 *Direct, explicit comprehension instruction*
2 *Effective instructional principles embedded in content*
3 *Motivation and self-directed learning*
4 *Text-based collaborative learning*
5 *Strategic tutoring*
6 *Diverse texts*
7 *Intensive writing*
8 *A technology component*
9 *Ongoing formative assessment of students*

Infrastructure improvements

10 *Extended time for literacy*
11 *Professional development*
12 *Ongoing summative assessment of students and programs*
13 *Teacher teams*
14 *Leadership*
15 *A comprehensive and coordinated literacy program*

(Biancarosa & Snow 2006, pp. 4–5)

Expanding decoding skills and fluency

Continuing to teach decoding at the secondary level is important for LLD students, as even those who have successfully completed well-regarded primary reading programs do not make the necessary decoding jump into secondary literacy. Their slower decoding impacts significantly on fluency and subsequently on comprehension, which is already a significant area of weakness for LLD students. Decoding rules taught earlier do not always generalise into multisyllabic or unfamiliar words. This base work can be made more interesting by using computer games before transferring the information to curriculum-based materials. Computer games enable students to complete many listening and sound sequencing tasks at a rapid rate while maintaining interest.

To generalise decoding skills from simple to more difficult words, students require explicit instruction. The following are beneficial for LLD students to learn, and most will be covered in good literacy programs. Skills are best developed using both reading and spelling tasks.

- In primary school, most students are taught the role of 'e' to change vowels from short to long sounds. They know it as 'magic e', 'bossy e' or 'jobs of e' when they see it in a word like 'take' but fail to generalise it to words like 'gene', 'fuse' or 'immigrate'.

- LLD students can be taught that 'c' and 'g' have two sounds, and will say 's' and 'j' respectively if followed by 'e', 'i' or 'y' as in 'nice' or 'page', but do not see the same application in words like 'cemetery', 'vice', or 'plagiarise'. Without explanation and the generalisation of earlier learnt skills, they freeze at words like 'pharmacology' and 'advocacy', seeing them as too big and unknown.

- Blends in initial and final positions need to be carefully taught. Blends containing 'l', 'r' and 's' can be problematic.

- S-blends, for example 'st', and final sound sequences with 'ts', present difficulties for many LLD students. These sounds are made in a similar position in the mouth and students struggle with sequencing them correctly.

- The five 'er' sounds ('er', 'ir', 'ur', 'ear', 'wor') also do not generalise easily into multisyllabic words. Despite earlier decoding skill with words like 'bird', they do not apply this sound knowledge to words like 'skirmish'.

- Closed syllables with short vowels like 'inject' and 'abstract' do not cause many difficulties but words with 'y' as a vowel in closed syllables such as 'analytic' cause more difficulty.

- Open syllables, where the syllable break is after the vowel (as in 'o-pen') and where the vowel says its long sound, require direct instruction if words like 'im-pro-vise' are to be decoded.

- Syllable division between vowels needs direct instruction, as does the teaching of prefixes, roots and open syllables. Difficulties can be encountered with words like 'ambiguity', 'diabolic' and 'biological'.

- Revision is needed for the single consonant versus the doubling of consonants, such as 'hopped' and 'hoped'.
- Confusion occurs when 'ch' says 'k'. Words like 'school' are automatic but a word like 'chaos' can be very confusing.
- Multiple phonograms or two-letter vowel combinations like 'ou'/'ow', 'aw' and 'ea' remain problematic in words like 'pronounce'.
- Direct instruction in syllable division helps with decoding and memory, as chunking small numbers of letters together is easier for LLD students.
- Teach the expansion and contractions of words like 'you are' to 'you're'.
- Teach the patterns in prefixes and suffixes, and highlight any of these patterns that cause decoding difficulty in texts. Suffixes are particularly important for connecting sound knowledge to grammatical knowledge.

Improving fluency

To ensure generalisation (taking earlier learnt skills in simple decoding and using them with new words and in more demanding texts), LLD students need to use their decoding knowledge on a variety of texts. For very weak students who are completing systematic phonics programs, text needs to match the patterns they are learning. For those students who have mastered basic phonics knowledge and are trying to move their sound and pattern recognition to more demanding text, using classroom materials, set texts and novels is best. Errors can then be discussed in context, and scaffolding of more demanding text can be provided to support students as they make the jump to more difficult decoding.

In text analysis, students have to find evidence to support the development of a character. Students can write their notes in a chart similar to this example—from *Lord of the flies*—where pages and key quotes are identified, so the same passages can be used for decoding and fluency training. This enhances the students' comprehension, as well as their recall of key quotes to be used when writing an essay.

Page	Actions: what Ralph does	Dialogue: what Ralph says and how he says it	Reactions of other characters to Ralph	What this reveals/implies about Ralph

Fluency training ideas for adolescents

While we need more research information regarding the best way to improve fluency, most researchers agree that significant practice is required and that teacher assistance and feedback is critical. Shaywitz (2003) uses repeated reading of the same passage with feedback on errors until an acceptable rate of fluency is obtained.

The end goal of this is to free students to concentrate on the important goal of reading comprehension. Research summarised by Stahl (2004) suggests that repetition of the same material is not as significant as practice, practice, practice on any and every text. Either method will give improvement for most LLD students. They make significant gains especially when measured as personal bests, but they do not necessarily catch up to their peers in fluency rate.

Listening to tapes of class texts is more effective if students know that after listening to the tape they will have to read a particular section aloud to a peer or adult. For text that requires a significant increase in decoding skills, it is helpful to analyse words, especially highlighting any patterns to aid recall when reading the text independently.

Spelling and the 'schwa'

LLD students' difficulties in generalising sound–symbol correspondence in multisyllabic words when reading also impacts their spelling. Weak phonological processing can also play a part. Even when consonant sounds are well known, vowels may still cause problems. Spontaneous speech, which is fast, often collapses the vowel, so a word like 'yesterday' sounds like 'yestuday'. This reduced, short 'uh' sound representing many vowels in spontaneous speech is known as the 'schwa' and causes LLD students enormous confusion, not to mention frustration. 'That's not how they say it!' students often cry when confronted with the difference between oral production and written spellings. Discussion of the schwa in spontaneous speech can be beneficial and relieve some of the students' frustration. While students may not always spell longer words accurately, especially if their phonological difficulties are more severe, a greater understanding of the schwa gives them an explanation for their errors and the confidence to at least try more difficult words with closer approximations, enabling them to use the spellchecker independently.

Accurate spelling requires a good match of the visual appearance of the word, knowledge of spelling conventions, and the ability to say the word accurately for spelling. Unfortunately for many LLD students, this taps into their underlying phonological (sound sequencing) deficit and it is very important that any new word is said carefully, with accurate syllable breakdown, and any sound patterns marked with highlighter pens.

Confusion as a result of the schwa is particularly noticeable in:

- ure
- an/en/in/on
- al/el/il
- tle/tal
- ple/pal
- ous/us/ice
- ary/ory/ery
- ent/ence/ant/ance
- able/ible.

> Annette, an LLD student with problems with the storage and sequencing of sounds, often had trouble remembering the exact word when speaking and writing. Sometimes she would talk around in circles, never seeming to get to the point as she valiantly searched for the word she wanted. Other times she produced some very amusing short phrases, such as 'birdie foot rests' for 'perch' and the potentially very embarrassing 'genitals' for 'gentiles'.

Connecting sound knowledge to grammatical knowledge

The theoretical model of language in the brain developed by Shaywitz (2003) (see Chapter 1) has, at its lowest level, the phonological module that processes the sounds of language. These sounds in words have to be broken down into their parts so that they can be stored and retrieved as necessary. Weaknesses at this level impact significantly on both the listening and decoding skill of LLD students. Difficulty here, along with short-term memory and working memory deficits (see Chapter 7) also affect the upper language module which deals with semantics: vocabulary and word knowledge (see Chapter 4) and syntax and discourse; and grammar and writing (see Chapter 5).

Words that are inaccurately stored by sound or by the chunking of syllables are more difficult to retrieve from memory. That is, LLD students do not remember how to say them accurately in the correct sound sequence and as a result struggle to spell them. As well as saying and spelling the words accurately, they have to then match the correct word to the correct visual image to establish good comprehension. This is particularly so for many multisyllabic abstract words, like 'sarcastic' and 'ironic'. Having the wrong visual image—or, worse, no visual image at all—impacts significantly on the comprehension of text, film and oral language. To counteract this difficulty, subject-specific words or key words need to be given the detailed word treatment (see key word vocabulary analysis in Chapter 11).

LLD students find it difficult to identify and use a variety of abstract nouns, verbs and adjectives appropriately when writing: they rarely use them spontaneously in spoken language. Once the sounds and patterns of sounds are well understood for decoding and spelling, and particularly when suffixes are understood, then LLD students need to see how these sound patterns can help them identify if a word is a noun, verb, adjective or adverb. They then need to use this knowledge to write sentences using words in their various grammatical forms (see Chapter 5).

- *Noun*: –ment as in 'state*ment*' or –ery as in 'station*ery*'
- *Adjective*: –ous as in 'danger*ous*' and –ant as in 'compli*ant*'
- *Verb*: –ing as in 'jump*ing*' and –ate as in 'regul*ate*'

Then there is 'regulation' (noun), 'regulate' (verb) and 'regulatory' (adjective).

ESL teaching materials are a good source of word lists. Books such as *Learners companion to English vocabulary* (Davidson 2002) are invaluable.

Summary

Continuing to teach decoding and fluency is critical for LLD students because of underlying difficulties with phonology. The impact of these difficulties is greater as the complexity of reading increases in the secondary curriculum. Improving decoding and fluency are also part of improving the comprehension and grammar of LLD students.

Sally had enormous difficulties learning to read, write and spell despite an excellent phonics-based program and systematic instruction over her first three years at primary school. At the end of this time she could recognise a small bank of familiar words but could not read or spell blends accurately, and neither she nor her teachers could understand what she had written. In desperation, the speech pathologist and aide began an intensive training program of discriminating vowels and reteaching. This started with blending simple CVC (consonant–vowel–consonant) words and then moved to blends in every position, focusing on fluency and dictation at this level. This took 18 months of individual instruction, five times a week.

By Year 4, Sally could read, write and spell CVC words and blends accurately as single words and in short sentences to dictation. However, her skills were still tenuous and some days she would struggle with her fluency. After the school holidays, her skills were particularly vulnerable to regression. By Year 5, she was able to read simple chapter books but her spelling remained poor and computer software was used to help with her written language. Support staff felt that she would need to use voice-activated software to keep up with written work in secondary school.

However, by mid-June in Year 5, and after a significant amount of instruction, Sally's reading fluency increased, and her written language and her reading rate began to improve. This continued throughout Year 6. The difficulty then was to find a secondary school that could provide a comprehensive and coordinated literacy program to build on the enormous amount of work done in primary school. This proved virtually impossible in her local area. The literacy programs available did not provide anywhere near the intensity of instruction Sally needed and, at best, were group instruction sessions not targeting her special needs. No individual instruction was available. Most of the schools also expressed reservations about the computer software, and indicated that there was no one at the school to work with her to develop her competence in using the software. Sally started at the local secondary school and participated in their educational support program. She continues to struggle with decoding and no additional literacy support was provided.

Connections to Section 2

Any key words or reading materials, regardless of subject, can be used for decoding and fluency work. The key word vocabulary/grammar analysis used for vocabulary from Chapter 11 (*Animal farm*) can be adapted to any subject, and any reading materials can be used to check decoding and rate fluency.

CHAPTER 4

Enhancing comprehension and word power for LLD students

Comprehension of spoken and written language is one of the most difficult areas for LLD students, and it pervades all aspects of their lives at school. It is difficult for teachers to anticipate and notice comprehension difficulties in the quick, ever-changing classroom environment. Misunderstanding is so common as to be considered normal by LLD students themselves.

To improve their comprehension, LLD students need strategic analysis of information, but because of pressure to cover a lot of content in the classroom, very little time is generally spent on this. Covering more content is not the same as teaching comprehension.

Comprehension involves connecting to previously learnt material, as well as understanding vocabulary and grammar. Memory, decoding, social and emotional engagement, and anxiety all have important parts to play in comprehension. Comprehension is also affected by such factors as excessive or unexpected noise from other students, or the vibration or 'ping' of newly arrived text messages or emails. These noises interrupt the auditory system, which is especially weak in LLD students.

> Making meaning is complex ... [The factors that contribute are] relevance, emotions and context and pattern making.
>
> (Jensen 1998, p. 92)

Comprehension of typical texts and class handouts (for example, newspaper articles) can be extremely difficult for LLD students. These difficulties are part of their language disorder and can be due to either decoding difficulties (especially of unfamiliar and multisyllabic words) or to vocabulary and grammar weaknesses (for example, in understanding sentences containing several complex ideas, or written language in which nouns are replaced with pronouns).

This chapter will focus on how to detect comprehension difficulties and how to strategically analyse information in the curriculum using both direct instruction and strategy instruction (including metacognition).

The importance of written instruction in compensating for STAM and oral language weakness

Instructions and significant information given orally in the classroom are often not understood accurately or retained by LLD students. Most LLD students rarely ask clarification questions. They may not recognise specifically what causes them not to know what to do. Even if they are aware that they have misunderstood the instruction or missed key information, they may still not know how to clarify the situation. If they have missed significant information due to short-term auditory memory (STAM) problems, anxiety or weak vocabulary knowledge, they are often not aware that they have missed anything, and this makes it impossible for them to ask a question.

> It is hard to ask a question if you don't know that you don't know.

Clear written instructions, with built-in checks at the completion of each step, are necessary to compensate for weaker oral language. Even so, it must be remembered that the structure of a sentence or instruction can have a significant impact on comprehension. The simple subject–verb–object structure is most easily understood, as are instructions that are broken down into a 'one idea—one instruction' format. With careful attention to the language and sequence used in written instruction, it is easier and quicker to determine where students are stuck if they have not started work, and to model or reinstruct individually, in a small group or using a peer.

When steps are made clear and explicit, LLD students can then increasingly focus their attention on higher order thinking tasks, such as searching for meaning (Section 2 models this step-by-step structure). Students should also be given the opportunity for quality feedback and intensive practice.

> *Patterns can be forged and constructed only when enough essential 'base' information is already known.*
>
> (Jensen 1998, p. 96)

Written instructions should be available in handouts and online, so they can be accessed from both home and school. Parents and any others working with the student need access to clear information, as comprehension difficulties make it hard for students to explain the requirements of their homework tasks.

Building comprehension checks into the curriculum

When oral instructions are given in the classroom, and discussions take place, LLD students with comprehension difficulties miss key information because of the vocabulary and grammar difficulties that are part of their language disorder.

Their working memory limitations also add to this situation. Some ways to check comprehension are as follows.

- *Ask LLD students for an oral explanation of the task and its meaning.* Ensure LLD students can explain to you what they think they have to do, and what the purpose of the task is—if it is possible to do this in a way that will not cause embarrassment. Keeping purpose in mind is very helpful for LLD students.

- *Emphasise key words.* Write key words on a whiteboard before starting to speak, and draw attention to these when talking.

- *Incorporate pauses.* Pause every 10 minutes for summaries and checking. Rowe (1986) developed the '10–2' structure: the teacher teaches for 10 minutes, then stops for 2 minutes while students (working in small groups) share their notes and clarify anything they do not understand. During the pause, students help each other rather than rely on the teacher. This technique works well across disciplines and with audiovisual materials.

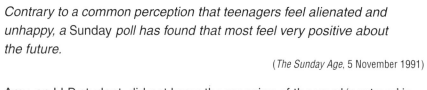

> *Contrary to a common perception that teenagers feel alienated and unhappy, a* Sunday *poll has found that most feel very positive about the future.*
>
> (*The Sunday Age*, 5 November 1991)
>
> Amy, an LLD student, did not know the meaning of the word 'contrary' in this paragraph of text. Even after it was explained to her, she still did not understand the paragraph. In answer to the question, 'How do teenagers feel about the future?' she replied, 'They feel alienated and unhappy'.
>
> The question required Amy to reorganise the information. The referent 'most', which refers to the previous noun 'teenagers', needed to be understood. The grammatical structure of the sentence was confusing to her as it did not follow the common sequence. A simpler sentence structure and sequence would be: 'A *Sunday* poll has found that most teenagers feel positive about the future. These results came as a surprise because many people think that teenagers feel alienated and unhappy.'

Additional steps to improve and monitor reading comprehension include the following.

- *Connect to previously learnt material.* For example, before students read a page, ask them what they already know about this topic or character. It is particularly important to connect a text to a student's general knowledge, and to other areas of the curriculum (including curriculum from previous years).

- *Identify text features.* Start by identifying the text type, structure, purpose and any distinguishing features of the text—even in a science lesson.

- *Check understanding.* Check to ensure students understand the question/s.

- *Provide comprehension questions requiring both literal and inferential interpretation.*

If their decoding skills are appropriate for the material, most LLD students will be able to answer literal questions, but will struggle with the inferential questions. If they do not understand literal questions, check decoding, vocabulary, grammar (for example, whether the LLD student can identify who or what a pronoun refers to) and whether there is any prior knowledge about the topic.

- *Provide one task where students have to generate questions.* This is very difficult for LLD students. Students who can generate their own questions about a text are involved with the text and are more likely to understand it.

- *Prepare summaries.* Complete written or pictorial summaries or graphic organisers for complex texts and plots. Examples of text summaries and cloze activities can be found in Section 2.

- *Monitor comprehension while reading.* This is very difficult for LLD students and requires considerable mental effort. Identify key passages, provide summaries and identify critical vocabulary for more in-depth work, and ask students to develop an individualised comprehension checklist from a base model provided by the teacher or peers. Using comprehension strategy checklists helps identify where the breakdown in understanding has occurred and is part of providing structures which lead to independence for LLD students.

- *Use comprehension checks with supplementary materials.* If a student with weak decoding listens to an audio book, better comprehension is obtained if they know they will have to read aloud a particular section of the chapter to the teacher once they have finished listening to the audio book. It also helps if the LLD student is alerted to key passages and quotes before listening to the tape.

Curriculum-based comprehension checklist for teachers

When preparing a new topic:

1. Allow time to connect the topic to students' pre-existing knowledge. Use detailed questioning: 'who', 'what', 'when', 'where', 'how'.

2. Identify text type: its purpose, structure and features. The same can be done for oral language presentations or discussions.

3. Read all articles before you give them to the students. Check for any difficult decoding, vocabulary and grammar. Alert students to these before they start reading.

4. Colour-code questions and relevant areas in the text. This helps students to complete reading comprehension tasks. Take particular note of literal versus inferential or interpretative comprehension questions to check comprehension. See whether students can identify the correct key words in the text that give them the answers.

5. Identify purpose, text type and structure for individual student responses. Reinstruct as for point 2 above.

6. Provide the additional step of 'having a go' orally with a scribe. This can help LLD students move on to writing independently themselves.

Using visual supports

While helpful, providing visual supports by using films and documentaries does not guarantee good comprehension for LLD students. To maximise comprehension, the following points need to be considered.

- A film does not always follow the narrative or characters in the novel. As a result, it is not suitable as a substitute for reading the novel but it can provide good support. In disciplines such as English, history and geography, assignments that compare and contrast a text and the movie based on the text are particularly good for checking comprehension and developing questions. Contrasting makes explicit the areas of potential confusion and develops thinking away from facts to be learned and toward different interpretations of events and characters. This is an important area to develop in LLD students and presents them with options and choices—a potential area of anxiety (see Appendices 1–4).

- It is very effective to play a scene from the film first without sound, then with sound. This enables students to analyse the visuals first and gives them one area to concentrate on before the addition of language. This is especially helpful for LLD students.

- Many LLD students struggle with visual interpretation and putting words to what they see. Compare the language and literacy devices with the visual techniques, for example, the description of feelings versus close-up camera shots (see Appendices 1–4).

- Students' experience and instinctive understanding is a good starting point. For example, if they discuss a character in terms of being a 'goodie' or a 'baddie', work on an analysis of 'how' or 'why' from this point.

The class was studying *Indiana Jones and the last crusade* but Thomas was completely confused. The humour in the scene in which Indiana rescues his diary from the Nazi book-burning during World War II, and Hitler signs it, was completely lost on him. Not only did he not understand the context, but the pace of the movie provided further confusion. Thomas struggled to connect the action in the foreground with the background, which largely provided the setting and much of the humour. In the end, he just concentrated on the foreground and summarised the viewing experience as 'people zooming around all the time'.

Checking written responses

Incomplete or inadequate written responses can be a sign of weak comprehension. If students do not write much in a response, it is worth checking if they understand the topic, purpose and audience. Before students start writing, it helps if they have a structured format for collecting their notes, and if these notes need to be handed in as part of their assignment. Structure the note-taking sheet in sections that require a summary statement of the main idea at the end of key points. Check also that sufficient scaffolding for the task has been provided. Include any key vocabulary and grammatical features that the student should use in the final presentation, such as present tense or the use of pronouns, as well as the usual text type, purpose and structure. An example from a peer with these features highlighted and labelled also assists comprehension of the task (see Chapter 5 for further discussion of written language).

Developing word power (vocabulary)

LLD students have poorer vocabulary knowledge than their peers and this contributes to their comprehension difficulties. Short-term and working memory difficulties result in weak storage of words.

It is both the sound patterns of words and their visual representations that are poorly stored. Unfamiliar words are often partially and inaccurately stored in the phonological module. Frequently, the sound pattern of the word and its syllable sequence cannot be reproduced orally, or read or written at the single-word level. In addition, LLD students have poor visual recall of spelling patterns, and many of the images and emotions that build up meaning and feeling about specific words and phrases are not well-established. When they hear a word like 'sarcastic', they have no image or example attached to this word to help them remember it. When they have to compare words like 'death' and 'slaughter', they cannot identify the subtle differences without help to establish visual images to determine connotations. They are stuck with words like 'big' or 'small' without access to the images and feelings for words like 'massive', 'puny' and 'wee'. Multiple word meanings (for example, 'order') are also the source of much confusion for LLD students.

Getting it right when writing

John was asked to write a sentence containing the word 'baffled'. He wrote: 'I was talking to a man who baffled'.

The dictionary said: 'Baffled: If something baffles you, you cannot understand it or cannot think of an answer to it'. John said, 'I probably didn't understand it'.

To improve understanding:

- Expand the sentence: 'I was talking to a man who baffled me by using unfamiliar words'.
- Find a familiar synonym, such as 'puzzled'.
- Point out that grammatical confusion can occur when a word can be used as both a verb and adjective.
- Give examples of both uses and place them on a chart.

Subject-specific vocabulary and key words

Unless there is direct instruction, subject-specific language rarely makes it into the written answers of LLD students, who tend to write in a general way. As well as traditional methods to develop vocabulary, LLD students need teachers to identify key and/or subject-specific words. These words need to be given in-depth treatment.

Students had been on a geography excursion to a beachside location where population density and the construction of a pier had impacted on the environment. Erosion, movement of sand along the beach and silting all played a part in the degradation. The students had been provided with a note-taking sheet and had completed class work preparing them for the excursion. However, on return, Matthew's notes were not sufficient for him to complete follow-up class exercises. No key geographical terms had been used; his language was general, and more appropriate to a tourist brochure describing the view and the coffee shops.

To counteract this, in preparation for the next excursion, key terms were analysed for sound and syllable patterns and then written under the relevant question on the note-taking sheet. The teacher explained to Matthew that he needed to use these words in his short answers, and in the follow-up essay and classroom test.

Specialised programs for visualising words, such as those developed by Nanci Bell (1986), can be used as a direct instruction method for weaker students, or as a simplified method of visualisation. Key words can be used to group adjectives, thereby building the images needed to understand and recall words.

Visualising and verbalising

If you are introducing a key word or new word to students, use related words on a continuum if possible (for example, 'We are going to visualise "death" and "slaughter"'.) Use cross-discipline examples where appropriate (for example, 'gorge'—geography use/English use).

Give students the following headings, with key adjectives under them:

- Size
- Quantity
- Shape
- Time
- Sound
- Taste and smell
- Appearance
- Feelings (positive)
- Feelings (negative)
- Condition

Build up an image based on these words. Ask students to identify words that match their image and describe these words. Remember to look for feelings and images that students know and that are relevant to them, as well as any patterns, and remember to contrast words and consider their connotations.

(Adapted from Bush 1979, pp. 66–8)

Good visualisation leads to an understanding of idiom and the connotations of words, and it assists with inference and understanding how language impacts on the emotions of the listener or reader. It also helps LLD students understand cartoons, how to   >>

arrange words with similar meanings on a continuum, and how to discuss the positive and negative connotations of words with reference to the images and the connections people have to them. Even names like 'Paris' and 'Homer' now have an extraordinary range of images and connotations attached to them. Nouns can become adjectives and verbs as a result: 'He was a Homer-style man', for example. Even 'Google', which started off as a noun, has now become an action as we 'google' information.

See Bell (1986) and Bell and Lindamood (1993) for more detailed instructions on visualising words, sentences and paragraphs. Davidson (2002) includes other useful word lists.

Specific work on synonyms helps to extend vocabulary and develops speed and recall of words. It also develops an understanding of multiple word meanings. Using a wider range of words with more subtle variation in meaning is a major problem for LLD students. The thesauruses available in computer programs such as Word help students by generating the word choices in the first place. Subject-specific synonym crosswords can be developed (for example, see Crossword Compiler, <http://www.crossword-compiler.com>) and if clues match the words in the thesaurus on the computer, students can quickly complete them. Adding the number of letters in the word in brackets at the end of each clue provides additional support in selecting the right word.

Use key words from a unit of work, or words that students will need to use in oral or written language tasks. Even a simple word like 'just' requires the student to consider the word's meaning, how the word is said and spelt, and whether it is used as an adjective or an adverb. Connecting words, such as 'however', can also be part of a synonym selection and can yield more options when writing. Clearly, such a task requires scaffolding and modelling tailored to the student's ability. A teacher who provides LLD students with several good model sentences using the specific target word is helping them to better consolidate vocabulary before they are required to say and write the word themselves.

Key comprehension and word-building strategies
Direct instruction

This includes the following strategies.

- *Detailed vocabulary work for both decoding and meaning.* This should be applied to specific texts, and include the structure of words, syllables, roots, prefixes, suffixes, the schwa vowel and word meanings. LLD students need to be taught the patterns (see Chapter 11). Many websites teach these skills: see, for example, The Resource Room, <http://www.resourceroom.net>.

- *Direct instruction in visualisation.* As well as specific programs, such as 'visualising and verbalising' (Bell 1986), adjective and synonym work can easily incorporate visualisations as students can visualise and consider the positive and negative connotations for words on a continuum (for example, from 'death' to 'slaughter' and from 'chubby' to 'obese'). Strengthening visualisations helps students to remember the word, and to understand the most appropriate time to use it.

- *Direct instruction in note taking.* This includes summarising, writing down main ideas and forming topic sentences. Note-taking sheets should be an integral part of research assignments. They need to be handed in and evaluated as part of the student's overall grade.

> With explicit instruction, 'students learn more, recall more and attitudes improve' (Jensen 1998, p. 97). With LLD students there is also a decrease in anxiety and an improvement in comprehension and vocabulary.

Strategy instruction

Explain to students what comprehension is, why it is important, and the strategies they can use to monitor and improve their comprehension. The key thing is to make overt the underlying strategies and thinking involved, and for the LLD student to understand that reading should make sense. For LLD students

> An LLD student, took notes and wrote: 'Cardboard— hard to stop breakages.' She reread her notes and wrote incorrectly in her essay: 'Cardboard is useful to use as it stops breakages because it is hard'.

it can be 'normal' to be surrounded by oral language that they do not always understand, and this can transfer to a similar expectation for reading.

A capable LLD student may appear to understand by answering questions directly from the text. However, if the questions are restructured or require inference, the extent of the difficulties becomes more apparent. The PROBE (Parkin, Parkin & Pool) is a reading assessment that has an emphasis on higher level comprehension (2002d). It includes materials with literal and inferential questions that gauge students' knowledge and understanding of vocabulary (2002b), and their ability to reorganise (2002c) and evaluate text (2002a) to answer questions. These materials also provide direct instruction in critical areas for comprehension and can be used with LLD students.

Metacognitive strategies, which require LLD students to monitor their thinking, demand enormous cognitive effort and often need an ordered and quiet environment. They also take a significant amount of time and so adequate time should be allowed for key curriculum areas.

> In the novel *The divine wind* (Disher 1998), the author sets the scene with a vivid description of Broome and the sea. When the LLD student, Cate, was asked where the novel was set, she said, 'In the Northern Territory near Alice Springs'. She pointed to Central Australia on the map, despite the fact that it was a long way from the sea.

Bishop (1997) has identified stages in the comprehension process. She starts from the individual sounds that make up words, and proceeds through to the level of connecting ideas and themes to the topic under discussion. In the table below, these stages have been expanded into a framework that can be used when designing curriculum to teach comprehension and to identify where student comprehension is breaking down.

Table 4.1 Strategies to improve comprehension for LLD students

Explicit sound recognition:
- Check the student can identify the individual sounds that make up a word.

How the sequence of sounds builds up to a specific word:
- Sequence the sounds in key words, break words into syllables, identify any sound/symbol patterns, and say and spell words correctly.

What words mean:
- Identify subject-specific words for direct instruction.
- Increase synonym work.
- Categorise and group words.
- Attach visualisations/images to words.
- Teach Greek and Latin roots.
- Teach prefixes and suffixes.

Groups of words go together to form phrases and then build to form clauses and sentences:
- Teach different phrases (especially noun phrases).
- Teach referents (often pronouns such as 'he' and 'she') and highlight the nouns they replace.
- Develop and create mental images.
- Connect ideas in different sentences.
- Consider sentence length and grammatical complexity, and rewrite if necessary.

Individual ideas in a sentence and the relationship between sentences in a text:
- Identify any areas of confusion in sentences.
- Check for multiple meanings or range of interpretations. (This is difficult for LLD students but important for understanding.)
- Make any inferences explicit.
- Draw a conclusion from the information in the text.
- Connect to mental images and visualisations.
- Teach structure of paragraphs (TEEL)—the topic sentence relates to what follows and contains the main idea of the paragraph. (See Chapter 5.)

Place topic in context and connect to existing information:
- Teach an overview of writing genres, e.g. what you usually see in a narrative, report, etc.
- Connect to previous examples in film, text, oral and practical work.
- Identify key themes and ideas.
- Connect any ideas not previously related.
- Identify audience and purpose.

Work with students using this list of comprehension strategies so that they can learn to identify where the breakdown in their own comprehension is occurring. This helps them to ask questions and identify where help is needed, thereby becoming independent learners.

> Jack had always done well with maths, but in Year 7 he was confronted with an increasing number of written maths problems and his scores plummeted. The PROBE provided some important information: it was noted that Jack had significant difficulty with sentences where the maths problem involved a sequence of steps with a referent (that is, where a person or place was referred to by a pronoun). Several people were introduced by name initially and then in subsequent sentences referred to using 'he, 'she' or 'they'. Jack often got the maths calculation correct but assigned it to the wrong person in the question.

Modelling

It is important that teachers demonstrate in class how they would approach a task or text. This usually requires teachers to model their internal thinking, so enabling students to understand implicit thinking and the importance of questions in ordering and developing ideas. Strategies include the following.

- *Questioning.* See examples in the question checklist box below.

- *Refining questions to clarify the task.* Note the decision-making questions in the question checklist. They range from the broader 'What do I have to choose between here?' to the narrower 'Which choice rates most highly overall?'

- *Predicting.* Here the teacher talks about possible hypotheses or predictions using the information that is initially available. In the process of doing this, students learn that predicting leads to further questioning, checking and gathering of information.

- *Grouping and summarising.* It is especially important for LLD students that teachers do not stop at listing or brainstorming ideas but that they verbalise the subsequent steps in their thinking by grouping and summarising. Seeing connections, and grouping ideas or points under headings, are significant areas of difficulty for LLD students. When teachers make this step explicit, it provides much needed support for LLD students producing summaries and topic sentences in oral or written presentations.

Question checklists

Making a decision

1 What do I have to choose between here?

2 What are the choices or alternatives?

3 What are the advantages and disadvantages of each choice?

4 From number 3, what are some relevant criteria for comparing the choices?

5 How does each choice rate with respect to these comparing criteria?

6 Which choice rates most highly overall?

Judging bias in a picture or report

The term **group** here refers to groups such as females, [particular cultural groups], and poor, weak or old people.

1 Is this **group** only shown in helping rather than leading roles?

2 Is this **group** only playing passive, safe games, rather than active, risk-taking games?

3 Is this **group** mainly placed in the background rather than the foreground?

4 Is this **group** mainly shown in non-professional roles?

5 Is this **group** mainly shown as being lazy or frightened?

Critical thinking

1 Where is the evidence for this?

2 What is the meaning of this …?

3 What is being assumed here?

4 What is the consequence of this …?

5 What is the opposite point of view?

6 What is the main point here?

7 What is an example of this …?

8 Are these reasons adequate?

9 How reliable is this source of information?

10 How consistent is this information?

11 How relevant is this factor, criterion, data …?

12 Is this information biased in some way?

(Langrehr 1993) (Reproduced with permission)

Langrehr also includes question checklists for the following: distinguishing facts from opinion; verbally summarising a reading; distinguishing an inference from a definite conclusion; solving a problem; judging the reliability of a report or statement; analysing the design of something; and visually summarising a reading.

Question checklists need to be adapted to specific tasks.

Generating questions

Once LLD students are familiar with the question checklist approach and have used a question checklist, they need to develop their own checklists and generate their own questions. This is a very difficult but valuable task. It checks both the comprehension of students and their independence as learners. It is simplest to start with visual prompts: for example, see the example of Standard of Ur note taking in *One in eleven* (Brent, Gough & Robinson 2001, pp. 53–5).

Scaffolding

At first, the teacher provides very detailed instructions or modelling for a task; then, as student competence increases, the scaffolding is gradually removed.

> ### *Scaffolding for note taking: highlighting key words*
>
> Without guidance, many students highlight chunks of sentences or text rather than honing in on key words in case they are 'wrong'. Give clear pointers about the type of words they should look for, linked explicitly to the intended purpose, such as:
>
> - adjectives
> - 'feelings' words
> - angry words
> - multisyllabic words
> - foreign words
> - unfamiliar words
> - words specifically to do with the topic
> - a specific, predetermined number of words
> - words related to a given starter word.
>
> Tell students directly that articles, for example, should not be highlighted. Prepare a highlighted copy of the text in advance so that they can see the proportion of words that are highlighted.
>
> It is very useful to follow up a highlighting activity by having students list the words they have highlighted. This allows connections and patterns to become apparent. It can be further refined by having them categorise their words under different headings appropriate to the topic.

Apprenticeship models

This model can be very reassuring for LLD students, particularly if the skills and the timeline are laid out. LLD students often panic if they perceive a task or unit of work as unfamiliar and outside their ability. It takes some anxiety away to know that they will be led by the teacher, as the content area expert, through the skills required to master a task. The teacher's role is particularly important in providing the scaffolding and questioning which leads the students to a greater understanding.

Realistic timelines are important. Some skills take years to develop, as do the independent metacognitive strategies which help LLD students understand how and why they are doing things, how to stay on task and how to check their understanding. Feeling secure enough to ask questions if they are confused—and knowing that it is acceptable to do so—saves a lot of time and anxiety for LLD students. Difficulties and embarrassment arise if they do not know that they have misunderstood.

Summary

Direct instruction and strategy instruction improve comprehension and enable LLD students to participate fully in the curriculum. LLD students should not be excused from individual and group performance tasks but, rather, should be offered scaffolding, modelling (from both peers and teachers) and practice instead. Increased time to complete comprehension and vocabulary work in-depth on fewer projects or topics improves comprehension.

Connections to Section 2

- Visualisation and imagery: Chapter 13, Step 5 (Romeo's speech); Chapter 11, Steps 4, 7
- Key vocabulary: Chapter 8, Step 1, Steps 3–5 (key vocabulary for note taking); Chapter 12, Step 1
- Idioms and metaphor: Chapter 9, Step 5; Chapter 13, Step 4
- Note taking: Chapter 9, Step 2; Chapter 8, Steps 3–5
- Thinking processes and reasoning: Chapter 13, Step 2

CHAPTER 5

Connecting oral and written language skills

The oral and written language of LLD students develops over time, but does so more slowly than that of their peers. For this reason, explicit instruction and expansion of the base skills of speaking and writing (including spelling, writing genres and plans) need to take place throughout secondary school. This chapter looks at the oral and written language that is needed for academic work. It outlines the oral language weakness of LLD adolescents, and suggests how we can teach the specific grammatical skills they need through oral and written language tasks embedded in the curriculum.

When talking to friends or teachers on a superficial level, LLD students' language can appear adequate. However, it is not sufficient for the more sophisticated, formal oral language that underlies written language development. When LLD students commit their ideas to paper, their concrete vocabulary, weaker grammar and comprehension become more apparent, as do the limitations these impose on cognitive development. Once the areas of oral language weakness are identified, however, they can be directly targeted through written language tasks to achieve maximum effect.

It is critical to teach LLD students to read, write and spell to the best of their ability, and to continue this instruction over years. It is also critical to expect LLD students will use their written language to complete curriculum tasks. In apparent consideration for their literacy difficulties, far too many LLD students are not expected to write paragraphs or even sentences, and their output is limited to visuals and unstructured oral presentations. While alternative response modes have their place in allowing students to 'show what they know', it is critical that their use not be exclusive.

> When Anna received her instructions for writing an introduction, she read them carefully, and her support person questioned her about them. Anna then discussed what she was going to include in the introduction. She was given 10 minutes to write the introduction, with the instructions alongside her to refer to if she needed. Her introduction was then compared to the teacher's instructions. Anna was amazed to find that what she had written did not match the instructions.

50

The curriculum for LLD students must include the use of written language skills. At the secondary level and into adulthood, it is written language that extends vocabulary, grammar and cognitive development. If taught well, it will develop pragmatic understanding, as it requires the LLD student to consider the audience—its point of view, age and background. Pragmatics (the effective and appropriate use of language in context) is often impaired in LLD students. This can be seen not only in social contexts but in their interpretation of texts, and in their own writing. Failure to teach oral and written language impairs LLD students' progress significantly, and limits their options and choices in adult life and work.

The differences between the language of LLD students and the language of their peers

The vocabulary of LLD students is more concrete, and lacks the variety seen in the vocabulary of their peers. LLD students have difficulty developing the grammatical skills they need for academic work. Specific areas of weakness are outlined below. More detailed information about adolescent language, and suggestions for language intervention, can be found in Paul (2006).

Vocabulary

- *Abstract nouns are rarely used.* Understanding emotions and intentions is an area of weakness for LLD students. They do not have a wide range of abstract nouns, especially those that describe emotions, ideas and feelings, and this lack of relevant vocabulary makes it difficult for them to identify and describe their feelings.

- *Multiple word meanings, synonyms and jokes are hard to understand.* As a result, the oral and written language of LLD students is characteristically very limited. They use repetitive vocabulary and choose words that lack the precision they need to convey their ideas.

- *'Teenspeak' is a challenge.* LLD students are not usually competent with 'teenspeak' and do not always use or understand the slang and asides of their peers. This impacts on their social acceptance at school and can cause distress and isolation, highlighting their sense of being 'different'.

Support vocabulary lists

Teachers can provide support for LLD students' written language by providing vocabulary lists, which students can then refer to when writing. Useful lists to provide include:

- lead-in sentences to develop a topic sentence
- lead-in phrases
- conjunctions—connecting words
- adjectives—grouped under headings to help with visualisation (see Chapter 4)
- verbs—divided into different tenses
- quotes—set out in a table format
- emotions—examples from good writers for this work.

Grammar

- *Many grammatical features are poorly recognised and inconsistently used in sentences.* There are many good texts and web sites (such as the BBC's Skillswise grammar site, <http://www.bbc.co.uk/skillswise/words/grammar>) that take students through basic grammar skills and provide clear written explanations, games and quizzes. This sets the groundwork for more detailed literate language instruction in the areas of subject-specific nouns, cognitive and linguistic verbs, relational words that link ideas, and idiom and figurative language.

- *Short sentences, with little detail added to nouns, are common.* LLD students need to be taught to elaborate nouns by first understanding the reason for elaboration, and the advantages of providing important information to capture the interest and improve the understanding of their audience. The LLD students' short sentences, with no noun elaboration, can be contrasted with sentences containing elaborated nouns, quickly showing the student that it is much easier to select the correct mental picture and/or understand an instruction if more information is included in the noun phrases. When students understand the advantages and the purpose, they can see the relevance of elaborating nouns using determiners (including 'the'/'a') and the value of giving more detail through number, quantity ('many', 'some'), possession ('their', 'your') and demonstratives ('this', 'that', 'these', 'those'). They can see the advantages of using adjectives ('the *cheerful* girl'), and phrases and clauses adjacent to the noun: for example, 'The girl with the *red* skirt'. Some students have enormous difficulty elaborating noun phrases. Further ideas for these students can be found in Paul (2006).

- *Development and use of conjunctions is limited.* It is common to find that LLD students use few conjunctions beyond the simple 'and', 'then' and 'but'. Thus, their sentence structure and literate language appear very immature: more at a primary school level than at a secondary or adult level. When students first try to write using more sophisticated conjunctions, their sentences may be overly long; they may contain many ideas and be confusing for the reader. Without further instruction, students are often discouraged and reluctant to commit much to paper or to improve their formal oral language presentations. This reluctance may lead to a false belief that LLD students cannot and should not do more demanding oral and written language tasks because they have a language disability. Instead, increased scaffolding should be applied to tasks, along with direct instruction in the underlying language skills to improve them (see Section 2).

- *Understanding and using adverbs is difficult.* In literate language, adverbs are needed to add emphasis, feeling and information, and to describe the tone of a verb or action: for example, 'He spoke *defiantly*'. Adverbs have an important function in guiding the reader through written language and in providing a logical sequence, thus aiding comprehension. Beginning new sentences and paragraphs with words like 'then', 'however', 'for a start'; adding emphasis through the use of 'really' and 'actually'; or even being a bit vague and using 'probably' if you are not certain are all features of literate language.

- *Maintaining verb tense is challenging.* This is evident within sentences, and at the paragraph and essay level. In particular, the following tenses cause confusion:
  - the two present tenses (happening now and happening generally—'walks'/'is walking')—see table below
  - past, present and future tenses (these are basic ones which can usually be mastered in structured grammatical exercises but break down in spontaneous writing).

Irregular verbs, and auxiliary verbs ('to be', 'to have', 'to do'), can also pose problems and impact on the correct tense. ESL materials used to teach verbs provide additional useful structure for sessions for LLD students. Charts also help LLD students to compare and contrast the tense they have selected, and to make changes if necessary.

Maintaining present tense in written work

Tense	Markers	Example
Simple tense	often shown by s, but not always	He walks to school.
Present perfect	has/have plus past participle This is an area of particular difficulty for LLD students.	He has jumped. He has swum. They have connected all the pipes.
Present progressive (present continuous)	formed with is/are and the present participle	She is looking.
Present perfect progressive	has been/have been plus the present participle	They have been watching the football. She has been sick for 2 days.

- *Pronouns are confusing.* LLD students often have difficulty understanding and using pronouns in oral language and are not clear about the noun that the pronoun replaces. LLD students also confuse their listeners, who are also not always certain who 'they' refers to. This oral language difficulty is clearly seen in reading comprehension beyond the sentence level and especially in novels and newspaper articles. More complex passages may need to be colour-coded, with the original noun and the pronouns replacing it highlighted in the same colour.

An LLD student, Angie, was asked to analyse an opinion piece by newspaper columnist Andrew Bolt about the supermodel Naomi Campbell: 'Oh that nasty Naomi. Well we knew she wasn't little Bo Peep' (Bolt 2000).

Example of Angie's writing without structure and key words

This article by Andrew Bolt is an opinion article. The structure of the article is found to have text that's been opinionated and has a bold and dark graphic of the subject. This is found to get the ideas across quickly of how the graphic is presented and the statement that is underneath it. Under the graphic of Naomi Campbell is the statement 'Oh that nasty Naomi. Well we knew she wasn't little Bo Peep.' Andrew bolts contention of Naomi Campbell is to argue that she is childish.

Angie's spontaneous writing immediately after a session on oral to written language, planning key words and paragraphs

The contention that Andrew Bolt explains to the viewers is that Naomi Campbell is a childish, rude and a famous model that we all love to hate one day. Through out his opinion piece he has a strong point of view and that the same time being entertaining the readers. He is an opinion writer in the Herald Sun on a regular basis. These articles he presents are for the general public rather than to be analytical.

The language that is used to support the viewpoint varies a bit such as the alliteration with 'Nasty Naomi'. Andrew Bolt uses this because it gives us the idea that she is mean and treats people badly to get what she wants. Another use is tone 'Don't make me laugh'. This is used so it comes across as sarcastic and negative towards her actions. Connotations are rarely used but there was one 'tantrum'. This is showing us that she is acting immature for her age and trying to get centre of attention by having them. Rhetorical questions occurred in the article such as 'Are people saying they are upset by the tantrum of supermodel Naomi Campbell?'. This is asked because it reinforces the idea that no one wants a model to act this way other wise they will feel upset and angry of the actions she is doing.

The audience's feelings can be persuaded by what Andrew Bolt does with his language.

The importance of developing oral and written language at the secondary level

The oral and written language difficulties of most LLD students fall into the areas outlined above. They need explicit instruction and practice in vocabulary and grammar skills, in a wide variety of subjects and activities, to develop their literate language (see Section 2). Westby (1989) identifies the following as particularly important areas:

- conjunctions
- elaborated noun phrases
- mental and linguistic verbs
- adverbs.

While conversation with peers is an important part of learning and can be highly motivating for students, it is not a replacement for direct instruction in oral language. Direct instruction develops more sophisticated (often subject-specific) vocabulary, sentence and paragraph construction, and essay writing. In primary school, oral language is seen as forming a basis for written language. This concept needs to expand to include the understanding that both oral and written language are important and that, in adolescence, written language is the vehicle to improve vocabulary, grammar and the structure of oral language.

For example, many LLD students begin a conversation without giving the listener any context. This leads to misunderstanding and confusion. Teaching simple written paragraph construction (as provided by TEEL) gives students a way of improving their oral language as well. Using TEEL (Ashton & Beardwood 2006), the first sentence of the paragraph tells the reader what the paragraph is about (**T**opic). This is followed by **E**xplanation and an **E**xample and, finally, a **L**ink back to the topic sentence (see also Appendix 4). LLD students can use this written language format to structure their oral language. If they notice, or are given feedback that their listener does not understand, they can use what they have learned about topic sentences in a paragraph and tell the listener what they are talking about.

One way that oral language and higher level thinking develops is through the more subject-specific, abstract vocabulary and ideas of written language. The late development of written language in many LLD students means that opportunities to revisit earlier skills need to be made available. Too many students with LLD miss out on the detailed instruction and the opportunity to complete written language tasks because of the mistaken belief that these tasks are too difficult for them. But LLD students need written language, at least to the paragraph level, so that they can succeed in their education and work.

Rebecca's class had been analysing a poem. They followed a highly structured unit of work that led to a written appreciation of the poem. A plan was provided, indicating exactly what should be included in the introduction, in each paragraph and in the conclusion. As the teacher talked the students through the plan, Rebecca repeatedly asked, 'But what are we meant to write?' The teacher repeated the instructions, but Rebecca still didn't 'get' what she was expected to do. A helpful classmate volunteered, 'It's pretty much like an essay'. Rebecca was still blank.

Although her language and comprehension skills were reasonable, she was experiencing executive processing difficulties that prevented her from putting together the information into a form that she could visualise. This is, in large part, a function of incomplete development of key areas of the adolescent brain. To solve the problem, the teacher rewrote the instructional prompts as questions that Rebecca could easily answer, and her answers provided the response.

At secondary school, there is often the assumption that students will make unspoken connections to new material without explicit instruction. This is usually not so with LLD students. They have difficulty generalising from, and connecting to, earlier learnt material. This means that even the simple narrative structure that they were taught in primary school needs to be analysed and applied to longer fiction texts, autobiographies and films. All require summaries and structural analysis so that LLD students see the connection and can better recall and understand.

> **Using written materials to support oral language development for LLD students**
>
> - Work with LLD students to identify and highlight key words and phrases used by an author to describe an emotion. Complete visualisation of these words and phrases. Use these phrases for students to write their own description and then report their feelings to a friend.
> - Have students read a short autobiography and biography prior to making a question sheet and interviewing a friend. Working in pairs, students can complete a short interview of each other.
> - Note any grammatical errors in students' written language. Develop a '20 questions' format where students have to answer using a particular grammatical structure or word. They get one point for every time they use this word or structure. The number of points can lead to a reward if this will provide a motivation for the student.

Oral language instruction that supports written language

Many teaching practices promote good development of oral language, and illustrate the interrelatedness of oral and written language at the secondary level.

Direct instruction in active listening

At secondary school, LLD students listen to instructions and information for lengthy periods, then take this information and produce an appropriate outcome. This may be in the form of recording information correctly in their diaries, following a sequence of steps in a science experiment, or following instructions in sport. Active listening can be taught through tasks that involve learning to give and receive instructions, and analysing what it means to be a good speaker and listener. Additional instruction in body language, such as showing interest when people are talking, turn taking and learning to interpret body language, can also improve the listening of LLD students.

Active listening is especially difficult and tiring for LLD students, as understanding and retaining oral instructions is a key area of weakness. It is difficult for the student to do and for the teacher to monitor, and will be discussed further in Chapter 14. It involves checking diaries and structuring students' listening by providing questions, summaries and note-taking sheets—often with categories, subheadings and key words. Note taking from longer oral presentations is almost impossible for LLD students without this initial structure and support.

Discussion groups

A 'book circle' approach, in which students are assigned specific roles, offers many opportunities for LLD students to be both speakers and listeners. The roles of summariser and/or elaborator, while difficult ones for them to fill (and usually taken by more language-competent students), give LLD students exposure to competent language models and explanations from their peers. Oral language (vocabulary and grammar) can be consolidated if LLD students are taken through quick written answers to the following questions, which follow a simple TEEL paragraph structure. The topic sentence can be provided instead of the first sentence if necessary. Students can do this at the end of a discussion, at critical points in the discussion or every 10 minutes.

- T: 'What was the main thing we talked about?'
- E: 'What did the elaborator (expander) say?'
- E: 'What two examples from the text support the above statement?'
- L: Ask the summariser to conclude.

Following this discussion, drafts of written language tasks need to be conferenced with peers or the teacher.

Peer and teacher modelling

This is a regular part of most classrooms, but more steps are necessary for LLD students: therefore it is necessary to 'walk the talk'. Most peers and teachers are comfortable and familiar with demonstrating a task, an experiment or a physical action to students, but are less familiar with discussing their thinking processes as they do it. But this is exactly what LLD students need, so that the steps taken in mastering a skill are made explicit.

The importance of questions

Because of their language disorder, LLD students struggle to use questions to clarify any misunderstandings, and to structure their thinking and written work. This is why teachers need to make explicit their own thinking and the inner questions they use to make decisions, to plan and to write. Any opportunity to incorporate questions into the curriculum well beyond the traditional reading comprehension format can provide enormous benefits for the language and cognitive development of LLD students. (See question checklists in Chapter 4.)

Debating

Debating, with its formal structure, provides good language models for students and, if well done, can be very entertaining. Preteaching the debating topic is important for LLD students' understanding and enjoyment. Debating provides a wonderful opportunity to see the argumentative or persuasive essay structure in 'action'. The first speaker is the introduction; the second speaker is the body of the essay; and the final speaker is the conclusion. The importance and nature of a rebuttal is more readily recognised when 'seen' in this way. Students can see the purpose—to convince the audience of a point of view—and, with their teacher's input, they can learn to analyse why one argument is more convincing than another. They often have the chance to see the power of humour to sway the audience. Simple debates in Years 7 and 8 can be used as models when teaching the more difficult argumentative and persuasive essay structure.

Structured oral presentations

Presentation tasks give LLD students practice in developing and using explicit questions to structure their thinking. For example, when talking about their own artwork or the work of others, their presentation can be structured by questions under headings such as:

- Why I chose this medium
- How I made the artwork
- What were the steps involved?
- Were there any problems?
- How I solved these problems
- Anything else?

Oral presentations also provide the opportunity to use subject-specific vocabulary. If LLD students are to develop vocabulary, they must hear the new words and recall them to use in oral and written presentations. Those LLD students who are anxious presenters may need to present to one person, then to several, and then to the group. With preparation and support, however, most should be able to present to the group. There is generally no reason why a student should not learn to give an oral presentation.

Structured note-taking sheets

Note-taking sheets provide support for reporting back to peers and teachers. In addition, they give students an opportunity to structure observations and thinking, and to use subject-specific vocabulary. Done well, they can also be sequenced to give a good paragraph or short essay structure. To ensure the use of appropriate vocabulary, subject-specific key words need to be included under the questions or headings on the note-taking sheet. LLD students need to know that they will be expected to use these words in their presentations and note taking tasks.

Brainstorming, categorisation, excluding, ranking and modelling the thinking involved in making choices

Brainstorming is important for LLD students. It uses a group to generate the language LLD students need but may find difficult to recall and produce themselves. This is especially so if a new topic is being introduced or if language needs to be recalled quickly. However, brainstorming needs to be followed by categorisation, exclusion and ranking of ideas: all significant underlying difficulties for LLD students. These language and thinking abilities form the basis of deciding what to put in a sentence, paragraph or essay. Including additional steps and detailed work on brainstormed materials teaches directly to the LLD students' areas of need, and prepares for better oral and written language structure and content.

Tasks for transferring oral language to written language

- Listen to an interview and analyse interview technique.
- Write a recount of an autobiography/biography from film or radio.
- Following a debate, use the order of the speakers and what they said to write a structured persuasive essay.
- Make up a narrative on the spot (each student contributes a sentence).
- Write eyewitness reports of a crime. Use or make a film, then write a description of the suspect under key headings.
- Use a 'synonym circle' (the first student says a word and the next student has to think of a similar one). Then complete a piece of writing using a selection of these words.

Why direct spelling instruction continues to be important for LLD students

Traditional methods of spelling instruction bring to mind the process of learning long lists of unrelated words, or lists of words grouped according to topic. These approaches, without context or follow-up, will often have minimal impact on LLD students' spelling. Without explicit instruction in vocabulary, grammar and written language plans, many subject-specific words never make it into the written responses of LLD students.

LLD students need to reach a level where spelling is as automatic as possible, leaving them free to concentrate on ideas, sentences structure and other higher order language skills. Other advantages of spelling instruction are as follows.

- Improvements in spelling often lead to improvements in decoding. Spelling instruction offers an opportunity to work again on the alphabetic principle, and to fill in any gaps in the LLD students' knowledge of sound/letter combinations, sound sequencing, and storage and recall of syllables and visual patterns.

- Spelling work allows discussion of pronunciation changes. When working on spelling across phonological, orthographic and morphological levels, pronunciation changes in related words such as 'child' to 'children' can be discussed. These changes impact not only on spelling but also on reading and meaning.

- Spelling can reflect where a student's major areas of deficit lie. While LLD students will generally not have perfect spelling, they can often become independent users of the spellchecker. As with decoding, it is important not to give up too soon with spelling instruction. A case study by Apel and Masterton (2001) found that 23 hours of group instruction with a student produced a measurable change in reading and spelling impairments.

While it is advantageous to continue spelling instruction for LLD students, they should not be given the impression that it is the most important part of writing: it is a means to an end. Communicating ideas to the audience is the important thing. Encourage students to put all their ideas down and have a go at any word they want to spell. They should concentrate on the syllable count first, then think about the most appropriate symbol to represent the sounds, especially if the spellchecker does not help. Often the goal is not perfect spelling but being able to select the correct word from the spellchecker.

Students who have very impaired phonological awareness and spelling, and who cannot make reasonable approximations for a word, may benefit from the use of voice-activated software. Sometimes, after a period of using the software along with instruction in phonological decoding, students' reading and spelling improves. With a positive attitude and adequate opportunity, it is possible to see continuing improvements in written language. If possible, do not stop instruction, but ensure it is based on the curriculum and on the student's interest.

> *Hi Mrs B*
> *his is Em*
> *How are you going?*
> *I'm STILL in homework overlode!!!*
> *Thank you for sending the perswasive essay plan,*
> *i just sat my outcome and it went pretty well.*
> *i was happy i wrote 5 1/2 pages, so that was good.*
> *but i didn't have time to proof read, so that was bad.*
> *Plese give me the email adress ro Mr Y ASAP.*
> *thanks a lot,*
> *Em*
>
> This highly motivated Year 12 student had four years' literacy instruction in primary school. She was able to read basic text at the end of primary school but could not spell well enough for others to read or to type on the computer. With further spelling instruction in Year 9 (two 40-minute sessions a week) and Year 10 (one session a week), she eventually achieved independence with typing and writing.

Spelling as part of vocabulary and grammar instruction

As well as the usual techniques for teaching grammar, further grammatical support for LLD students can be gained by teaching spelling, and by identifying the phonological, orthographic and morphographic identifiers that improve spelling. This instruction has the added benefit of lifting LLD students' confidence, and increasing their success in selecting and spelling more sophisticated and subject-specific vocabulary. It frees up working memory and cognitive space so students can concentrate on the ideas in written material, and the material's flow and structure. In addition, this type of instruction helps students identify whether a word is a noun, verb, adjective or adverb.

Errors in the spelling and spontaneous written language of LLD students give us a window into the underlying linguistic deficits of these students and provide us with a specific focus for both group and individual instruction. Spelling, as part of vocabulary and grammar work, can teach to the following areas that LLD students find difficult.

Phonological awareness

Phonological awareness—the ability to identify and sequence sounds in language—is a skill that is independent of meaning, but impacts significantly on the acquisition of more sophisticated vocabulary, especially at the syllable level. LLD students often do not have accurate syllable count beyond 2–3 syllables, and show difficulties producing and predicting rhyme and discriminating between similar-sounding words: for example, 'solute', 'soluble' and 'solvate' (see Chapter 3).

Weakness in the ability to discriminate similar sounds, or sounds at the end of words, also impacts on comprehension, spelling and grammar. This can be seen in vowels, blends, final 's', suffixes and verb tenses. For example, LLD students often omit the final 's' when reading. Matching sounds to letters in spelling can bring to a conscious level these phonological confusions. It is worth pointing out these patterns in words, so students can hear and see how a final 's' can sometimes be pronounced as 's', 'z' or 'iz'. The same applies for the past tense, where they will hear 't', 'd' and 'id'—as in 'jumped', 'loved' and 'handed'. The common vowel confusions for LLD students are 'e'/'i' and 'a'/'u'. These impact on the present and past tense in words like 'ran' and 'run'. If consonant and vowel sounds are poorly discriminated, they need to be directly taught, and examples need to be highlighted in texts.

Phonological decoding

Unless LLD students have had explicit, detailed and continuous phonological decoding instruction at primary school—that is, detailed instruction in sound–symbol correspondence—their knowledge of this area will not be firmly established.

Many LLD students are overwhelmed when they arrive at secondary school and encounter an explosion of new vocabulary. Even those who have received good phonics instruction find the pronunciation of so many new words daunting, and will struggle with accurate recall for spelling. On top of this, the comprehension of the new words is also an area of difficulty. Without further instruction and appropriate curriculum-based tasks, LLD students avoid using these words in their oral and written language. For LLD students, it really does matter that new words are pronounced carefully. A web site with decoding lists (from simple to advanced) for students is The Resource Room, <http://www.resourceroom.net>.

Orthography

Orthography is how we represent spoken language through spelling. For LLD students, the connection between spoken sounds and their letter patterns in spelling needs to be clear. LLD students, who already have poor phonological awareness, are further confused if spelling patterns are taught without reference to the sound they represent. This is especially true for vowels such as 'ea' and 'ow'. These letter combinations represent more than one sound, and this needs to be explained when completing letter pattern exercises. See the sample exercise below.

Sample exercise
The letter combination 'ow' makes two sounds. Place the following 'ow' words in the correct box according to the sound they make.

browse   allowance   know   below

'ow' as in 'cow'	'ow' as in 'snow'

Once students can match the sounds well, they are ready to look at the many different ways that the same sound can be written in English and to rank these spelling options from the most common to the least common. For example, 'a' (long) can be represented by 'a', 'ai', 'ay', 'ea' and 'eigh'.

Morphology

The study of morphology (how language is structured: prefixes, suffixes and roots) helps with pronunciation, spelling and semantics (meaning). Word endings can help identify whether a word is a noun, verb, adjective or adverb.

For example:

Noun	Verb	Adjective	Adverb	Related words
abuse	abuse	abus**ive**	abusive**ly**	abus**er**

- '–ive' is used to form nouns and adjectives.
- '–ly' is used to form adverbs and sometimes adjectives (for example, 'a friendly girl').
- '–er' is often a noun.

Looking intensively at words

The words that LLD students are expected to recall and use recurrently in their oral or written language need to be given systematic spelling attention in the areas of phonological awareness, orthographic knowledge and morphology.

For example:

Word family	Phonological awareness	Orthographic knowledge	Morphology and semantics
Act Acts Acting Action	• Segmenting e.g. 'ac tion' • Discrimination e.g. 'ts' on the end of words	• Sound–letter relationships • Letter patterns • Spelling rules	• Includes suffixes, prefixes, base words and roots
	Errors • Delete or omit letters and syllables • Confuse 'l' and 'r' and nasals ('n', 'm', 'ng') • Demonstrate vowel discrimination problems, especially with 'a'/'u' and 'e'/'i'	**Errors** • Generally break spelling patterns and conventions, e.g. ending words in 'u', selecting wrong sound/letter pattern	**Errors** • Often do not include morphemes in spelling—noticeable in rapid writing

Key vocabulary analysis

Key vocabulary that students need to understand and use in their writing should be examined in several ways. LLD students generally have a weakness in the underlying sound sequencing system. Combined with weak short-term auditory memory (STAM) and working memory, this means that it can be difficult for students to store key words accurately for spelling, meaning and correct grammatical use in sentences.

The following is an example using words from Chapter 11 *(Animal farm)* that can be applied to any 10 key words from a unit of work, regardless of the discipline.

Key word vocabulary/grammar analysis (Animal farm)

Comrade

In the chart below, divide each word into syllables and say the word carefully.

comrade	
comradeship	
comradely	

Use your dictionary and place the word in its word families.

Noun	Verb	Adjective	Adverb	Related words
comrade comradeship			comradely	comrade-in-arms

Highlight noun endings, like '–ship' in 'comradeship'. Use a different colour for different word families.

The prefix in this word is 'com–'. Fill in this table.

Word	Prefix	Meaning	Other words which use this prefix
comrade	com–	with, together	community

Use your computer thesaurus to identify synonyms (words with similar meanings).

Word	Synonyms
comrade	friend, buddy, pal, companion

Write a sentence using each of the words in the word families.
(Note that ESL dictionaries also have good examples of words in sentences.)

Grammar instruction to improve the writing of LLD students

Grammar is notoriously difficult for LLD students because of their language disability. It is a bit like trying to play tennis when your dominant hand doesn't work well, and wondering why it is so difficult to hit the ball over the net. Grammatical terms are often confusing and hard to remember for LLD students. Colour coding is often a good way to help them: for example, have the noun phrases highlighted in yellow, adverbs in blue, etc. Grammar can also be daunting for teachers, especially if English is not their subject. Web sites such as the BBC's Skillswise grammar site, <http://www.bbc.co.uk/skillswise/words/grammar>, give the basics from which to build more instruction. A well-written web site for teachers and support staff, with good explanations of grammatical terms as well as examples, can be found at the University of Ottawa's HyperGrammar site, <http://www.arts.uottawa.ca/writcent/hypergrammar>.

When teaching grammar to LLD students, the key things are as follows.

- State the purpose of the grammatical device.
- Have examples at the sentence and paragraph level, and examples from the work of other students.
- Follow grammar instruction with targeted written language work that specifies the audience, purpose, person and verb tense. LLD students need individual or very small group instruction to monitor their comprehension of grammar tasks. They rarely do well with larger group instruction, even if it is written down, because the language used to explain this type of task is complex.
- Follow grammar instruction with structured written language tasks at the paragraph and essay level.
- Provide written language tasks that specify the structure and specific grammar needed. This gives the opportunity to teach grammar and gives much-needed practice in writing for purpose and audience. While there is a place for spontaneous oral and written responses, they should not be the only way LLD students present their work, as they do not always provide the opportunity to teach the formal grammar needed to improve oral and written language.
- Engage in oral conferencing with the teacher upon completion.
- Analyse feedback. Often LLD students do not read comments or understand what to do to improve their work next time. This is why the additional step of analysing feedback is important, whether it is individually, with peers or as a group activity (see Chapter 14).

Key grammatical areas to develop

The written language of LLD students is limited when compared to that of their peers in the two grammatical areas of elaborated noun phrases and literate conjunctions (Westby 1989). LLD students also benefit from further work on verbs, adjectives and adverbs beyond the single-word level to the phrase and clause level. Explicit instruction on these grammatical areas gives the LLD student the skills to improve their work.

Noun phrases—tell the reader more

The term 'noun phrase' is abstract, so if you ask an LLD student to use a 'noun phrase' the terminology can cause confusion. But if you say that the purpose is to tell the reader more, then contrast written work that does not use noun phrases with written work that does, then LLD students often understand what to do. Their ability to develop these phrases is hampered by underlying deficits in vocabulary and the ability to formulate questions. This is why modelling and the use of questions is critical in good curriculum planning and needs to be part of note taking, brainstorming, comprehending text and effective listening.

Develop noun phrases in the following ways.

- Add in the underlying questions for the LLD student.

- Give an oral example to show how to expand the sentence.

- Identify the lead-in words after the noun—a preposition, 'wh' word, '–ing' verb or that/which.

- Provide a written pattern to follow.

- Contrast sentences with and without noun phrases.

For example, if the student writes, 'The dog ate the bone', ask the student to 'Tell us more about the bone' and 'more about the dog' by adding the questions 'which?' and 'where?'—'Which dog?', 'Where was the bone?'—to produce a sentence like 'The border collie from the dogs' home ate the bone on the deck'.

To help LLD students identify noun phrases in a sentence, give them a question and ask them to answer by highlighting the noun phrase.

For example:

> Sentence: 'The girl wore the dress to the ball.'
> Q: 'Where did she wear the dress?'
> A: '… to the ball.' This is the noun phrase. Highlight this in the original sentence.

Adjectival phrases and clauses

Adjectival phrases add information and variety and help the reader visualise what you mean. Lead-in words for adjectival clauses are 'who', 'whom', 'which' or 'that'.

For example:

> Sentence: 'The boy who wore the red jersey kicked the goal.'
> Q: 'Find the lead-in word.'
> A: 'Who.'
> Highlight 'who' and the words that help the reader visualise the boy.

Adverbial phrases and clauses

Adverbial clauses and phrases give more specific information about the action. They ask 'how', 'when', 'where' and 'why'. Clauses often lead with conjunctions such as 'because', 'through', 'before' and 'when'.

For example:

> Sentence: 'The team was beaten because it had not trained for three weeks.'
> Q: 'Find the word "because".' Highlight this word and the words that tell us why the team was beaten.
> A: '…because it had not trained for three weeks.'

Conjunctions—connecting ideas and guiding the reader through your writing

LLD students are often taught the common conjunctions: 'and', 'but' and 'because'. However, to improve their literate language, they need more instruction in what are called the most common conjunctive adverbs, such as 'also', 'consequently', 'finally', 'furthermore', 'hence', 'however', 'incidentally', 'indeed', 'instead', 'likewise', 'meanwhile', 'nevertheless', 'next', 'nonetheless', 'otherwise', 'still', 'then' and 'therefore'. This can be done prior to the essay draft, as part of a structured written plan where students have to select a connecting word (see Appendix 4).

Adjectives—describing and visualising

It is useful for LLD students to have a chart of adjectives under key headings such as size, shape and sound, as well as words to describe positive and negative feelings. As they have word-finding problems, lists like this quickly give them the word they want or a possible synonym (see Chapter 4 and Section 2). Many web sites provide word lists like this, for example <http://www.paulnoll.com/Books/Clear-English/English-adjectives-1.html>.

Adjectives task

Fear

At least when you're frightened you know you're alive. Energy pumps through your body so hard that it overflows as sweat. Your heart—your heart that dies, the pumping—bangs away in your chest like an old windmill on a stormy night.

I think I've felt every strong feeling there is: love, hate, jealousy, rage. But fear's the greatest of them all. Nothing reaches inside you and grabs you by the guts the way fear does. Nothing else possesses you like that. It's a kind of illness, a fever that takes you over.

(Marsden 1995, p. 1)

Visualise and brainstorm more images of fear:

- voices—screaming, bouncing, swirling
- mouth—dry, burning
- heart—pounding
- legs—trembling, weak
- stomach—turning, burning
- head—spinning, confused.

Paul, writing about his feelings after falling from a bike, completed the following written piece after analysing the John Marsden text, above, and completing visualisation of adjectives and work on conjunctions:

I heard a crunching sound in my leg. I ached all over as I sat there trembling and everything spinning around me. I was sobbing and calling out but no one heard me because they were far away on the tracks. My head was pounding and the wind was ricocheting around my head but I felt nothing. I looked down at my leg and it felt detached from my body. Fear raced through me as I thought no one would find me. My mouth was dry after all my yelling.

Verbs—holding tense and using verbs which tell about thinking and feeling

There are two major areas of difficulty for LLD students in the use of verbs.

- *Using verbs which tell about thinking or feeling.* A small chart with a range of options for the student to use depending on the task provides support for this work.

- *Holding tense in longer pieces of writing.* This can come from an underlying difficulty with the understanding of time. Some students who are able to hold tense consistently at sentence level in typical grammar exercises may not be able to hold tense at the paragraph level. They need more practice at the paragraph level.

The following web site (from the HyperGrammar site mentioned above) is too difficult for LLD students to use independently, but teachers and support staff will find useful examples for maintaining tenses in a sequence: <http://www.arts. uottawa.ca/writcent/hypergrammar/vbseq.html>.

Simple verb tense sheet

Verb tense sheets can help LLD students maintain tense once the teacher has identified the tense they want used in a written piece. LLD students find it very difficult to maintain tense. They require direct instruction and assistance with editing. Understanding tenses and the aspect of time they represent is at the core of a language learning disability, especially once students move from simple tenses to the tenses used in written language. It helps if there is a written example from another student where tense is maintained throughout the piece and LLD students can use this as a model.

On a written exemplar:

- Colour-code the verbs and discuss the tenses.

- Give a brief explanation as to why the piece is to be in the present, past or future tense, as the formal grammar terms used to describe tenses are confusing for LLD students.

- A simple explanation, used by speech pathologist Rebecca Brown, is to divide tenses into those that go for a long time and those that happen just once. Use a long line for the tenses that go for a long time, and a cross for tenses that happen just once. For example: 'I was sitting on the park bench in the park [long line] when a tree fell on me [cross]'. This timeline concept also works well to explain the use of past, present and future tenses, and even different points of the past as they imply different points in time. Give a simple oral example. LLD students may find it helpful when writing to use a check sheet for the tenses. They can refer to this when writing their own material or editing.

- Use the auxiliary table on page 70 to assist LLD students to match or recall auxiliaries. Give oral examples and assistance in selecting the correct auxiliary. A significant area of confusion for LLD students in sequencing tenses comes from the perfect tense, which is formed by adding the auxiliary to the past participle.

Verb tense check sheet

	Simple present		Present with 'to be'		Present with 'to have'		Present with 'have been'	
Present	I	jump	I	am jumping	I	have jumped	I	have been jumping
	you we they	jump	you we they	are jumping	you we they	have jumped	you we they	have been jumping
	he she it	jumps	he she it	is jumping	he she it	has jumped	he she it	has been jumping

	Simple past		Past with 'to be'		Past with 'to have'		Past with 'had been'	
Past	I	watched	I	was watching	I	had watched	I	had been watching
	you we they	watched	you we they	were watching	you we they	had watched	you we they	had been watching
	he she it	watched	he she it	was watching	he she it	had watched	he she it	had been watching

	Simple with 'will or 'shall'		Future with 'to be'		Future with 'to have'		Future with 'have been'	
Future	I	will watch	I	will be watching	I	will have watched	I	will have been watching
	you we they	will watch	you we they	will be watching	you we they	will have watched	you we they	will have been watching
	he she it	will watch	he she it	will be watching	he she it	will have watched	he she it	will have been watching

Past participle—key verbs that cause confusion

Present	Past	Past participle
am	was	been
are (plural)	were	been
do	did	done
has	had	had
is	was	has been

>>

A full list of past participles can be found at the UsingEnglish.com web site, <http://www.usingenglish.com/reference/irregular-verbs/>.

Auxiliaries

Auxiliaries include 'be', 'can', 'do', 'may', 'must', 'shall', 'will', 'has', 'have' and 'had'. As noted above, most confusion in sequencing tenses comes from the perfect tense—that is, adding the auxiliary to the past participle. For example:

- present tense (present perfect): they have jumped
- past tense (past perfect): they had jumped
- future tense (future perfect): they will have walked.

Auxiliaries	Present tense auxiliary plus past participle (third person)	Past tense auxiliary plus past participle (third person)	Future tense auxiliary plus past participle (third person)
be	He is beaten.	He was beaten.	He will be beaten.
can			
do			
may			
must			He must be beaten.
shall			He shall be beaten.
will			They will be beaten.
has	He has visited. He has beaten.	He had visited.	
have	They have known. They have broken.		They will have known.

Teaching inference, humour and idiom

Underlying vocabulary and grammar difficulties make 'reading between the lines' and understanding jokes (especially those that play on double meanings) very confusing for LLD students. These impact not only on their understanding of curriculum but also on their relationships with their peers as they do not always understand the jokes and meanings of 'teenspeak': the language that separates adolescents from adults and from those younger than themselves. LLD students may use non-'cool' words or, even worse, continue to use old, ex-'cool' words when their peers have moved on. They may not fully understand where and when to use 'teenspeak' or that the real meaning is often the opposite of what their peers say.

Added difficulties are that the vocabulary of slang and 'teenspeak' is constantly changing, and the grammar does not follow set rules—in fact, it breaks most of them. Invention of sounds, words and grammar is the norm. Units that explicitly study the purpose, audience and meaning of 'teenspeak' have advantages for LLD students and can also be a lot of fun.

Supporting LLD students' writing

To move students from spoken to written language requires careful preparation and teaching, as shown in the unit on *Animal farm* (Chapter 11). It is important for new words and concepts to be introduced, and for comprehension to be as well developed as possible (see Chapter 4). The benefits of taking the time and effort to teach LLD students to write are enormous. Writing expands and consolidates comprehension and vocabulary, enables students to tap into higher order thinking skills, and gives them tangible structures in which to place ideas and arguments. It gives support and practice for STAM and working memory, and is also significant in retrieval, a process in which students relearn by consolidating what they know. Without this retrieval and higher level work, students may function well below their level of ability.

> *When I was in Year 8, I thought that the teacher would not know that I had not read the book. Now I am in Year 10, I realise it must have been very obvious.*
>
> (A comment from a student learning essay writing)

LLD students often have significant memory weakness. This means that it can be difficult for them to hold an idea in mind and connect it to existing information without losing the sentence completely. In addition, their ideas can easily be lost if they are also concentrating on spelling and grammar, or if there is too much noise or distraction in the environment. This is why it is best for them to concentrate on meaning and what they want to say as a first step, then edit for spelling and grammar later. It is also best if they can use a computer (either typing or by using voice-activated software) to make the many editing changes needed. Poorly developed handwriting skills, both in letter formation and in speed of writing, can also limit their written output.

Anxiety also impacts here. Apart from not seeing themselves as writers (at least initially), the beginning process of writing can feel very mentally taxing and confusing for students. As ideas and structures swirl around in their heads, they often struggle to pin them down to an order and find the words they need. A quiet environment and adult support are important here.

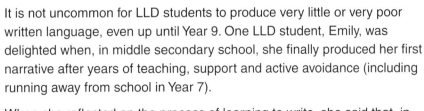

It is not uncommon for LLD students to produce very little or very poor written language, even up until Year 9. One LLD student, Emily, was delighted when, in middle secondary school, she finally produced her first narrative after years of teaching, support and active avoidance (including running away from school in Year 7).

When she reflected on the process of learning to write, she said that, in the beginning, she didn't know what to do. When she compared her work to that of other Year 7 students, she felt angry because she didn't seem to be able to write much and what she did write was 'pointless' and 'pathetic'. She described feeling more and more angry as she sat there, watching everyone else write, with the anger inside her getting worse.

A good starting point for developing the written language skills of LLD students is a note-taking exercise. Notes can be gathered from visuals—see, for example, the Standard of Ur exercise in *One in eleven* (Brent, Gough & Robinson 2001)—or from texts. Including questions and key words in the note-taking exercise adds more scaffolding (see Chapter 12). Additional scaffolding can be provided by structuring the questions in the exercise so that they naturally follow a TEEL structure—topic sentence, explanation, evidence, link. Then it is possible to move quickly to work on a paragraph or on a highly scaffolded essay. Provide word lists of adjectives and verb tense charts as needed.

PowerPoint presentations are a good way for students to learn to put key ideas from notes into a format, then use them as a memory prompt to expand an oral presentation. The language skills underlying PowerPoint presentations are quite complex—they require the ability to extract key ideas from an array of research sources and summarise them. To use the medium well and produce good slides which inform the viewer, students require these underlying language skills, as well as explicit instruction and a good knowledge of a topic. Appendix 5 provides information on the language skills that are needed to prepare a PowerPoint presentation and an example of the detailed instructions required.

Supporting oral responses in LLD students

Students are often allowed to select tasks in areas they perceive to be their strengths. This has many benefits and can be highly motivating, but the language skills underlying these tasks need to be explicit. Without modelling, scaffolding and explicit instructions, LLD students will often select tasks that they perceive have minimal written language content, even if the underlying oral language and questioning skills are substantial.

For example, a task may be: 'Draw a portrait of yourself as an ancient Egyptian using the artistic conventions of ancient Egypt: e.g. colour, positioning of head and body, etc. You will then give a short oral presentation to the class.'

Even though the presentation is an oral one, a task like this requires students to identify the key words that describe artistic conventions. There may be pre-existing knowledge that students need to recall, and a significant amount of categorisation of ideas and information required (often a key area of difficulty). A presentation, whether oral or PowerPoint-based, requires language skills including key words, summaries and the ability to answer questions such as:

- What were the steps involved in this task?
- What did I enjoy?
- What was difficult about the process (with reference back to the key artistic conventions of ancient Egypt)?

Summary

Checklist: Literate language in curriculum

Teacher	Student
Give clear instructions with a plan and scaffolding depending on student's ability with written language. Provide sequencing ideas and actions.	Follow plan. Organise. Sequence.
Instructions should include audience and purpose.	Orally identify audience and purpose.
Brainstorm key words and ideas. Categorise these ideas. Sequence as a basis for paragraphs.	Categorise words following brainstorm. Give name to each category—e.g. fruit: apples, oranges, bananas—or the name of the character/idea, along with the words and examples used to describe them.
Provide note-taking sheets with questions. Include subject-specific/key words.	Use subject-specific/key words to answer questions.
Specify tense, along with a written example. Highlight key verbs. Discuss their use and any distinguishing visual or phonological clues.	Identify tense of piece, and use this as a model for written responses. Use verb tense chart if necessary. Understand how tense will work in a writing piece, e.g. editorials: report events in the past tense but make paper's comments in the present tense.
Abstract verbs: select five or six appropriate verbs for the task. Establish meaning and memory for words through spelling, word analysis and visualisations. Make clear any positive or negative connotations.	Use these new words in oral and written language tasks. Recall and use them at a later date. Develop a visual image attached to the word.
Model three options for sentences using task or subject-specific key words—demonstrates teacher's thinking.	Attempt sentence orally. May first need oral practice with a scribe/support person.
Model subordinate clause.	Use check sheet for subordinate clauses when writing.
Model conjunctions.	Use conjunction checklist.
Model noun phrases, and the underlying 'wh' question that develop them, to expand students' writing. Assist with making these explicit to the task.	Use model from the teacher to expand written language. Identify underlying questions.

>>

Model adverbs—to describe tone. Establish meaning and memory for words through spelling, word analysis and visualisations. Make clear any positive or negative connotations. Read aloud so LLD students can 'hear' and 'see' tone. Exaggerate. Ask students to select tone from a short list of seven words (any more is too confusing).	Select the tone of an oral presentation and then a written text from a list of approximately seven words.
Provide key vocabulary or subject-specific vocabulary.	Use vocabulary list, and include words in note-taking tasks, and paragraph- and essay-writing exercises.
Provide check sheets with underlying questions for oral and writing tasks.	Answer questions on check sheets. Eventually, make own question check sheet for a task.
Provide group editing sheet for class. Develop an individual editing sheet for LLD student. Many LLD students have their own unique errors in grammar and spelling which need to be clearly identified. Provide individual support for editing.	Use group and individual editing sheets. Seek assistance with editing from adult or peers.
Give specific feedback on ideas, structure, grammar (including use of noun phrases, conjunctions, verbs, etc.), and use of group and individual check sheet. Highlight words in students' writing for vocabulary expansion, e.g. synonym work on computer.	Make changes to work following feedback. State what was done well and the areas that need to be developed in the next piece of work.

Connections to Section 2

- Considering the audience: Chapter 11, Step 6
- Emotive language: Chapter 9; Chapter 11
- 'Teenspeak': Chapter 9
- Empathy: Chapter 8
- Spelling and syllabification: Chapter 13, Step 2
- Connecting to existing information and experience: Chapter 10, Step 2; Chapter 8
- Summary: Chapter 13, Synopsis, *A midsummer night's dream*
- Nouns and adjectives: Chapter 11, Steps 4, 8
- Mental and linguistic verbs: Chapter 13, Steps 2, 5

- Holding verb tenses: present tense: Chapter 11
- Active listening check: Chapter 12, Step 2 (direct instruction)
- Comprehension checks and following direct instruction: Chapter 12, Step 3
- Debating connection oral to written language: Chapter 11, Step 8
- Structured note-taking sheets: Chapter 9; Chapter 8
- Brainstorming, categorising and excluding: Chapter 13, Step 2
- Highlighting key words: Chapter 12; Chapter 10; Chapter 13 (Mark Antony speech)
- Inference and idiom: Chapter 11; Chapter 9
- Opening sentence(s) to get started with writing: Chapter 11, Steps 6, 8
- Structuring an essay: Appendix 4
- PowerPoint presentation: Chapter 8

CHAPTER 6

Nurturing self-awareness, empathy and resilience

LLD students need the opportunity, within the curriculum, to develop self-awareness and empathy, to improve their interpersonal skills, and to nurture their own resilience and self-reflection. These are often areas of significant weakness. Combined with the still-developing cognition and emotions of adolescence, they make for a confusing and at times volatile mix. LLD students who are more severely impaired in these areas may not see the need to interact and can be very passive when communicating.

The key areas to be considered in curriculum planning include:

- assessing the presenting language difficulties
- developing and maintaining relationships with teachers, support staff, peers, family and significant adults
- implementing a curriculum that builds self-awareness and empathy
- developing persistence in tasks
- creating the environment that enables LLD students to achieve their potential.

There are many excellent programs that foster social skills and group work, but the focus of this chapter is on building reflection and feedback into curriculum tasks. It must be acknowledged that insight, self-control and emotions are not fully developed in adolescents, and continue to develop well past the secondary school years. Even with excellent curriculum and encouragement, skills in these areas may not be achieved by LLD students until the post-school years.

How language disability impacts on the development of self-awareness, resilience and empathy

Adolescents with LLD have difficulty with oral language comprehension and expression due to underlying problems in vocabulary and grammar, including difficulty understanding abstract words and ideas. These problems also impact on their reading, spelling and written language. In the areas of self-awareness and empathy, LLD students often struggle because they do not effectively use language to question, clarify, persuade or sustain conversation. When they try, often it is interpreted negatively by others. Throughout their lives, LLD students find it hard to express emotions and explain their point of view through language. They are often the children who become withdrawn or act out at primary school because they cannot explain themselves or the reasons behind their actions. When working in the curriculum, LLD students express this in a number of ways.

- They find it hard to take the point of view of others.

- They have a black-and-white view. This means they become quite agitated with paradox—where two or more opposing ideas can be equally valid. Most of their lives they have struggled to understand and find the 'correct' answers, and have suffered embarrassment due to their failures. They often feel insecure when they must consider many options and when there is no definite right or wrong position. This insecurity may be directed as anger towards teachers, or as enormous reluctance to begin or complete a task.

- They feel it is impossible to argue for a point of view which they do not believe.

- Humour is something LLD students struggle to understand. This is apparent in the general classroom, with peers and in literature. The students themselves may come across as humourless, socially inept and ungracious.

Laura struggled to understand and enjoy the humour of *A midsummer night's dream*. She felt that it was not humorous and, to make matters worse, it was stupid. She was particularly critical of the behaviour of the two main female characters and of the dialogue, where exaggeration plays a part in the humour. After teaching the unit in detail, the teacher divided the class into small groups. Each group prepared a section of the play and then performed it, in sequence, for the class. Through this process, Laura finally understood humour and exaggeration in a way that was impossible to describe. In the end, she liked the play and was prepared to concede it was a comedy—although she declared her intention never to tell any man she would be his lap dog!

- Tasks that require imagination are difficult. Empathy for others requires reorientation to the other's point of view and a leap of imagination, and also requires a capacity to deal with complex grammar and thought processes. LLD students' concrete rather than abstract vocabulary knowledge means that they require explicit instruction, and sufficient time to establish the emotional connections and personalise feelings in such tasks as the analysis of films, novels and texts.

- They struggle to classify and group ideas. LLD students can get lost in the breadth and complexity of the language involved in researching and systematising information. Limited self-awareness means that they do not always realise that the confusion they feel is what makes them disengaged and sometimes angry.

- They often do not have the language to describe or understand the range and subtlety of emotions.
- If ideas do not match their social experience and world view, LLD students reject them and quickly switch off.

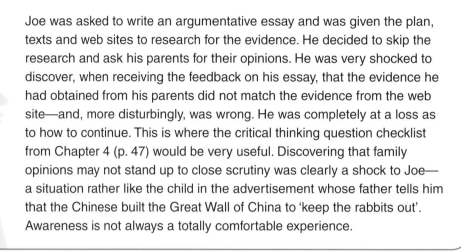

Joe was asked to write an argumentative essay and was given the plan, texts and web sites to research for the evidence. He decided to skip the research and ask his parents for their opinions. He was very shocked to discover, when receiving the feedback on his essay, that the evidence he had obtained from his parents did not match the evidence from the web site—and, more disturbingly, was wrong. He was completely at a loss as to how to continue. This is where the critical thinking question checklist from Chapter 4 (p. 47) would be very useful. Discovering that family opinions may not stand up to close scrutiny was clearly a shock to Joe— a situation rather like the child in the advertisement whose father tells him that the Chinese built the Great Wall of China to 'keep the rabbits out'. Awareness is not always a totally comfortable experience.

The story of Dan, and the importance of parents

One reason for depression and anxiety in LLD students at secondary level is poor skill development. This is why it is important to continue to develop skills as discussed in previous chapters. However, the emotional resilience that LLD students need can rarely be achieved without the support of significant others, including counsellors and parents.

Counselling for feelings of depression is not enough on its own and, to be effective, should be accompanied by changes to the learning environment, and the involvement and support of parents. Those students who cope best are realistic about their difficulties, prepared to seek help and, ideally, have wise parents.

Many LLD students can manage to hold themselves together at school in front of their peers, but at home it is their parents who bear the brunt of their feelings of failure, expressed through tears, moodiness and a pervading sense of hopelessness. It is very difficult for a parent (usually the mother) to constantly encourage a son or daughter experiencing these feelings and to keep their self-esteem high.

Resilient: *People and things that are resilient are able to recover easily and quickly from unpleasant or damaging events.*

(Collins 2001)

Adolescent LLD students need time, adult mentoring and practice that leads to success before they can develop resilience.

Dan is 21 years old. He is the youngest in a family of five, and is a very handsome man with dark hair, dark eyes and olive skin. He retains the quality of reliable persistence that has been the hallmark of his character from childhood. As a young boy, Dan had major comprehension and memory problems, and he often masked the confusion he felt with a broad smile. These problems persist today. Although his difficulties were quite evident to his parents, he passed unnoticed through the early years of primary school because he looked no different from other children, and was blessed with excellent coordination and good social skills. However, by secondary school, he was struggling with the curriculum and comprehension.

Dan's parents do not have a tertiary education and have limited financial resources; however their optimism and their capacity to realistically assess options enabled Dan to get on with life and be positive in handling adversity. It especially helped when he was not able, despite high motivation and application, to achieve his dream of becoming a builder or carpenter, because of his disability.

Parents talking: encouragement

[Dan would] get depressed and say, 'It's not fair. Maria and Bernard [his siblings] don't do any studying and they're at the top of the class.'

And I said to him, 'Well, love, we're all born with gifts.' I said, 'They've got that gift.'

He looked at me and said, 'What are my gifts?'

I said, 'Your gifts are that you stick at things. You have the ability to work hard and you stick at things. You don't get sidetracked.' I said, 'That is a gift.'

'Oh, I'd prefer to have another gift, one that I didn't have to study.'

I said, 'Yeah, okay, you may prefer that, but a lot of kids that are born with these gifts waste them.'

(Dan's mother)

The experience of Dan's mother helped Dan in:

- decision making
- helping him face his problem
- encouragement
- timing
- watchful supervision
- preparation for the next step in his life
- planning his education and career
- not assuming guilt and blame.

It's not the boss's fault, it's my fault, and I can't help it. This is the way I am.

(Dan's comment when he realised he could not be a carpenter because of his language disorder—he could not retain the instructions from his boss)

Some parents need a lot of support themselves to be able to assist their children. It can be particularly difficult for parents who have not understood the extent of the comprehension and memory problems of their children until secondary school. Over the years, they may have blamed teachers and schools for the significant behaviour and learning difficulties they have had to deal with at home.

Parents talking: support

Interviewer: How would you describe Dan's problems to someone?

Dan's mother: Well, I'd just say he was born with a language disorder and that means without the ability to learn how to express himself properly, and so he had to be taught how. And they usually said, 'Was he really? You wouldn't think so now. He speaks all right now.' I said, 'Yeah, but if you listen to him you realise how limited his language is and if he's trying to explain something to you or trying to tell you something, he gets a bit tongue-tied because he can't think of the right words.' And they would say, 'Well, I didn't notice that.' And I don't think they would. I don't think that they believed me—some of them, even his bosses, say, 'No, no, not Dan— no, he speaks all right.'

Interviewer: And what about the understanding? That was a problem for him, wasn't it? He's an intelligent person.

Dan's mother: Yes. Well, to this day, if I'm telling him about something that's happening, I look at him and I say, 'Do you understand that? Do you know what I mean? Do you know (whatever word it was that I thought that he might have trouble with), do you know what that means?'

And he'll say, 'No. I haven't got a clue.' And then I'll go and explain it to him, and he'll say, 'Ah, is *that* what you said.'

Interviewer: He still has comprehension problems?

Dan's mother: Yes, yes. Things that have happened at work and he's told me about them, and he'll say he didn't understand at first. But in time he's understood. He won't come out and say, 'Explain that to me' at the time.

The importance of relationships in the development of self-awareness and empathy

The development of self-awareness and empathy in LLD students relies extensively on modelling and explicit instruction from significant adults, followed by practice. The school contact person for individual LLD students needs to be highly adept at relating to these students and the range of people involved with them. It should be clear to the student that this support person is 'on their side' and will act as an advocate for them. The support person should have the opportunity to explain to staff the impact of comprehension and other difficulties on behaviour and should also be present when the student receives appropriate discipline so that misdemeanours and consequences can be reinterpreted and reinforced.

Students who are very vulnerable in this area need individual work with an experienced counsellor, and ready access to a support person.

> From Year 7 onwards, Helen, an LLD student, suffered extreme anxiety with the change of teachers. This anxiety showed in a very hostile manner toward any new teacher who was invariably described from day one as 'not as good as the old one'. Helen was convinced that the problem lay totally with the teacher and, as a result, was impossible to fix. Hours were spent with the counsellor discussing the difficulty. This continued for several years and the pattern became very predictable.
>
> Part of Helen's work with the counsellor and school support staff involved bringing to her an awareness that her problem was one of anxiety, then practising how to ask questions and clarify expectations with new teachers using role plays. This led to a decrease in the verbal attacks on teachers. Feedback and practice increased Helen's self-awareness, but change in her behaviour was slow. Clearly, the school would not be able to achieve all that is necessary here, and life and work experiences will have to play a significant role.

While it is important that students have their point of view heard, it is the follow-up practice and feedback that will bring about the most change in self-awareness and empathy. Careful instruction in finding evidence in a text, finding explanations for the motives of characters or predicting what might happen next in a character's development all provide opportunities to develop awareness of the validity of individual differences. Connecting behaviours with the reasons for the behaviours helps LLD students understand their own motivations as well as the motivations of others. Then, rather than answering questions by adding information from their own experiences—which may have no direct relevance to the question or task, and which can be very embarrassing—LLD students can then be more relevant in their comments.

Giving and receiving feedback

Clear guidelines about how to give and receive feedback with peers and with adults should be included in group work tasks for LLD students. This is important in developing self-awareness and empathy. LLD students frequently have difficulties with peer acceptance and peer interaction, and often misinterpret both verbal and non-verbal cues. Both negative and positive interaction is often misinterpreted. For those who have weak social skills, even friendly overtures can be seen as unfriendly. If anxiety, anger and frustration build up, then students project these feelings onto others, particularly onto their teachers and mothers. In general, comments that explicitly state or imply blame of others signal this type of difficulty.

Terry had been in trouble since he started school. He was defiant and angry, and had a short temper. He would not abide by uniform rules and had to be constantly monitored for attendance. He had normal IQ and was a wonderful sportsman, although he often got into fights in casual sport because he could not cope if rules were interpreted or changed. When he was asked to explain himself, he could not. Words would not come out, and he would often swear and storm off, in trouble again.

When his language comprehension was tested, it was found that Terry had great difficulty understanding what people said to him; in fact, he could not accurately understand the instructions and information he heard. To help him understand, sentences had to be kept short and repeated. He had a severe language learning disability that affected his learning at school and his personal development.

Curriculum planning to support self-awareness and empathy

The following general principles of curriculum planning can assist in developing LLD students' self-awareness and ability to empathise.

- *Keep a long-term focus.* Opportunities for repetition and skill development should be included in the curriculum over several years. This allows time and charts progress so that LLD students can see how far they have come.

- *Engage in teamwork.* Engaging in teamwork should occur across year levels and between faculties, especially in the practising of group roles, and in giving and receiving feedback.

- *Give detailed instructions.* To encourage persistence, instructions should break down tasks, and allow students to check off sections as they are completed.

- *Use group work.* Areas such as debating, drama and public speaking are underutilised as methods for teaching self-awareness and empathy, especially to LLD students.

- *Include clear statements and check understanding.* Always check LLD students' understanding of audience and purpose.

- *Continue long-term, systematic instruction in literacy.* This will increase the opportunities for LLD students to develop more sophisticated language skills. Failure to achieve in literacy makes students feel ashamed and often angry. Angry, embarrassed people rarely show empathy and self-awareness.

- *Allow enough time.* Allow the necessary time to develop the skills of organisation, written language and complex comprehension. The cognitive effort involved to reorganise and develop more sophisticated thinking is exhausting for many LLD students, and the effort involved needs to be acknowledged.

- *Give individual, face-to-face feedback.* Feedback from peers and teachers is the key to self-awareness and change in the long run, but it can be very threatening initially.

Strategies and explicit instruction to deal with both compliments and criticism are necessary. Personalised and respectful feedback within clearly explained parameters assists in the development of resilience for LLD students.

- *Encourage success and positive self-image.* Engineer success early on to build self-image. Successfully completing tasks and feeling that skills are developing builds confidence that problems can be tackled (even if at first this only means knowing where to seek help or clarification). It is important to experience some successes initially, so that LLD students develop resilience when inevitably things do not go well, and they fail a task, are reprimanded or meet an unsympathetic teacher.

- *Work on anxiety and motivation.* Include specific programs to help students understand their own anxiety and motivation. This especially relates to negative self-talk and subsequent anger or avoidance (see Chapter 2).

Empathy and interpreting social situations

One approach to engaging LLD students and increasing their understanding is to provide tasks based on texts that appear to match LLD students' experiences. However, this will not automatically lead to engagement or understanding of the motivations of characters. Making connections to existing knowledge and experience requires systematic teaching.

LLD students tend to interpret social situations in a relatively unsophisticated way. This results in difficulty understanding and predicting what characters will do in complex texts, and in recognising that characters' responses will differ from what they would do themselves in a similar situation. Some popular teen literature and movies use a conversational style typical of the everyday interactions of teenagers: they use simple sentences, and tend to keep character development minimal and emotional intensity high. This is what makes them appealing to students. To develop insight, however, LLD students need exposure to more complex character development and the inherent paradoxes in people to improve their understanding of the nuances and detail in social situations. Very short stories, such as in *Paper windows* (Baines 2001) and *Paper families* (Baines 2000), and drama studies all contribute to understanding people and social situations.

Explicitly identifying students' current knowledge and belief system

- What do I already know about this?
- Is this totally new to me?
- Does the character behave in ways that make sense to me?
- What do I find confusing about the behaviour of the character?
- What emotion do I feel for the character? (Provide a short list to select from if students have significant difficulty in this area.)
- Why do I feel this?

Then go on to find evidence in the text.

LLD students need help to move from their personal understandings to the wider viewpoint, and to move their focus from self to community and then to the wider global perspective. They are not always ready to take a broader world view, and can quickly disengage if curriculum is taken too quickly or too far from their personal understanding of the world. Understanding and empathy continue to develop as they mature, particularly after they leave school and move into work.

Teaching empathy through ethics modules

Successful and challenging modules which have developed empathy and awareness in LLD students, and extended thinking beyond self to broader social issues and consequences, can be found in the ethics and morality units in the Victorian (VCE) curriculum. While written for the senior years, these types of units can be a beneficial part of a Year 10 program, although some LLD students will require modification to the content and outcomes. The ethical decision-making module challenges students to at least be aware of different perspectives, including what they themselves bring to the understanding of the ethical dilemma.

Experienced teachers say that at Year 10 level, LLD students need to be carefully led into the language and thinking involved in ethics, especially as the language and concepts move from concrete to abstract. It is necessary to spend time discussing what 'abstract' means and contrasting examples like 'the sky', which can be seen, with the emotion of 'love', which cannot. Without careful introduction to this more complex work, LLD students can become anxious and decide too quickly that they cannot do the work; their confidence drops and they give up. At first, LLD students may say that they 'don't understand and will never understand'. One student expressed her initial anxiety and lack of confidence by saying that she was 'not going into that way of thinking'.

Supporting LLD students by providing overall themes and categories, allowing them to stand with their group when presenting an individual section of work, increasing teacher time and feedback (both face-to-face and via emails), and carefully structuring oral and written responses has enabled LLD students to participate in these more demanding but cognitively stimulating lessons. Interestingly, teachers say that in the second half of Year 10, students show significant improvement in their ability to deal with the more complex language and thinking of ethics. This coincides with an increase in abstract language across all curriculum areas, which, although demanding, allows LLD students to begin the difficult but important task of learning to detach their reason from their emotions.

This process, in turn, enables them to be sufficiently emotionally removed to tackle a difficult topic like euthanasia. For example, they may be able to understand the perspective of a terminally ill teenager (as in the video *Someone had to be Benny* (1997)) by focusing instead on the process of ethical decision making. In another example, before they study the novel *To kill a mockingbird*, students might look at photographs taken during the Great Depression and analyse the emotions of the faces of the people. Both these units provide challenging material and at the same time connect to wider concerns. The BBC 'Ethical issues' web site presents arguments for and against many ethical issues, and can be very useful for developing key vocabulary and structuring responses: see <http://www.bbc.co.uk/religion/ethics>.

> After a significant amount of class work on an ethics topic, a Year 10 student, Anna, had the task of working through an ethical decision-making model to reach her ethical decision on an issue. She arrived for her individual session very agitated and reluctant to work through the steps. Her belief was that she was not a person who could make an ethical decision.
>
> By very slowly working through the teacher's instructions and steps, she finally came to the last question and, to her surprise, spontaneously came out with her opinion. The look of amazement on her face was a delight to behold. The speech pathologist quietly said, 'That is your ethical decision ...' And just to keep the understanding that it was possible to change an ethical decision, she added, '... with the knowledge and understanding you have at this time'.

Feeling comfortable with different points of view

LLD students need curriculum that helps develop awareness of different points of view and familiarity with the idea that there may be more than one way to look at a problem or issue. LLD students benefit from explicit instruction in the purpose and use of thinking strategies such as those in Bloom's *Taxonomy of educational objectives* (1984), Gardner's *Theory of multiple intelligences* (1983), De Bono's 'six thinking hats' (1992) or Ryan's *Thinker's keys* (1990). Many of the processes underlying these thinking techniques require the understanding and generation of questions—a key underlying difficulty with LLD students. However, they provide wonderful opportunities for LLD students to practise and hear quality questions. Dalton and Smith's (1986) work provides excellent ideas for questions: see the web site at <http://www.teachers.ash.org.au/researchskills/dalton.htm>.

Resilience and persistence

Resilience comes from persistence and a sense of hope that achievement is possible. Develop persistence by:

- working at individual skill level, with a focus on skill development
- explaining the purpose and restating this as needed
- providing achievement feedback and timelines to help LLD students see their progress

- physically ticking off steps as students move through tasks—assignments need to be carefully sequenced
- setting core work that looks manageable, and modifying as necessary
- developing and expecting a 'completer–finisher–hand it in' mentality.

Parents can be an enormous help to schools in developing the 'completer–finisher–hand it in' mentality. Tom, and several of his classmates, had not completed their term's work, despite extra time and classes provided for them to do so. With the support of Tom's parents, in the first two days of the holidays the school ran a 'finishing course', where students came in school uniform and completed any outstanding work. At first, Tom was shocked that he would be required to go to school in the holidays to complete work, and surprised that his parents thought it was a very reasonable request. The same problem did not happen in the next school holidays, because Tom took advantage of the homework club and extra classes during term to hand everything in.

Connections to Section 2

- Teaching mental and linguistic verbs, and thinking and feeling verbs: Chapter 13, Step 2
- Taking the point of view of others: Chapter 11, Step 6; Chapter 9; Chapter 8
- Teen language: Chapter 9

CHAPTER 7

Memory: helping LLD students remember what you teach them

Students with LLD often find it difficult to remember information, and to identify and remember overall themes and ideas. In most psychological assessments, students with LLD have short-term auditory memory (STAM) or working memory (WM) results significantly below those of their peers. STAM is defined as 'information you need to remember for just a few seconds or minutes' (Nelson 2005, p. 2) while WM is 'a form of short term memory that is a bit more complex. [It] comprises information that you hold in mind for a brief time to use for some specific purpose' (Nelson 2005, p. 2). Although our understanding of working memory and our application of this knowledge is still in its infancy, it is currently conceptualised in the following way.

Working memory and LLD students

Models of working memory identify several parts of the brain that are involved in the overall storage, processing and retrieval of information. Assessment of LLD students consistently finds difficulties in this area.

Figure 7.1 The Baddeley and Hitch working memory model

Central executive

Selective attentional control

Planning and decision making

Phonological loop	**Episodic buffer**	**Visuospatial sketch pad**
Short-term storage of verbal material	Short-term storage of event complexities	Short-term storage of visual and spatial images
Rehearsal of words	Binding together things not previously associated	
Numbers (7+/−2)		

(Baddeley 2006)

87

According to the Baddeley and Hitch model, the central executive coordinates information coming in from three subsystems: the phonological loop, the episodic buffer and the visuospatial sketch pad. In its coordination role, the central executive decides what is relevant, and supervises and directs the subsystems. It also accesses long-term memory. Its role in maintaining attention is critical, as tasks usually require more than one subsystem of working memory.

The phonological loop has to do with remembering sound. Accurate memory for verbal information decays rapidly, so articulatory rehearsal of words—a component of the phonological loop—actively works to prevent this decay by repeating the information. Repeating a phone number or information over and over to remember it before writing it down is an example of the phonological working memory in action, and an example of how important competent literacy is in managing any weakness in this subsystem. In LLD students, the phonological loop is particularly vulnerable to interference from other noise or distractions.

The visuospatial sketch pad is involved in establishing the meaning of what we see, and how and where this information is located. For example, a watch is a watch no matter how it is located in space—upside down, sideways, etc.—or where it is (on the wrist, or the table). However, in real life, the working memory subsystems rarely function in an isolated fashion. If the object we see is known to us, we recall the past representations and associated meanings related to this image that are stored in long-term memory. By giving what we see a name, we also involve the functioning of the phonological loop. The episodic buffer temporarily holds information from the other two subsystems and makes connections between these areas of information.

LLD students generally have difficulties in all four areas of working memory: the phonological loop, the episodic buffer, the visuospatial sketch pad and the central executive (Gathercole, Lamont & Alloway 2006). Good articles on working memory, and a teacher- and parent-friendly overview, can be found at the University of York's 'Articles on working memory' web page: <http://www.york.ac.uk/res/wml/ArticlesTeachers.htm>.

> *You will conquer the present suspiciously fast if you smell of the future but stink of the past.*
>
> (Hein 1968, p. 21)

Working memory deficits have a significant impact on academic performance (Pickering 2006). The classroom places heavy demands on working memory. For LLD students, who perform significantly below their peers in tests of working memory, difficulties begin to surface from the moment they have to listen to a teacher's instructions and then carry out tasks. These difficulties follow through to written language. When LLD students are required to read instructions and then write a response, they may forget the question they are answering and rapidly digress, or they may find it hard to write anything at all. Working memory deficits impact on all areas of the curriculum, from vocabulary acquisition to oral and written comprehension, and mental arithmetic.

Modern school environments are very busy places where multitasking is the norm. Students have to rapidly swap between listening, writing and talking while holding the overall task or goal in mind. In highly verbal and rapidly changing school environments, it is common for original instructions to be modified while a task is in progress. In school settings, information is often held for a short time in working memory while one task is completed, then working memory is wiped clean for another completely different task. Sometimes, students are then asked to return to the earlier task. Working memory deficits make these rapidly changing learning environments very stressful for LLD students, whose anxiety is further heightened by the fact that many of them are well aware of their memory difficulties.

This chapter will outline general steps involved in memory acquisition with specific comments on LLD students related to the Baddeley and Hitch model. Principles of curriculum planning designed to maximise the initial storage of information, improve organisation and allow for recall, repetition and pattern identification will be discussed. Examples of the application of these principles are given in Section 2.

Steps involved in memory

Nelson (2005) suggests that the following sequential steps are crucial for recall from memory.

1 Acquisition of the information

This is the first critical step in the function of memory. Given their STAM and WM difficulties, it is frequently a struggle for LLD students to get information into memory in the first place. Comprehension is critical. Continuous checking needs to be built into the curriculum here so that 'deep' rather than 'shallow' learning takes place. LLD students' ability to remember is supported with increased structure in the curriculum, and by showing any patterns or grouping of sounds, words or ideas which will lead to better categorisation and storage of information.

Time for rehearsal, and access to examples of concepts or good work from other students (such as essays written by peers), are helpful, as is the opportunity and time to relate curriculum material to LLD students' personal experience. When using written material, there are benefits in the teacher explicitly identifying key words, sentences or paragraphs that are critical for understanding and recall, and using highlighter pens to identify them. An overview is best done before adding in more detail.

2 Consolidation to retain information over time

Repetition of tasks and periodic review are critical for LLD students. Repetition of tasks allows for increased comprehension, and periodic review helps consolidate memory. It helps if there is some novelty in the repetition, as LLD students do not always see the advantages of repetition, recall and review. While it is standard practice to recap key information and terms at the beginning of every lesson, these need to be reinforced throughout the lesson and at its conclusion.

In a crowded curriculum, LLD students do not get the repetition they need to consolidate skills before they are moved on to the next step. As it is, they have difficulty shifting information from working memory to long-term memory. The shaky foundations of their initial learning can crumble when further layers of complexity are added to a weak base.

3 Retrieval—'taking it out of storage'

Key skills need to be used regularly at first, and then intermittently to ensure consolidation. This is where long-term curriculum planning is important—it needs to factor in the years taken to acquire key skills and build them from a simple to a complex level. LLD students will retrieve information better if they can connect it to previously learnt material and build on what they have established already, rather than learn information as discrete units. LLD students must be called on to retrieve so there is a chance to check learning and reconsolidate.

Retrieval is very vulnerable to anxiety, fatigue and distractions. With this in mind, it is important to encourage students to retain carefully organised notes and complete written tasks. It is not only LLD students who swear that they have never written an essay or report before, when we know full well that they have. A concrete reminder can be helpful.

4 Forgetting

No one retains everything they learn. Everyone forgets, but LLD students have a greater chance of forgetting—particularly the language and sequence of tasks—than most of their peers. Forgetting is part of learning for everyone. The rather depressing statistic from research is that up to 90 per cent of new learning is forgotten within 24 hours (Sousa, 1995). Further discussion of the susceptibility of STAM to forgetting can be found at the SparkNotes web site: <http://www.sparknotes.com/psychology/cognitive/memory>.

Given that this level of forgetting is normal, it becomes important to plan curriculum in ways that consolidate memory. If particular skills and information are critical in the mastery of a subject, then they need to be firmly established in the long-term memory of LLD students. For key or complex material, LLD students need a quiet environment to listen to what they have learned, and to reorganise and consolidate it. The weaker auditory system in LLD students is particularly vulnerable to interference and distraction in noisy environments.

Long-term memory and recall can be checked using the following strategies.

- Revisit a task no sooner than 24 hours after learning. Good programs for LLD students incorporate knowledge of their working memory difficulties. They require students to demonstrate mastery of the same task at least three times, with at least 24 hours between each trial, to increase the chances that students will be able to store and recall important information in long-term memory.

- Test exactly what has been taught.

- Give brief quizzes with no warning. This approach is generally only helpful for LLD students after a significant period of teaching, and when the teacher is reasonably confident that most of the language and concepts are familiar to a student.

> *Consider repeating key ideas within 10 minutes of the original learning, again 48 hours later, and then tie it all together 7 days later.*
>
> (Jensen 2005, p. 141)

School-based assessment of working memory

Given an increased awareness of the significant impact of working memory on learning, some schools are administering screening tests to evaluate students' working memory capacity. The Automated Working Memory Assessment (AWMA) (Alloway 2007) is a computerised test available to teachers. This test provides a screening assessment of three key areas of the Baddeley and Hitch model mentioned previously: the central executive, the phonological loop and the visuospatial sketch pad. At the time of writing, researchers are still to identify a range of tasks to assess the episodic buffer. The task of sentence repetition, which students with LLD perform particularly poorly on, provides some measure of episodic buffer (Alloway & Gathercole 2005).

The working memory model and the difficulties of LLD students

Central executive

- LLD students have difficulties in areas such as:
  - attending to key words and ideas when presented orally or in reading
  - selecting a topic to write about
  - making decisions about what information to include or exclude
  - keeping the topic in mind and staying on task when completing written work.

- Many LLD students do not consciously or spontaneously use memory strategies, such as memory hook devices (for example, PQRST—Preview, Question, Read, State, Test). These devices can be very effective if they are used, and can help LLD students to recall what they need to do, how to prepare for exams, or how to edit and check their work (Crowe 2006). For effective use, these strategies need to be part of study notes or material that LLD students have studied and are expected to recall.

- They have problems organising, grouping and structuring information. These problems also make information, vocabulary and ideas difficult to recall.

- Swapping strategies when the strategy being used is not working, or changing from a habitual way of doing things to a novel way, are very demanding for LLD students. They often continue to use the same strategy despite its ineffectiveness, and their previous failure with it. This is often quite clear in organisational and written language tasks.

The phonological loop and listening difficulties

- LLD students have more limited ability to take in information presented orally. While we know that STAM storage is, by definition, short, it is even shorter for those with LLD because of their problems in the phonological loop. Decay occurs quickly (in less than 20 seconds) unless there is an opportunity for repetition and practice.

- LLD students do not process all of the auditory material. This means that in conversations and when processing instructions, nouns and verbs are generally processed but other language features will not be within the capacity of the STAM. These features include adjectives, adverbs and complex embedded sentences.

- Poor storage of auditory information leads to difficulties with recall and—like holes in cheese—information falls through. LLD students are often not aware that information has been lost or not stored in the first place. They may be genuine in saying that they did not 'hear' the information and rapidly become confused, especially if it is key information that has not been stored. Confusion precipitates anxiety and anger.

- LLD students need to support weak working memory through literacy. With an already weak working memory, these students are doubly disadvantaged if they are not given detailed literacy instruction, starting with simple sound–symbol correspondence and working through to decoding multisyllabic words. The best practical support for weak working memory is literacy.

- Deficits in memory show in limited variety in language. LLD students go on to reflect deficits in the storage of oral language in their own oral and written language. They do not store the full range of language features and subsequently need direct instruction in identifying patterns that their peers find much easier to store.

The episodic buffer and difficulties connecting ideas

- LLD students have difficulty making connections to existing information. This is either because of poor initial storage, or slower than average retrieval. LLD students need a lot of teacher modelling where teachers make explicit the thinking processes that underlie their conclusions, as well as make explicit connections to existing information. The importance of preteaching has been discussed in *One in eleven* (Brent, Gough & Robinson 2001) and involves taking students through key vocabulary and ideas in a small group before the topic is introduced to the larger class. This allows the additional time needed to make connections and understand vocabulary.

- As a result of poor connections to previously learnt material, many tasks seem completely new, so an overview or revision is required to make the necessary connections.

> As part of a review of LLD students' research skills in Year 9, students were asked to find books in the library when given a call number. Significant numbers of students had not consolidated this skill. The same difficulty was found with refining terms to find information using search engines. Reinstructing across disciplines in this skill needs to be done over many years.

- Understanding inference is impaired. Because LLD students have difficulty connecting previously learnt material with new material, and with seeing connections within the material currently being presented, they often draw erroneous conclusions or fail to draw a conclusion at all.

- Sentence and paragraph recall is limited. The recall of sentences and paragraphs is highly dependent on understanding context and prior knowledge, as well as on linguistic ability and attention. This is a particularly difficult task for LLD students.

The visuospatial sketch pad

- A frequent problem for many students with learning difficulties is accurately connecting visual images to language, and recalling them for future use. This is the result of a deficit in their short-term storage of visuospatial information (Gathercole & Alloway 2006).

- Students do not develop visual representation for words. This poorly developed visual representation applies to images of the meaning of the word, and to the letter sequences used to write the word. Because of this, words—abstract words in particular—are poorly understood. The students do not have images for words like 'sarcastic' or 'slaughter'. Forming accurate and firm images helps with both storage and the accurate use of words.

- Storage of the visual patterns of words for both reading and spelling is weak. This is especially so if students have not been exposed to detailed phonics instruction which matches sounds to letter strings, such as 'igh' and 'ea'. Detailed phonics work gives support for visual recall. The way in which words and sentences are recalled when spelling and writing gives a window into the phonological and visual memory difficulties of LLD students.

Working memory speed

As task demands increase, working memory can slow down. The following strategies can assist LLD students in this area.

- Give students additional time to process information.

> *Without the quiet processing time much learning is never transferred to long term memory.*
>
> (Jensen 1998, p. 109)

- Realise that time pressure will decrease performance of information processing, especially in complex tasks.

- Allow five seconds for retrieval of information for students who are slow processors (Rowe 1986). This increases time for retrieval. If questions are asked and answered too quickly, students will stop trying to retrieve information. LLD students need to learn to retrieve to complete many school and work tasks. Quick retrieval of language is needed when writing notes and essays, and is also a way to check their comprehension.

- Check comprehension and storage of information. Improvement in comprehension and the storage of information results in significant gains in recall and therefore performance.

- Provide a detailed, systematic way to approach tasks. Having a consistent plan is very helpful when approaching a task, as it allows LLD students to focus on the content and meaning.

- Consider using computer-based training programs. Computer-based programs are being developed to improve working memory, but these programs need further research. Currently, it is hard to tell which students will improve by using these programs, and in which ways or areas they will improve. However, we can still use current software to provide support to LLD students for their working memory difficulties. We already have technology that allows for the provision of notes, summaries, assignments and worksheets online. Voice-activated software has improved remarkably, as has the software which enhances literacy acquisition and enables LLD students to try their hand at writing more complex ideas.

Student strategies

To accommodate slow processing speed, LLD students should use the following strategies.

- *Be aware of their processing speed deficit.* When students understand that they process information more slowly than others, they can then form an accurate idea of the time they need to complete a task, and what they can realistically achieve under time pressure. When language processing is slow and effortful, it takes time to understand the task and to make decisions about what will be included and what will be omitted. All areas of language, from selection of vocabulary to the sequencing of ideas in paragraphs and sentences, take longer than for other students.

- *Undertake subject-specific and task-specific planning and organisation.* Teachers can compensate for slow processing speed by detailed planning that organises material into a sequence and hierarchy. Good examples or practical models from other students can also be helpful. LLD students can then rehearse the plans (for example, for the structure of an essay) without time pressure. Then, when they are under timed conditions (such as in exams), they need to use the critical skills of preplanning, organisation and rehearsal to achieve success and complete their work.

- *Rehearse tasks.* Practising important skills increases speed.

- *Record key information in a form that is easily accessible under exam conditions.* Notes in dot points, or, even better, in table form will support slower processing. Good examples can be found in the *Macquarie study guides* series in Victoria (Macmillan 2008). Study notes set out in this way can more easily transfer to a structured written format at either the paragraph or essay level.

- *Colour-code and highlight key words.* Identifying key words in both questions and notes can provide an opportunity to check comprehension.

Teacher strategies

To accommodate slow processing speed, teachers need to use the following strategies.

- *Include timelines in students' assignments* and projects, and monitor progress.

- *Be aware* that it may take LLD students a lot longer to complete work than their peers, and set homework accordingly.

- *Modify the work if necessary.* With thoughtful curriculum planning, it is often not necessary to modify all work in all subjects for LLD students.

- *Provide structure for oral and written presentation.* If a student runs out of time (under timed conditions), planning and structure enables students to at least write key words or a topic sentence, with several points underneath, to show understanding of the question. This is particularly important in external exams when little modification or additional time is allowed and students still need to show what they know.

- *Provide an overview of the subject and summaries of key points.* Study guides provide these, as do many class texts. Teachers should take LLD students through these summaries rather than set them as an independent homework task.

- *Integrate information from class discussions into an overview.* Key concepts and ideas discussed in class need to be recorded in point form. Teachers need to provide notes or appoint a competent student as a note taker or summariser of oral discussions so there is a written record for the LLD student at the end of the process.

- *Factor in rehearsal followed by writing under timed conditions.* This is especially important in the planning processes for essays.

- *Discuss past exam papers in detail and practise how to approach them.* Consider the essay structure and the sequence in which to approach it, but also where to start and what to do first. Also, work with students on organising the timing of answers, reading time, etc.

- *Provide examples of lead-in phrases and key starting sentences.* These also increase speed, especially under timed conditions like exams.

Curriculum planning that supports STAM and working memory

As mentioned earlier, all four areas in the Baddeley and Hitch model of working memory can be implicated in the learning difficulties seen in LLD students. To support their difficulties with processing and storing information across the different areas of working memory, the curriculum units in Section 2 pay careful attention to providing short and clearly expressed instructions in a step-by-step manner. There are opportunities to check comprehension, and the LLD student's ability to accurately rephrase or repeat instructions. There is also an emphasis on vocabulary—from the accurate storage of the word for reading and spelling, to attaching visual images to the word (see the curriculum-based comprehension checklist, Chapter 4, p. 39).

Additional supports, providing the key words for those students who need them (such as in cloze activities), are included. Storage difficulties increase retrieval problems. Information may not leave short-term memory and go into working memory and long-term memory: instead the incomplete fragments may be lost. It helps if information is held accurately in STAM in the first place.

In busy classrooms, working memory difficulties are most likely to occur when:

- information is lengthy and/or not organised or chunked for the student; for example, when a lot of information is presented orally, when a student has to recall long lists of numbers or words, or when copying from the board

- multitasking, which is a constant requirement; for example, listening while writing in the diary or record book
- the task requires rapid switching between tasks or modalities, which occurs frequently in classrooms; for example, when a teacher gives one set of instructions, then alters the instructions while the student is carrying out the task. This is especially difficult if changes are not clearly signalled.

> Peter was a student with severe working memory limitations, particularly in the area of executive processing. He struggled to write essays, and had to be reinstructed at every paragraph of the essay to keep the purpose in mind. However, if he was given a sequenced set of questions, and ticked each one off as he completed it, he was able to work independently and stay on task.

Feedback and check sheets

Given their working memory difficulties, it is critical that LLD students have regular feedback so that learning, especially in complex tasks, continues to progress. Feedback is critical to improving learning, especially for LLD students who may not have processed all the key ideas the first time and need a more interactive approach with feedback. By receiving and discussing their feedback, LLD students have a chance to refine and enrich their memory for key processes. Then, with repetition, they can consolidate their memories. Chapter 14 discusses ways to give feedback and Chapter 15 describes changes to school organisation to allow teachers more individual and small-group time with students to provide the level of feedback needed.

Check sheets can be a useful regular addition to curriculum planning as well. After receiving feedback from the teacher at each stage of the learning process, LLD students then tick off the relevant section as completed. Consultation and feedback from the teacher at each stage is critical. When first using check sheets, students should be given regular feedback at significant steps along the way before being expected to use them independently.

Learning environment

Distractions and interruptions have a severe impact on weak working memory capability, and 15 minutes may be needed to regain concentration after a disturbance (Crowe 2006). LLD students find it hard to get to the 'deep' learning state needed for higher level integration of ideas. Providing the right environment and regular feedback is what keeps them on task and maximises their learning opportunities.

Use diaries to assist organisation and develop priorities, and build regular monitoring of diary use into the learning environment. Encourage LLD students to do little things straight away before they have a chance to forget them.

The avoidance and anxiety discussed in Chapter 2 means that LLD students can be slow to start tasks even when they know how to do them, thus increasing their chances of forgetting.

Chunking

LLD students find smaller chunks of information (2–4 bites) more manageable. However, despite the advantages to them of putting information into smaller chunks, many LLD students do not spontaneously use this strategy themselves. They need direct instruction and modelling of chunking, with the teacher stating specifically why they are putting things together. In addition to working memory deficits, their underlying difficulty with language makes it hard to identify the ideas, words or actions that go together.

One simple test of working memory requires people to repeat numbers forward and then backward. Most people in the normal population can store approximately 7 items, with a range of 5–9. This is often written as STAM capacity of 7 digits (+/– 2). However, assessments find that LLD students store well below this: some times in the range of 3 or 4. And even this lower figure does not easily translate into a useful working memory limit for LLD students. The fact that LLD students do not chunk numbers, words or ideas spontaneously adds to their working memory limitations.

While chunking is a recommended strategy to assist LLD students, significant and long-term practice using this strategy is necessary. For example, when spelling multisyllabic words, many LLD students continue to try to sound out each letter as they would in a single syllable word, rather than to work out each syllable in the word. As a result, they rapidly lose the sound and letter sequences. When they chunk by syllables, their spelling improves but this skill requires a lot of practice and is easily lost in complex tasks like essay writing.

Other curriculum strategies

The working memory difficulties of LLD students also require us to pay particular attention in the curriculum to the following areas.

- *Reading instruction in comprehension, fluency and decoding throughout secondary school.* This instruction needs to be part of the teacher's program (see Chapter 3), and some students will require more intense individual or small-group instruction. LLD students are doubly disadvantaged if reading has not been well taught. Instruction needs to target all areas of the Baddeley and Hitch model. It is best started in the first year of school and continued throughout primary and secondary school.

- *Explicit instruction to improve comprehension.* Comprehension—such a key area in adolescent literacy— is critical in memory as information stored accurately from the beginning is information that will be better recalled (see Chapter 4 and Section 2).

- *Vocabulary.* Work on vocabulary should identify linguistic patterns to improve storage at this critical phase (see Chapter 11).

- *Careful, concise and clear oral instructions.* Instructions need to be concise and grammatically straightforward to compensate for the working memory difficulties and grammatical limitations of LLD students. Chunking information and instructions also helps. The *Collins Cobuild English dictionary for advanced learners* (2001) pays particular attention to the grammatical structure in definitions, and in practice has real advantages for LLD students.

- *Carefully sequenced and clear written instructions.* Students have a strategy to check their memory and comprehension if they can consult clearly written instructions. These are best given to the student in a typed format rather than copied from the board where working memory difficulties can lead to inaccuracies in the LLD student's copying.

- *Metacognitive checklists, explicit instruction, repetition and recall.* Metacognitive checklists make thinking skills explicit and structure thinking by using questions. Along with explicit instruction, repetition and recall, they improve base skills in decoding, organisation and planning. This decreases anxiety and frees up the limited working memory capacity of LLD students so that they can focus on more cognitively demanding tasks.

- *Summaries and overviews.* Prepare summaries and overviews of completed topics. These can be left displayed on the classroom wall for several weeks.

- *Stimulation, repetition and novelty.* According to Jensen (1998), these are key to the brain's growth and remembering. Teach what is new first and summarise at the end. Material presented in the middle is more likely to be forgotten. In current curriculum, not enough repetition is built in for LLD students. Repetition and spaced rehearsal can check how much LLD students have remembered. Jensen (2005) advises to first teach and then repeat ideas within 10 minutes, then within 48 hours, and then within 7 days.

- *Increased opportunities for recall.* These should be included both orally and in practical tasks to check that information has been well stored and can be used in a timely and accurate way.

- *Connections to feelings and emotions.* Connecting feelings and emotions to topics of study improves memory. Humour and stories are also effective memory aids.

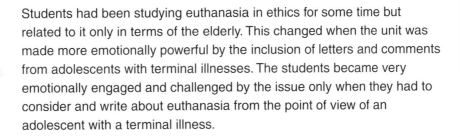

Students had been studying euthanasia in ethics for some time but related to it only in terms of the elderly. This changed when the unit was made more emotionally powerful by the inclusion of letters and comments from adolescents with terminal illnesses. The students became very emotionally engaged and challenged by the issue only when they had to consider and write about euthanasia from the point of view of an adolescent with a terminal illness.

- *Note taking and brainstorming.* Turn note taking and brainstorming into class or small-group activities. Contrast different opinions and present them in simple charts. Contrasting is effective for memory, and is a way to check comprehension and identify any gaps in the LLD student's understanding or information. It also gives a good representation of information visually and encourages decision making and choices. This process develops thinking for LLD students and takes them into problem solving, thinking things out and developing their own ideas. It is also very useful in helping LLD students deal with more complex issues and in considering arguments for and against an issue. The BBC religion and ethics web site, for example, provides information on a range of ethical issues. The decoding level is within the grasp of many LLD students, enabling them to concentrate on comprehension and higher order thinking. See <http://www.bbc.co.uk/religion/ethics>.

- *Mnemonics and memory devices.* Trial mnemonics or different memory devices and use them with individual students to determine their effectiveness. The 'Using memory effectively' web site provides a summary of memory devices which can be used across different subjects: <http://www.studygs.net/memory>.

> In a health and human development class, the students were learning the names of the female and male sexual organs for a short quiz. One of the students used a mnemonic device in which car names helped her to remember the different parts of the body (for example, 'Volvo'/'vulva'). She shared this with an LLD student with significant problems in the phonological loop. Unfortunately, it was not a good method to use for a student with sound sequencing difficulties, as the LLD student recalled 'vulva' as 'volva', a mixture of the sounds from the mnemonic device and the original word. A simple sentence with the first letter as the memory hook may have been a better strategy.

- *Monitoring comprehension and anxiety.* While new and challenging experiences can improve memory, LLD students may, at first, become extremely agitated in a new situation. Sometimes preparation the day before can help—give questions to think about in advance, highlight key ideas and so on.

- *Thinking time.* Build in thinking time with discussions. Give questions in advance, even if only briefly, so that answers can be prepared. All students benefit from thinking time so that they avoid hasty, unconsidered responses.

Further information regarding working memory with an educational focus can be found at the Centre for Working Memory and Learning web site: <http://www.york.ac.uk/res/wml>.

Checklist: Planning curriculum that makes the most of working memory

Teacher	Comment
Is there an aspect of the task I can rehearse, or make rote or automatic?	This will free up more WM for cognitive tasks.
Have I given clear written instructions? Have I reduced sentence length where necessary?	LLD students with WM difficulties forget and find complex sentences difficult to process and comprehend.
Have I remembered not to give instructions orally, at the end of the lesson or with a lot of background noise?	
Have I written the purpose of the task?	This is particularly important for students with WM difficulties.
Have I connected this new information to previously learnt material and asked students to show connections?	
Have I checked comprehension of the task?	This can be done by asking students to repeat what they have to do. At its most simple level, it may be asking if the student can remember the task that has been set.
Have I built in opportunities to reinstruct and review?	If the task is complex or the assignment is long, the student is likely to lose focus without reinstruction and review.
Have I given a task to help with better storage of key vocabulary?	This could be, for example, note taking with key words provided in the question. With this, storage in long-term memory should be better. Target the phonological loop, as this is believed to be most impaired in LLD students.
Have I provided the student with a clear, well-sequenced plan to approach this task?	This is advisable to increase the efficiency of completing tasks, and to make planning and process conscious so that students can apply the experience to similar tasks in the future.
Are there points in the task where students can reflect on their learning?	
Is there an opportunity for students to repeat skills for consolidation?	
Can I add in a visualisation task to check comprehension?	
Have I given choices, and will these choices build the skills needed?	
Do students understand clearly what is expected from them at each stage?	
Are students aware of the outcome to which all their work is leading?	

SECTION 2

Skills and strategies embedded in the curriculum

The units of work in this section are designed to show how a range of texts and tasks can be made more accessible to LLD students within a mixed-ability classroom. The intention is not necessarily to provide a fully developed unit of work—although some units do—but to use texts and tasks as exemplars to illustrate a suggested working method.

They are also designed to explicitly state the teaching goals, vocabulary and tasks for a unit of work. This makes it possible for support staff to plan the content and goals of their individual and small-group sessions using curriculum-based materials, and teaming with subject teachers to achieve the systematic development of language skills. Support staff can clearly identify areas for preteaching, the specific focus for vocabulary and written work, and potentially challenging areas for comprehension. It also enables them to identify areas outside the curriculum that may need to be addressed, including additional literacy instruction.

A step-by-step approach

Students of all abilities and at all age levels will benefit from the highly structured approach suggested in Section 2. By following such approaches we reduce the need to modify work, and create a truly inclusive classroom. Some of the texts are challenging, particularly to the students we have discussed in Section 1, but the step-by-step approach is designed to securely support students through various levels of challenge. They move from concrete to abstract tasks, engaging in higher order reading and thinking skills in a highly structured framework. At the same time, they benefit from the richness of challenging texts and concepts, with no patronising 'dumbing down' of materials.

Far too often, teachers feel under pressure to motor through whole texts and tasks quickly, not allowing themselves enough time to thoroughly teach the essential skills. This is, in part, due to the demands of externally imposed curricula and cannot be avoided. However, by using a text thoroughly to teach a wide range of skills—which can, with constant reinforcement, be applied to other tasks—we equip our students to work efficiently and effectively across the curriculum.

The notes that accompany each unit are designed to be used by both teachers and support staff. Additional or extended activities are suggested where students have the benefit of individual tuition by support staff. As well as elaborating on the instructions to students, they explain the ways in which the tasks support and reinforce student learning.

An icon shows which material is specifically intended for students, and another icon indicates notes for teachers.

 Student material

 Teaching notes

Teaching specific skills

How often do we ask students to complete procedural tasks on the assumption that they already have the skills? When we ask a class to make lists or complete tables, do we know that they have the skills to isolate and organise the relevant information? Key terminology, essential to successful understanding, is often so familiar to us that we forget to check that we have the same understanding of it as our students. The units that follow are designed to make the teaching of such skills specific, and to show how constant reinforcement is needed to consolidate them.

Consequently, there is a strong emphasis in every unit on the teaching of vocabulary. Research shows that this is a difficult but essential area to develop. The intention here is to show how vocabulary teaching can be integrated into a unit of work. Explicit teaching is essential; students cannot successfully read for meaning if they do not fully understand the connotations of key vocabulary. There is also an emphasis on expanding students' working vocabulary and fostering more precise use of language. For these reasons, all units begin with an emphasis on the necessary key vocabulary and provide ways to reinforce this throughout. This method of working should be applied to every area of study.

Reducing anxiety

The anxious student, as we read in earlier chapters, is quickly and frighteningly overwhelmed by challenging tasks, lengthy blocks of text and long lists of instruction. Their need to feel that they can attempt one little part of the task, even if what follows may prove too difficult, often leads to the confidence to attempt tasks of a complexity that might otherwise be beyond them. Not uncommonly, students will commence with the view that they can only do a small part of the unit but end up successfully completing all of it. Anxiety flashpoints are identified throughout. If these can be anticipated, they can often be avoided or defused before problems set in.

Checklist: Strategies for structuring the teaching of any text or task

• Break down tasks into steps. Encourage the 'one step at a time' approach.
• Provide essential background information. Try to link the subject to students' own experience.
• Highlight key words from both the text itself and from the instructions. Explicitly teach their meaning within the context.
• Break down complex or unfamiliar words. See if students can identify parts of the word that are familiar and will help them to derive meaning.
• Encourage students to guess meaning by reading in context.
• Teach dictionary and thesaurus skills, including the computer dictionary and thesaurus. Don't assume that students know how to use these.
• Teach students how to collate and organise information effectively. Show them how to use highlighters to group words and ideas, and how these can be organised into lists and tables, and under headings.
• Encourage an explicit awareness of audience and purpose. A writer needs to know who they are writing for so that they can adopt an appropriate style.
• Reinforce word knowledge and understanding of key terms by constant repetition and revision, quizzes, crosswords, games, and so on. Remember that if the students can say words correctly and write them, they have a powerful aid to memory.

CHAPTER 8

Working as an historian: using historical texts in the mixed-ability classroom

About this unit

This unit leads to a written report on the impact of colonisation on early Australian society in the years following the arrival of the First Fleet. It asks you to consider how Australia's beginnings as a penal colony made a difference to the early development of Australian society.

You should refer to the source material you have studied on the European settlement of Australia. The timeline below will remind you of the key events and dates.

Timeline of key events

1788	Arrival of the First Fleet
1790	Beginning of Pemulwy's campaign
1803	First British settlement in Van Diemen's Land
1808	Rum Rebellion
1824	Wiradjuri resistance defeated
1825	Settlement established at Moreton Bay, Queensland
1827	First attempt by the British to settle in Western Australia
1832	Surviving Aboriginal Tasmanians placed on Flinders Island
1834	Attack on Pinjarra people, Western Australia
1835	Settlement established at Port Phillip, Victoria
1836	South Australia founded
1838	Myall Creek massacre
1842	Native Police established in Port Phillip
1851	First gold rush
1853	End of convict transportation to eastern Australia
1856	Beginning of colonial self-government
1891	Constitution produced
1898–99	Australians vote for Federation

Ⓢ Step 1: Vocabulary

Key word	Definition	Synonym
Aboriginal	Indigenous (native) Australian	
authority	those in charge or the powers they hold	
civilian	free settler, not a member of the army or navy	
colony	outpost, a place governed by a foreign country	
colonisation	the taking over of land by a foreign country	
convict	person found guilty of a crime	
establish	set up	
impact	the difference something makes; the effect	
Indigenous	native	
liveable	suitable to live in	
officers	officials in charge	
pardon	release from charges	
penal	to do with punishment	
settler	person who comes to live in a colony	
settlement	new community	
social order	the way society is structured	
transported	shipped by force from Britain to Australia	

Task: Key vocabulary

Synonyms

1 Read the definitions above, then find a synonym (a word with the same or a similar meaning) for each one by using a thesaurus.

Fill in the gaps

2 Use the vocabulary list and the timeline to complete the following sentences so that they make sense.

Britain t_____ 11 shiploads of c_____ to Australia in the First Fleet. They arrived in Australia in 17__ __. The first p_____l c_____y was set up in Sydney in 1788.

This was the beginning of European s_____ in Australia. The
o_____ were in charge and had complete a_____y
over the convicts.

The first settlement began to evolve over time. C_____ settlers
came to Australia of their own free will, where they hoped to
e_____ farms and new industries. In time, many of the convicts
were able to obtain a p_____ and live as settlers in the colony.

The new settlers had to find ways to live with the native A_____
people, whose lands they had taken in the process of c_____.
The i_____ of this created huge difficulties in the relationships
between the new settlers and l_____s people. These
difficulties had to be overcome if the new society was to become
li_____.

Ⓢ Step 2: Thinking about effects

We can divide early Australian society into three groups:

- **Indigenous** Australians, the Aboriginal people who are native to Australia
- **convicts**, the prisoners who were transported to Australia
- free **settlers**, such as governors, officers and civilians. These people came to Australia of their own free will. Some came to govern the convicts, others to set up and run the colony.

Task: Impacts on settlement

Your first task is to identify the **impact** of European settlement on the lives of each of these groups. Our guiding question at this stage is:

*What was life like for these people as a result of
European settlement in Australia?*

But first, let's pause. Think about your own life, and what is important in your day-to-day living. With a partner, discuss which aspects of daily life (that you take for granted) are most important to you. Which, if any, could you live without? For example:

- home
- availability and variety of food
- keeping in touch with friends
- the support of your family
- entertainment (TV, books, cinema, theatre, etc.)
- sports and hobbies

- religious worship
- access to clothes
- furniture, bedding, etc.

Find someone who has come to live in Australia from another country, who is willing to talk to you about their experiences. What were the differences in **society** that had the greatest **impact** on them?

Compare your discussions as a class, then remind yourselves that all aspects of daily life would have been affected for the early European **settlers** in Australia. The daily lives of the **Indigenous** Australians living in or near the settled areas would also have been turned upside down.

Below is a checklist to help you to think about the many ways in which the lives of all three groups of people would have been affected by European **settlement**. Add some of your own ideas to the list.

Checklist: Effects of European settlement

• Homes, houses and shelter
• Use of the land to grow or gather food
• Use of the land to hunt for food
• Religious worship and practices
• Contact with family and friends
• Relationships between **convicts** and **officers**
• The **impact** of **authority** on daily life
•
•
•

Ⓢ Step 3: Indigenous Australians and settlement

What was life like for **Indigenous Australians** as a result of European settlement in Australia?

Copy out a chart like the one on the following page. Make notes on the impact of settlement on the Indigenous people. Use the checklist you completed in Step 2 to guide your thinking. Some important aspects of daily life are suggested to direct your note taking.

Working Together © Brent and Millgate-Smith 2008

Indigenous Australians

Guiding question	Your notes
How did European **settlement** affect **Indigenous** Australians' use of the land?	hunting grounds restricted: sacred: culture:
How did **Indigenous** Australians' relationships with **settlers** evolve?	weapons: language:
How did the arrival of European **settlers** affect the **Indigenous** Australians' relationships with each other?	trust: communication:

⑤ Step 4: Convict settlers and settlement

What was life like for convict settlers as a result of European settlement in Australia?

Copy out a chart like the one on the following page. Make notes on the **impact** of **settlement** on the **convict settlers** using the checklist you completed in Step 2 to guide your thinking. The idea of this task is to help you to develop your understanding of what life would have been like in the early days of European **settlement,** and what kind of **society** would have grown out of this.

Convict settlers

Guiding question	Your notes
What **impact** would the initial punishment have on the **convicts**?	transported: distance: separation:
How might the hope of a **pardon** affect their lives?	behaviour: future:
How did living conditions in the **colony** differ from those in their home countries?	authority: liveable:

⑤ Step 5: Free settlers and settlement

What was life like for governors, officers and civilians as a result of European settlement in Australia?

Copy out a chart like the one on the following page . Make notes on the impact of settlement on the free **settlers** and governing **officials** using the checklist you completed in Step 2 to guide your thinking.

Working Together © Brent and Millgate-Smith 2008

Governors, officers and civilians

Guiding question	Your notes
What sort of control and power did free **settlers** have over the **convicts**? Consider: • governors • officers • civilians.	punishment: power: assigned labour:
How would the fact that they had this **authority** affect their lives and their attitudes to the convicts?	employers: rules: freedom: work:
How did they attempt to **establish** the **colony** as a **liveable** place that reflected some of the laws and values that they had brought from England?	rule of law: buildings: roads: food and agriculture: pastimes: clothing:

⑤ Step 6: Reporting on your findings

Use the drafting frame below to present a report on the impact of European settlement.

Your report could be presented orally or in writing. Your teacher will direct you.

1 The most significant **impact** of European **settlement** on the lives of **Indigenous** Australians was on _____. This was caused by _____. It affected their lives in many ways, including

_____

_____.

> You might find some of these words useful:
> *culture   hunting   sacred   rituals*

2 For the **convicts** who were transported to the colony, the most significant impact of European **settlement** was on _____. This was caused by _____. It affected their lives in many ways, including

_____

_____.

> You might find some of these words useful.
> *authority   liveable   social order   settlers   transported   penal*

3 The free **settlers** found that the greatest **impact** of European **settlement** on their lives was _____. This was caused by _____. It affected their lives in many ways, including

_____

_____.

> You might find some of these words useful.
> *establish   officers   authority   liveable   social order*

Using PowerPoint

If you decide to present your report orally, you could use a PowerPoint presentation. If you do, remember that each slide should include a brief summary of your findings. It should not include all of the information you have found. The words should be your own.

For example, it might be useful to your audience if you include a bullet-point checklist of the effects of colonisation on each group of settlers. These will be elaborated (explained more) in your talk.

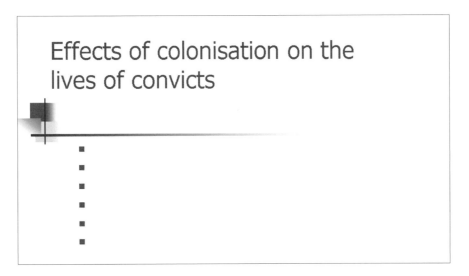

Writing a report

Below is an extract from a student's written report on the same question. Read it with a partner and discuss how well Josh has completed this task. What more might he have included (if anything) to extend his report?

The impact of colonisation on Indigenous Australians

The impact in which the first fleet had on the Indigenous Australians (Aboriginal people) land use was drastic. As most people know the Indigenous Australians were the first people on Australian soil. The First Fleet carried the first ever European people to invade Australia and start a settlement. As soon as the First Fleet arrived in Australia they decided Sydney Harbour was a good place for the convicts to be stationed. So the Indigenous Australians were more or less thrown off their own land in order for the white invaders to set up their penal colony. The Indigenous Australians' way of living was abandoned by the invaders; the invaders started to build their own jail, farms, docks and stores to meet their food needs, whereas the Indigenous Australians used to hunt animals for their food.

Although the British intended to have friendly relations with the Aboriginal people, the Indigenous people and the white settlers did not get on very well for obvious reasons: the invaders just came into Australia without consulting the Aboriginal people, as soon as the First Fleet got into Australia they started to do things their own way, they did not pay any respect to the Aboriginal people and finally they brought with them some diseases, for instance smallpox, which the Aboriginal people had no resistance to.

Ever since the First Fleet landed the aboriginal ways of life were altered dramatically. Before the invasion Aboriginal people moved around in tribes and hunted animals in order to eat. Each tribe had its own separate area of land. It had a special relationship with that area but when the white settlers came that relationship was broken up. The tribes were broken up and their way of life was gradually ruined. This is because they were unable to do the things that they usually would, for instance they could not hunt food as easily.

Notes to teachers and support staff

Key skills for History in this unit

By completing this unit, students will build on their research into a period in early Australian history using primary and secondary sources. The skills focused on include:

- broadening subject-specific vocabulary
- interpreting visual and textual information
- empathetic thinking skills
- note making
- report writing
- individual and collaborative oral skills
- forming questions.

It builds from the preteaching of vocabulary that is essential to the completion of the unit. Explicit teaching is essential; students cannot successfully read for meaning if they do not fully understand the connotations of key vocabulary. There is also an emphasis on expanding students' working vocabulary and fostering more precise use of language.

Vocabulary tasks in this unit include:

- a glossary of key words, both concrete and abstract
- synonym research
- a cloze procedure requiring the use of those words in context
- reinforcement of the key words in headings and questions
- encouragement to use key words in a planning/writing frame.

Connections to Section 1

- Anxiety: Chapter 2
- Vocabulary and comprehension: Chapter 4
- Oral and written language skills: Chapter 5
- Empathy and self-awareness: Chapter 6

This unit builds on the historical study of the early convict settlement of Australia. There are, of course, many textbooks and course books available on this subject. The Internet will also provide useful websites.

🅣 Step 1: Vocabulary

- The vocabulary grid should be established here as a resource that will provide support throughout the unit.

Working Together © Brent and Millgate-Smith 2008

- The search for synonyms could be completed as a group activity but ensure that every student is allocated an individual task.
- Definition/synonym posters could be produced and displayed on the classroom wall to provide reinforcement. Alternatively, a class booklet of synonyms could be copied and provided for each student.
- The cloze procedure requires students to reread the key words and process definitions.
- The completed cloze procedure provides a summary of salient facts that can be retained as a resource.

ANXIETY FLASHPOINT

In the cloze activity, it may be necessary to provide some students with more than the single initial letter of omitted words, especially when more than one word shares the same initial letter. In these cases, the first syllable or last letter of each word could be offered. This could be extended as needed.

❶ Step 2: Thinking about effects

- The definitions at the beginning of this step act as an extended glossary and should be referred back to throughout the unit.
- An important element of this section is to establish an understanding of what is meant by 'impact'. By asking students to broaden their thinking about the effects of migration we aim to extend this.
- The words 'impact' and 'effects' are both used to encourage students to understand the close connections between the two. They need to be prepared for the interchangeable use of these words.
- By interviewing migrants within their community we encourage students to think of historical experiences in a way that is more immediate and relevant to their lives. The use of tape or digital recorders eliminates the need to write answers down under time pressure. It will also serve to develop the skill of question formulation.
- The recorded interviews could be used by support staff for a variety of purposes, including:
  - transcription practice
  - finding key quotations to support oral or written presentations
  - summaries
  - checking comprehension and questions for grammar and content.
- The consideration of students' own values and culture nurtures the development of empathy. For some LLD students, it can be challenging to take the point of view of others, and they may become agitated and even angry as they struggle to see that there may be an equally valid—if opposite—point of view.

- Key words are highlighted in bold print. The intention is to draw students' attention to the word and alert them to its importance. The glossary can then be consulted if necessary.

🅣 Steps 3 to 5: Indigenous Australians, convicts, free settlers and settlement

- The research focuses on three discrete elements of society. These are separated into three steps to avoid overwhelming learners.

ANXIETY FLASHPOINT

Introduce each focus in turn, and encourage students to deal with one research question at a time.

- The use of a chart is designed to aid students in organising their note making.

- There are three charts, one for each group of inhabitants, to promote clear distinctions in thinking and note making.

- Provide limited space for notes within the chart to encourage conciseness in note making.

ANXIETY FLASHPOINT

Formulating questions is a potential anxiety flashpoint. The questions that are provided in this section of the unit are designed to act as models from which students can be encouraged to formulate further questions. They could be asked to practise turning an issue or point into a question by returning to the list of 'effects' discussed at Step 2 and formulating questions from them.

- Students should be taught that it is unnecessary, and indeed inefficient, to write notes in full sentences. A reminder about audience and purpose would be valuable here—the intended user of the notes is themselves.

- The key words in the note-making sections are designed to direct students' gathering of information.

- The vocabulary list and glossary should be referred back to as needed.

ANXIETY FLASHPOINT

If the task needs to be modified, this can be achieved by requiring completion of two (or even one) of the groups of inhabitants instead of all three.

ⓣ Step 6: Reporting your findings

- Note that the planning frame is designed for use in preparing either an oral or written report.

- Oral reports will work only as well as the structure provided. As in written responses, a clear framework is essential.

- The use of a planning frame, such as the one featured here, has wide application to any extended piece of writing. Students who are extremely daunted by the requirement to produce extended written responses need help with the basic structure of paragraphs, and even of sentences.

- Providing an opening phrase, sentence or even word can set students off in the right direction.

- Closer instruction and guidance should be provided on the first section, which can subsequently act as a model for completion of the remaining sections.

- The use of PowerPoint (see Appendix 5) to aid oral presentations can be beneficial to students who are very self-conscious, because it diverts the gaze of the audience from the speaker to the screen. However, bear in mind that the demands of effective PowerPoint presentations are considerable for LLD students, who must be guided to read, process, condense and summarise. Prescribing a limited number of words per slide can help to set the parameters. Encourage the use of bullet points. Most importantly, the teacher should model the process. The class will be entertained and enlightened by a deliberately awful presentation, in which the text on each slide is dense and unprocessed, and the speaker whips like lightning through the reading of it. You would probably want to follow up with a better model!

- An extracted sample of a student's written response is included. Reading such models with students provides opportunities for explicit discussion about the qualities of an effective response, as well as identifying shortcomings and discussing how they could be remedied.

ANXIETY FLASHPOINT
Avoid presenting academically outstanding examples of written work to the general class, as these might provide a model of excellence but can also intimidate the insecure learner, who sees them as yet more evidence of their own shortcomings.

Inside the covers: teen magazines as an approach to media studies in the mixed-ability classroom

About this unit

This unit leads to the creation of a magazine for teenagers. It asks you to think about how the needs and interests of young people are catered for in magazines.

Ⓢ Step 1: Vocabulary

Photocopy the table on page 121. Cut out the words in the left-hand column and match the words to their definitions. Use a dictionary or thesaurus to help you.

The bolded words are **core words**—start with these as the most important.

Ⓢ Step 2: The front cover

Have you noticed the number of different magazines that compete for your dollar on the shelf at the newsagent's? Obviously, this means that the front cover must grab your attention and make you want to buy the magazine. Let's look at how the designers do this.

Analyse the front cover of the teenage magazine you have chosen, using the chart on page 122 to record your impressions. Identify the strategies the publisher has used to make the **layout** attractive and appealing to the potential buyer and reader.

anecdote	a type of essay in a newspaper or magazine
appeal	a part of a magazine regularly devoted to a particular interest or theme, e.g. gossip column
article	the main point argued, or **contended,** by the writer
caption	the attraction or interest for the reader
colloquial language	an article written or approved by the editor
column	text which describes or explains a photograph
connotation	a little story or personal experience
contention	a cartoon, graph, diagram, etc.
editorial	a writer employed by the publication
graphic	the significance and meanings implied by a certain choice of word or image
headline	the everyday language of a particular group in society
imply	everyday, informal spoken language
infer	the arrangement of text, graphics, headlines, etc. on the page
journalist	a heading in the body of the text which highlights the content of that section of the text
juxtaposition	to draw a conclusion from an implication
layout	to suggest or hint at something without directly stating it
subheading	this might be described as the 'speaking voice' of the piece
tone	the effect created by placing specific and often contrasting words, images, phrases, etc. side by side
vernacular	the main title of an article, set in large, bold font

Element of cover	What is its appeal to the buyer?
Main image	
Title	
Headlines (descriptions of content)	
Text (font, size, colours, shape, etc. of lettering)	
Layout (how everything is arranged on the page)	

Working Together © Brent and Millgate-Smith 2008

⑤ Step 3: Range and appeal of articles

Now that you have given some thought to what teenagers hope to find on the front cover of a magazine, what should be inside the covers? Conduct a quick survey of your friends to find out what sort of topics or subjects would interest them: for example, music, clothes, books, cars, films, sport, etc.

Now it is time to consider how much of this the magazines deliver.

When studying media, we often talk about the **appeals** they make. By this, we refer to the ingredients of an article that might appeal to the interest of the reader.

An article may **appeal** to the reader in different ways and on different levels. We are looking for some element that would naturally be interesting to the reader.

- An article might **appeal** to the reader's interest in music, clothes, football, a particular actor, gossip or sex.
- It might **appeal** to our curiosity, to our concern for less fortunate people, or to our desire to look better, overcome shyness or find out how our bodies work.
- It might **appeal** to our need to know—to know that we are like everyone else, and not the only one to have problems or feel anxious.
- Or it might just **appeal** to our sense of humour when we need a little fun!

Task: Exploring language

There are many shades of meaning in the word 'appeal'.

1 The verb: find synonyms for the word **appeal** as a verb.

pl_____d   req_____t   be_____   entr_____t

bes_____ch   imp_____e

2 The noun: find synonyms for the word **appeal** as a noun.

att_____tion   pl_____   all_____e   int_____t   entr_____ty

Now check the answers (provided in Appendix 11).

Task: Articles and appeal

1 Compile a list of the articles contained in your magazine. Identify the issues and interests that each one addresses. Discuss why each of these articles would be expected to **appeal** to the intended teenage reader. (Draw up a chart like the one below.)

Article title or headline	Content (issue or subject)	Appeal to reader (why would teenagers want to read this?)

2 As a class, discuss how effectively the magazine's editorial board understands what teenagers want to read, and whether the magazine meets those needs.

3 Read the following statements and decide which most reflects your own findings.

The teenage magazine I have surveyed:
- presents the range of teenagers' interests pretty fairly
- presents only a small fraction of teenagers' interests
- focuses on many areas of interest for teenagers but leaves others out
- shows little understanding of teenagers' interests.

4 Suggest ways in which the content of the magazine could be improved to satisfy the readership better.

Ⓢ Step 4: Advertisements

Task: Analysing an advertisement

Find a full-page advertisement in your magazine. It should feature a male or female model. It might be promoting a mobile phone or computer, clothes or cosmetics.

1 How would you describe the impression that the model in this advertisement gives about his or her feelings?

Choose three adjectives from the list below to describe the way the model is presented. Give reasons for your choice.

happy	*ecstatic*	*delirious*	*amused*	*intimidating*
refreshed	*clean*	*attractive*	*powerful*	*wholesome*
confident	*moody*	*alluring*	*smug*	*self-conscious*
brooding	*seductive*	*protective*	*strong*	*arrogant*

Adjective	Reason for choosing this

2 What are we expected to **infer** about the product in this advertisement?

Working Together © Brent and Millgate-Smith 2008

Task: Advertising audit

1 Look through your teenage magazine page-by-page and complete an audit of the advertisements that it features. Use a chart like the one below to record the products advertised.

Page number	Product	Main image	Key words

Hidden advertising

2 Now look through the magazine again and try to find examples of hidden advertising, where products are promoted through articles. List them.

Celebrity promotions

3 How many examples are there of celebrities being used to promote sales? Why do you think advertisers would be willing to pay them to do this?

4 What kinds of celebrities are employed for this advertising, and how would each celebrity appeal to the reader?

5 By checking the total number of pages in the magazine, do a rough calculation to work out what proportion of the magazine is occupied by advertisements.

You will find that a large proportion of the magazine is devoted to advertisements. The publishers charge the advertisers large sums of money for this. This is how they make a profit; the price you pay to the newsagent would not even begin to cover the costs of producing a magazine. In order to persuade the advertiser that the cost is worthwhile, the publisher has to convince them that many people will read the magazine and be influenced to buy the product. So, you see, magazine publishing is big business!

Ⓢ Step 5: 'Teenspeak' language study

Teenage magazines are speaking to a teenage audience. They try to use the same language that teenagers use. This tends to include lots of terms popular among the age group, including slang and abbreviations. We call this the **vernacular**: 'the commonly spoken language or dialect of a particular people or place' (Collins English dictionary).

This particular vernacular is often **colloquial** in style, which means that it is chatty and informal, and draws on language that is used in speech rather than in formal writing.

Task: Editor profile

The extract below is taken from an **editorial** in *Dolly* magazine. An editorial is an opinion piece written by the editor or, more likely, by a senior journalist. Before reading it, spend a few minutes thinking about the kind of person you would expect to be the editor of a popular girls' magazine. Jot down a profile of the person's:

- age group
- qualifications
- work experience.

Task: Editorial

Now read the editorial below and highlight the **colloquial** words and expressions used.

School is a double edge sword

One day it's the best place in the world, and the next, one of your 'friends' is being a complete cow and turning the rest of the group against you. Or worse, someone sent a horrible SMS/IM/email about you to the WHOLE grade. Sound familiar?

This month in the DOLLY office we got talking about our experiences at school— and the first thing that came to all our minds was the school bitch. We couldn't recall the names of a lot of our teachers and even some of the last names of the girls we hung out with every day, but the name of the school bitch rolled off our tongues without hesitation (and have you noticed how the school bitch is always referred to by first AND last name, like Susie Peterson, rather than just Susie? LOL). There were days when my high school bitch (who shall remain nameless) was so foul to me I'd go home feeling sick in the stomach and terrified at the thought of having to return. Then, other days, this girl acted like my best friend and school was the coolest place ever—a total rollercoaster. And you know what? Every girl in the DOLLY office went through the same thing.

(*Dolly*, September 2006)

Not much chance of a 15-year-old landing a prestigious job like this, is there? Yet the language used seems to give the impression that the writer is 'one of us'.

1 How is this achieved?

2 Why do you think this **colloquial** style of language is used?

3 Does it improve your enjoyment of the magazine? Or would you prefer a more formal style of writing?

⑤ Step 6: Opinion and debate

Teenage magazines often provoke heated discussion among adult commentators. Some support the role they play in teenagers' lives, but others question their value.

Task: Arguments and contentions

Below is a series of extracts from articles and letters that have appeared in newspapers and periodicals on the subject of teenage magazines.

- Read each carefully, in turn.
- Work out whether the writer supports or challenges teenage magazines.
- Use a highlighter to identify the **argument**.
- Rewrite the main **contention**, or point of view, in your own words.

Note that **arguments are reasons**. You may say, 'Snow Patrol is a great band because …' The 'because' is your reason, and therefore part of your argument.

> *Girls are encouraged by these magazines to see themselves as bimbos, interested only in boys, clothes and make-up. They do nothing to challenge the notion that this is all that matters in the life of the teenage girl.*
>
> The writer's main **contention** is …

> *Okay, so teenage mags are not high literature, but don't we all need some downtime? Which of us doesn't love to flick through the pages of the glossies in the doctor's waiting room? Kids are smart enough to know that they only represent part of their lives, but, hey, we all need a little light relief. Get over it.*
>
> The writer's main **contention** is …

> *What on earth are we parents thinking when we buy this trash for our kids? These publications are badly written, frivolous and misleading. Buy them a good book instead!*
>
> The writer's main **contention** is …

>>

>>

The most worrying aspect of teen magazines is their relentless focus on the body beautiful. How many 14-year-olds are aware that actually even models get spots, which the wonders of airbrushing can transform into flawless translucent skin on the cover photo? How does it make the hapless boy feel when he looks from mag to mirror and sees the reality of teenage hormones?

The writer's main **contention** is …

True, teenage magazines often appear to promote undue obsession with sex. But ask yourself this: would kids be any less interested in sex if they didn't read them?

The writer's main **contention** is …

Well-meaning parents and teachers approach sex education responsibly. They encourage young people to discuss their concerns frankly. 'Ask me anything', they say, and they mean it. But the reality is that most teenagers find it excruciatingly embarrassing to ask the questions they really want answers to. Teenage magazines give answers to the questions that kids want to ask. They provide a genuine forum for information. We may cringe, but kids need to know.

The writer's main **contention** is …

How many eating disorders are created by images of stick-thin models pouting from the pages of the latest teen magazine?

The writer's main **contention** is …

Task: Letter to the editor

Write a letter to the editor of the magazine you have studied, expressing your opinion about it. Make sure you have a clear contention, and that you support it with arguments. You might select one of the contentions below if there is one that closely matches your views, or you can come up with your own contention.

Contentions:

- Teen magazines are just for fun and shouldn't be taken too seriously.

- The images of young women presented in _____ can cause serious damage to girls' self-esteem.

- Boys and girls are presented as stereotypes in _____

- There is too much emphasis on appearance in _____

- Teenagers can learn a great deal from reading _____ that they might not otherwise discover.

Ⓢ Step 7: Ask the doctor

The letter below was sent to a girls' magazine. It is from a reader who is asking the magazine's consultant doctor for advice.

Read the doctor's reply and answer the questions that follow.

> Dear Doctor,
>
> A few months ago I started to borrow big bruv's razor to shave my legs. Sometimes my legs are really smooth straight after, but recently I've started to get an ugly red rash on my calves. I use shaving cream but this hasn't helped. What can I do? Summer's coming and I don't want to be stuck in jeans the whole time.
>
> From Annie, 15

> Dear Annie,
>
> It sounds as though you are suffering from classic shaving rash. Make sure that the razor you use is sharp—being dragged over manly stubble will blunt it so buy your own. There are lots of pretty coloured razors for girls in the shops.
>
> After shaving, rinse thoroughly and gently pat your legs dry with a soft towel. Then be sure to rub a cooling moisturiser into your legs to calm down the inflammation.
>
> Meanwhile, the rash should only last a day or two so you'll soon be able to uncover those pins for summer!
>
> Good luck!
> From the Doctor

1 According to the magazine's doctor, rashes and skin irritation can be caused by:

   A shaving

   B waxing

   C depilatory cream

   D all of these.

2 The rash usually lasts:

   A 2–3 weeks

   B a couple of hours

   C a day or two

   D forever.

3 Shaving can cause irritation when:

   A the razor is blunt

   B the skin is dirty

   C the skin is scratched

   D the razor is too sharp.

4 One solution is:

   A do not shave your legs

   B shave less often

   C shave more frequently

   D apply a moisturiser after shaving.

Discussion

How valuable do you think this advice is to the teenage reader? For instance, does the doctor in any way challenge the notion that it is necessary to shave one's legs?

⑤ Step 8: Extending our understanding of the issue

Catalyst, a program on ABC TV, aired a report on 25 May 2006 on hair removal that would be of interest to many girls and boys. It applied scientific research techniques to the question of hair regrowth and came up with some interesting findings.

Working in small groups, allocate a part to each person so that you can recreate the script. Read it aloud like a play script. You will need to read the following parts:

- Dr Paul Willis: reporter

- narrator (this person reads the narration, or 'voice-over')

- Professor Claude Roux: forensic scientist

- David Salinger: trichologist (hair specialist)

- waxist.

Answers: 1 A; 2 C; 3 A; 4 D

Read the transcript in sections, stopping to discuss the questions and make notes.

Hair regrowth

Reporter: Dr Paul Willis
Producer: Gabrielle Betteridge
Researcher: Gabrielle Betteridge

Your mother always told you that if you shave a part of your body the hair will return with a vengeance, causing you to look like a gorilla. And the beauty therapy clinics all promise to rid you of unwanted hair forever with just a few sessions of waxing.

Are either of these true or just old wives' tales? Reporter Paul Willis offers his body to science once again to test the effectiveness of both shaving and waxing and to find out what really goes on beneath the skin during hair removal and regrowth.

1 What is the **hypothesis** that is to be tested in the experiment?

Part 1

Narration: We rip, pluck, shave, and even chemically burn in an effort to rid ourselves of that unwanted menace—excess hair. We're told 'wax this and you'll never have to shave again', 'shave that and it'll encourage even more growth'.

Dr Paul Willis, reporter: But is there really any scientific proof that shaving your hair will make it grow back thicker and darker—or that waxing it will make it grow back thinner and fairer? Well I'm handing my legs over to the professionals in a Catalyst-designed experiment to find out the truth—and I think it's going to hurt— Owwwww!

Narration: Before I put myself through that torture, I succumbed to another, so that we can do a precise measurement of whether the hair density changes as well. It required tattooing four markers on each leg to enable a precise hair count in that 2 square centimetre area.

2 Draw a labelled diagram to show the **method** used to test the hypothesis. Indicate the **materials** used.

Then it was off to a hair growth specialist to take 'before' photos for later comparison.

Dr Paul Willis, reporter: My left leg we've waxed well and truly over the test area— and beyond. I'll keep this for later analysis. My right is being shaved so that we can compare what happens with the different treatments.

Narration: Leg hair, underarm hair, nasal hair or scalp hair, it's basically composed of the same stuff—mostly a high sulphur protein called keratin. And it's so strong, if you ate it even the acid in your stomach couldn't break it down which probably explains why it's so tough to get out! Each hair grows from its own follicle in the skin and you've got about 5 million of those on your body, all growing at different rates independently.

Narration: While the scalp hair grows fastest, the hair on my legs will grow back at a slightly slower rate—about 0.3 of a millimetre a day, so I should have it all back in about four months. Luckily I'm not having my eyebrows done as they're slower growing still.

Waxist: Okay Paul, that's it.

Dr Paul Willis, reporter: Thank you very much. Now let's see if the hair grows back.

Narration: Later in the show we'll reveal the results— and find out just what goes on deep down during the regrowth.

Part 2

Dr Paul Willis, reporter: I think I've done a pretty good job of regrowing my hair. But now I'm taking my original hairs and regrown ones off for a little forensic investigation—ouch!

Prof. Claude Roux, University of Technology Sydney: Side by side you can see here, pre-waxing and after waxing—the two hairs have a very similar structure, very similar colour and the same width. Next, the shaved hair and regrown ones freshly cut from the same area.

Dr Paul Willis, reporter: So the shaved hairs, same again?

Prof. Claude Roux: Yeah, that's it. In my opinion there is no significant differences between these two hair samples.

3 What **result** did Paul Willis notice?

Dr Paul Willis, reporter: So shaving or waxing doesn't affect hair thickness or colour. But are my legs actually hairier? David Salinger knows all about that. He's a trichologist who specialises in hair loss—and replacement.

Dr Paul Willis, reporter: I notice as the waxed leg grew back it didn't seem to grow all at the same time. It seemed to be more slow. What's going on there?

David Salinger: Well there would be a mixture of growing hairs and resting hairs.

Dr Paul Willis, reporter: That's because hair grows in a three-stage cycle and the timing differs from hair to hair. A hair plucked at the beginning of its cycle will take longer to grow back than an old hair that's up for replacement. Now a lot of people say, and I'd have to say that I agree with them, that as shaved hair grows back it seems to be thicker than hairs that have been waxed.

David Salinger: Okay, so let's take another shot and I can show you a comparison of now and four months ago.

Dr Paul Willis, reporter: It looks like exactly the same density to me. That comes as no surprise to you though, does it?

David Salinger: No, I mean, as far as you can see, certainly the number of follicles are exactly the same. You are not going to create new hair follicles. The follicles you have are the ones you're born with and they're certainly not going to increase.

Dr Paul Willis, reporter: There is evidence that repeated waxing may eventually damage the follicle enough to prevent it reproducing hair—but that would take years. But when it comes to my legs it looks like there's no significant difference between waxing and shaving, they're just old wives' tales. So for the shavers among us, rest in peace, it's not going to turn you into some kind of gorilla.

4 What **conclusion** is drawn from the experiment?

(*Catalyst*, 25 May 2006, <www.abc.net.au/catalyst/stories/s1647527.htm>
Reproduced by permission of the Australian Broadcasting Corporation and ABC Online. © 2006 ABC. All rights reserved.)

⑤ Step 9: Testing the hypothesis

Complete the **glossary** to make sure you clearly understand the words used in the transcript.

Word	Definition
density	
analysis	
keratin	
follicle	
regrowth	
forensic	
trichologist	

After completing the reading task on the *Catalyst* investigation, you should now be able to answer the questions you discussed while reading the transcript:

1 What was the **hypothesis** that was tested in the experiment?

2 What **method** was used to test the hypothesis? What **materials** were used?

3 What **result** did Paul Willis find?

4 What **conclusion** was drawn from the experiment?

⑤ Step 10: Responding to the issue

Use the information you have gleaned from the transcript of the *Catalyst* program to complete these tasks.

1 Write a letter to the 'doctor' page of your magazine. Ask the question that was researched by Paul Willis: does hair removal make hair grow back more strongly? (Remember to use some colloquial language, or 'teenspeak', but not too much.)

2 Then write the reply that the doctor might offer. Base it firmly on the results of the experiment. (You should write in standard English here. Make it as clear as possible but use the findings available.)

Ⓢ Step 11: 'Reading' photographs

Read the analysis of the photograph below.

Sample photograph analysis

Camera angle	The low angle, looking slightly up at the subject, makes him look in control.
Background	The completely black background acts as a foil for the subject by making him stand out clearly. Our attention is drawn to his face.
Appearance	His hair looks neat but natural, giving the impression that he doesn't need to spend too much time on his appearance to look good. He is wearing a casual shirt, which adds to the impression of calm contemplation.
Expression and gesture	The eyes looking to the side suggest that there is something outside the frame of the photograph that is engaging his attention. It gives him an intriguing appearance, as though he is thinking deeply. The subject's lips are full and slightly parted, suggesting a sensuous side to him. We suspect he would have a great smile.
Symbols in the photograph	The sunglasses add a touch of casual style. The subject chews on them absently, reinforcing the suggestion that his mind is elsewhere. This makes him rather mysterious and we want to know what he is thinking about.

Working Together © Brent and Millgate-Smith 2008

Now select a photograph from your magazine. Complete an analysis of it, using the example given above as a model. Copy out a chart similar to the one below and fill in each category.

An analysis of my photograph

Camera angle	
Background	
Appearance	
Expression and gesture	
Symbols in the photograph	

Ⓢ Step 12: Using technical terms

Find an article in your magazine. (Hint: these are often presented as readers' real-life experiences.) With the help of the glossary you completed, use arrows to label the following components:

- headline
- subheading
- caption
- colloquial language
- graphic
- column
- anecdote.

Ⓢ Step 13: Produce your own teenage magazine

Teen mags are okay to flick through as long as you don't take them too seriously. The problem is, you can end up feeling that you're the only 14-year-old with pimples, homework and no boyfriend. The image of girls is not realistic.

(Kate, 14)

What worries me most about guys' magazines is that they make us feel we should all be primitive man, treating girls as sex objects and pumping iron. Most of my mates are much more rounded than that.

(Josh, 16)

Where are the articles about the sport we play, the footy teams we follow, the problems of juggling homework and part-time jobs? This is the stuff that takes up most of our time. Yeah, relationships are important but I like to think of myself as an independent girl with a brain, not an ornament to dangle off some guy's arm.

(Alex, 15)

Read and discuss the comments above, which were recorded by a number of teenagers. How valid do you think their points are? Could you produce a magazine that would be more appropriate or satisfying to your peers' needs?

Task: Make your own magazine

Work in groups to produce a mini-teenage magazine. Your magazine should include a front cover and between 2 and 4 pages (4–8 sides).

Imagine that you are an editorial team of journalists who produce a monthly teenage magazine. Its target audience is teenagers (boys, girls or both—you choose). You will need to spend some time **brainstorming**, **planning** and **allocating tasks.**

Present your written work in the style of a teenage magazine with a **front cover**, **title**, **date**, **table of contents**, **editorial**, **articles**, **illustrations**, **photos**, **quizzes** and **advertisements**. Remember to set it out using **headings**, **sub–headings** and **columns**.

You may decide that your magazine will have a **theme,** to which everything in it relates. Themes could include health and fitness, Christmas, relationships, study, family, body image, the fashion industry, food, spring, etc.

Each member of the group should be responsible for a distinct area of the magazine. The journalists' names (yours!) will appear on their articles.

Like professional journalists, you are working towards a fixed deadline. It is a vital part of any journalist's brief to be able to meet deadlines. Publication cannot be delayed because your article is unfinished.

Agree with your teacher on a deadline and stick to it.

Notes to teachers and support staff

Key skills for media studies, science and literacy in this unit

By completing this unit, students will be given an introduction to the study of print media and pursue a scientific investigation. The skills they will develop include:

- broadening of vocabulary
- interpretation of ideas
- interpretation of scientific data
- understanding of editorial and authorial purpose
- analysis of standard and non-standard English
- creative responses that employ the techniques identified
- individual and collaborative oral skills.

The step-by-step approach is designed to securely support students through various levels of challenge. They move from concrete to abstract tasks, engaging in higher order reading, thinking and creative skills in a highly structured framework.

There is considerable emphasis in this unit on the teaching of vocabulary. As previously mentioned, research shows this is a difficult area to develop. The intention here is to show how vocabulary teaching can be integrated into a unit of work. Explicit teaching is essential: students cannot successfully read for meaning if they do not fully understand the connotations of key vocabulary. There is also an emphasis on expanding students' working vocabulary and fostering more precise use of language.

Vocabulary tasks in this unit include:
- a step-by-step approach to identifying and defining key words
- emphasis on words within the jargon of media
- reinforcement of the scientific lexicon
- work on connotations and visualisations
- grouping activities.

Connections to Section 1
- Anxiety: Chapter 2
- Vocabulary and comprehension: Chapter 4
- Oral and written language skills: Chapter 5

This unit can be taught in media studies or in English, and possibly in conjunction with science. It requires students to have the use of a teenage magazine.

Preteaching: ways into the text
- Draw on the students' prior knowledge of teenage magazines to encourage discussion of preferences, etc. Get them to consider how and why their tastes have changed over time.
- Allow time for them to browse without direction. Follow this up by asking which sections of the magazine drew their interest and which did not.
- Students could be asked to compile and conduct a questionnaire or survey into the magazine reading habits of their peers.

T Step 1: Vocabulary
- After completing the task, students should be asked to paste the correctly completed chart onto paper for future reference.

- A glossary, providing answers to this task, is provided in Appendix 6. This could be suitable for students who work more slowly. Most of the words included in the vocabulary exercise are used in this unit. It should be referred to regularly.

- The task could be set up in groups and completed as a team activity, with pairs of students working together.

- These key words should be reinforced frequently, both at the start and throughout the lesson. Further activities can be built around them: for instance, they could be used for a spelling program.

ANXIETY FLASHPOINT

Not all students will complete the task. Reduce the pressure on anxious or slow-working students by encouraging them to complete the bolded core words.

🅣 Step 2: The front cover (beginning analysis)

- If students find it difficult to judge the appeal to the broad readership, remind the class that they are the intended audience. Ask them to record what appeals to them personally.

- To broaden this awareness of appeal, ask them to consider what might appeal to a reader of the opposite gender, or to their friends or classmates.

- Refer students back to the vocabulary exercise/glossary for definitions.

🅣 Step 3: Range and appeal of articles (developing analysis)

- Ensure that students have a clear grasp of what we mean by appeal. The synonyms task provides opportunities to track word roots and connections.

- It is highly likely that students will confuse advertising features with articles when completing the audit. Point out that this is a deliberate ploy by the advertiser.

- The provision of statements, from which students are asked to select the one closest to their own views, is often helpful to students who have difficulty formulating their own responses, and can be used for many purposes. The last task in this section, for example, could be addressed in this way. Students themselves could be asked to devise a list of suggestions for their partners to select from.

🅣 Step 4: Advertisements (developing analysis)

- The adjectives task is designed to extend vocabulary. Encourage the use of a thesaurus or dictionary to promote precision of choice and usage.

- The hidden advertising task should initially be modelled by the teacher using an example and discussing the techniques employed to disguise its purpose.

- Advertisements are increasingly sophisticated in their efforts to conceal their intentions so that young readers often take them for independent articles or believe that celebrity endorsements are altruistically motivated. Further, articles often incorporate product promotion. Students need to be aware of this practice while also understanding that advertising is crucial for magazine publishers to meet production costs.

ⓣ Step 5: 'Teenspeak' language study

- To reinforce understanding of the vernacular, students could be asked to compile a list or class dictionary of colloquial expressions used within their age group.

- This could be developed into an enrichment or extension task by asking them to compile similar lists for a different demographic, for example, older people or those with different accents or dialects.

- Highlighters are an effective device to encourage close reading and the identification of information. Students who are uncertain about this task tend to highlight slabs of text rather than focus on key words. The editorial could be highlighted as a class model to use later.

- The use of the word 'prestigious' presents an opportunity for extending word attack skills through discussion. If students can be guided to see the core word 'prestige', they will probably be able to define it by linking to their prior knowledge; most will know what a 'prestige' car is, for instance.

ⓣ Step 6: Opinion and debate

- As always, key vocabulary is isolated for definition at the start of the task, in this case 'argument' and 'contention'.

- This step presents a challenging reading task—although each extract is quite short, students are asked to read for inference and deduce authorial intentions. It is advisable for the teacher to read the extracts aloud, as using an appropriate tone in the reading voice will support the communication of opinion.

- The task is structured to encourage the identification of arguments and contentions progressively.

- Highlighting is recommended to encourage students to hone in on key words and phrases.

- The contentions should be summarised in the student's own words. This is an essential step in processing the information, and omitting it will usually lead to unprocessed regurgitation without comprehension of meaning.

ⓣ Step 7: Ask the doctor

- This section is designed as a cross-disciplinary task, as it draws on and consolidates students' knowledge of the writing up of scientific experiments.

- The quiz is designed to test reading comprehension in a light-hearted way.
- The follow-up discussion should encourage students to make judgments about the underlying assumptions and values implicit in the letter and reply.

🅣 Step 8: Extending our understanding of the issue

- The *Catalyst* transcript has been 'chunked', with questions posed at strategic points in the body of the text to allow readers to locate information one step at a time.
- By setting up group reading of the transcript, students who struggle with reading will be unobtrusively helped by their partners. The allocation of parts may need to be determined by the teacher to avoid giving poor readers more than they can handle.

🅣 Step 9: Testing the hypothesis

- Make sure that the glossary definitions are completed using a dictionary and/or thesaurus before the report is written up; readers need to understand these key terms.
- Reinforce the word definitions by discussing their meanings in a variety of contexts and by focusing on the word root/prefix/suffix, etc. 'Density', for instance, will be related back to 'dense'; students might think about what they would envisage as a dense forest.
- The answers to the guiding questions, if they are written in full sentences, create a fluent narrative report. This is an example of how asking questions can stimulate a developed piece of writing.

🅣 Step 10: Responding to the issue

- Here students are required to apply the knowledge they have gained, both about language conventions and about social assumptions.
- The letter and reply at the beginning of this section should be employed as a model for the students' own writing.

🅣 Step 11: 'Reading' photographs

The example of photograph analysis notes serves as a model for this task. Students follow the same approach to analyse a different photograph.

ANXIETY FLASHPOINT
Students who might feel anxious about the complexity of the task should be encouraged to approach it step by step, looking at each component in turn.

T Step 12: Using technical terms

- Here is another opportunity for embedding newly acquired vocabulary.
- Students should be referred back to the glossary to help them complete this task.

T Step 13: Produce your own teenage magazine

- See Appendix 7 for further work on maintaining consistent verb tenses.
- This task can be expanded or reduced as required—alter the number of pages to be completed.
- Refer students back to the work completed in Step 5. They should be encouraged to recreate the particular 'voice' of the magazine they have studied.
- It is a good idea to designate a certain amount of writing to be completed to prevent students from taking the easy option and simply producing advertisements. However, for students who struggle to write at any length, this is a valuable opportunity for them to produce a finished product for a specified audience.

CHAPTER 10

Understanding the problem: breaking down the language barriers in maths

About this unit

This unit deals with aspects of area. You will learn how to find the area of a rectangle. The area is the amount of flat surface that the figure (shape) covers. Please note: shapes that include measurements are not drawn to size.

Ⓢ Step 1: Essential vocabulary

The table (chart) below gives you the definitions of the key words you will need to know. Have it handy to look at when you are completing the tasks in this unit.

Word	Definition
quadrilateral	plane (flat) shape with four sides and four angles
rectangle	oblong shape a quadrilateral with two pairs of equal and parallel sides and four right angles
square	quadrilateral with four equal sides and four right angles
area 5 cm / 4 cm 5 cm x 4 cm = 20 cm²	the amount of surface or the size of a surface, measured in square units

>>

>>

length	longer side from end to end
width	shorter side from end to end
formula	an equation that uses symbols to represent numbers
pronumeral	symbol which represents an unknown value in an equation e.g. $6x = 18$; $2a = 8$ $x = 3$ $a = 4$ x and a are pronumerals
substitute	use something else
calculate	work out
dimension	measurement
squared units (e.g. metres, kilometres, centimetres) shown as ^{2}	the area within an enclosed space e.g. $1\,cm \times 1\,cm$ the area is 1 square cm
convert	change into another form
unit of measurement	could be centimetres, kilometres, hectares, millimetres, etc.
subtract —	take away, find the difference
divide ÷	share
perimeter	length of the outside edge
face	(in a three-dimensional shape) the flat part of a surface that is bounded by the edges; a cube has 6 faces and a tetrahedron has 4 faces

Task: Crossword

Use the information from the table on the previous pages to complete this crossword.

CLUES

Across

3 Change a sum or number into a different form

4 Share out

7 Shape with four sides of equal length

8 Oblong

9 Longest side of a rectangle

10 A unit of measurement

Down

1 A plane figure with four sides

2 A symbol which represents a number

3 Work out

5 The outside edge of a figure

6 Take away

ⓢ Step 2: Identifying rectangles

Abbreviations for units of measurement

millimetre	mm
centimetre	cm
metre	m
kilometre	km

A rectangle:

- is an oblong shape
- has two long sides opposite each other
- has two shorter sides opposite each other.

long side

short side   short side

long side

Task: Perimeter

1 The **area** is the space inside this rectangle.

Measure each side in centimetres, and write the length and width in the spaces below.

2 The **perimeter** is the distance around the edges.

Measure the perimeter of the rectangle above and write the measurement in the space below.

Width (shorter sides) in cm =
Length (longer sides) in cm =
Perimeter (distance around the edges) in cm =

Task: Rectangles

1 Find a rectangular object in the classroom.

2 Draw a diagram of your object.

3 Measure the length of each side.

4 Measure the width of each side.

5 Measure its perimeter.

6 Show the measurements on your diagram.

Are both **lengths** (long sides) the same as each other?

Are both **widths** (short sides) the same as each other?

If so, you have successfully identified a **rectangle**.

Ⓢ Step 3: Area squared

- **Area** is the amount of surface that a shape covers.

- It is measured in square units.

- In Australia, the standard area unit is the square metre.

The term **square** indicates the space enclosed by the sides. For example, one square metre = 1 m^2. This is the area enclosed by a square that has sides of $1 \text{ m} \times 1 \text{ m}$.

Unit of measurement	Symbol
1 square millimetre	1 mm^2 (or 1 sq mm)
1 square centimetre	1 cm^2 (or 1 sq cm)
1 square metre	1 m^2 (or 1 sq m)
1 square kilometre	1 km^2 (or 1 sq km)
1 square hectare	1 ha

Use graph paper (with squares of one centimetre) to test this out. Draw a rectangle using these dimensions:

- length: 6 cm

- width: 2 cm.

Now shade it. How many squares does the rectangle cover?

⑤ Step 4: Investigating the area of a rectangle

1 On a sheet of graph paper (with squares of one centimetre), draw four rectangles of different sizes.

2 Make sure the length and width of each rectangle is in a whole number of centimetres.

3 Calculate the area of each rectangle by counting the squares (cm^2).

Example

My pencil tin is 14 cm in length and 9 cm in width.

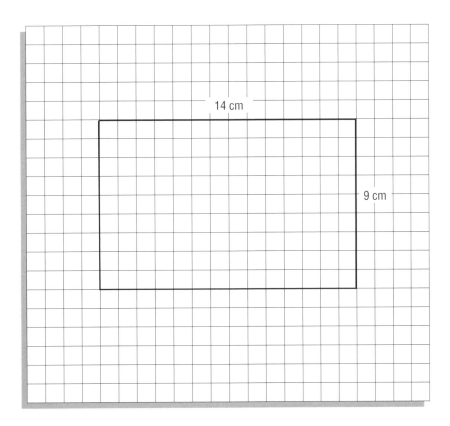

Now copy and complete the following table to record the results for your four rectangles.

Rectangle	Length in cm	Width in cm	Area in cm^2
1 *Example* pencil tin	14 cm	9 cm	126 cm^2
2			
3			
4			
5			

4 With a partner, can you work out the link between length and width and area? Complete this sentence:

We can work out area by multiplying (times) l_____ by w_____.

⑤ Step 5: Using the formula A = lw

Learn the formula for finding area. You will be able to use it to find the area of any rectangle. The letters stand for:

- A = area
- l = length
- w = width.

The formula is usually shown as **A = lw**. (You do not need to show the multiplication sign.)

Example

- A = lw
- A = 5 cm (length) × 4 cm (width)
- A = 20 cm^2

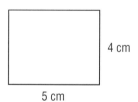
4 cm
5 cm

You try this one:

2 cm
7 cm

HINTS

- Remind yourself of the formula for the area of a rectangle by completing the gaps. A = ___ × ___
- Substitute the value 7 for length and 2 for width. A = ___ × ___
- Calculate the result. Remember to answer in the correct units (cm^2). A = ___ cm^2

Ⓢ Step 6: Having a go

Task: Finding the area

Find the area of the following rectangles.

 HINTS
- Use the formula A = lw (area = length × width).
- Set each calculation out as shown in the examples above, for example:

  A = __ × ___

  A = __ cm^2

- Show your working out.

Show your working out.

1   A = _____ × _____

   A = _____ cm^2

(rectangle: 6 cm wide, 3 cm high)

2   A = _____ × _____

   A = _____ cm^2

(rectangle: 12 cm wide, 3 cm high)

3   A = _____ × _____

   A = _____ cm^2

(rectangle: 8 cm wide, 4 cm high)

4   A = _____ × _____

   A = _____ cm^2

(rectangle: 10 cm wide, 3 cm high)

Task: Drawing and finding the area

Read the measurements of the rectangles below. Draw a diagram for each of the rectangles and then find its area. Show your working out.

1 length 10 cm; width 4 cm

2 length 8 cm; width 4 cm

3 length 13 cm; width 5 cm

4 length 20 cm; width 4.5 cm

HINT
Use the formula
A = lw (area = length × width)

5 length 7 cm; width 4 cm

6 length 26 cm; width 10 cm

7 length 12 cm; width 8 cm

8 length 19 cm; width 7 cm

Ⓢ Step 7: Units of measurement

So far we have completed all of our measurements in centimetres. This **unit of measurement** is useful for relatively small objects. It would take a long time to measure a paddock in centimetres!

We have to choose an appropriate **unit of measurement** depending on the size of the area.

- **Square kilometres (km^2)**: used to measure a very large area such as a town, state or country.

- **Hectare (ha)**: used to measure a large area such as a farm.
  (A **hectare** is 100 m × 100 m, or 10 000 m^2.)

- **Square metre (m^2)**: used to measure an area such as a room, window, tennis court or whiteboard.

- **Square centimetre (cm^2)**: used to measure quite small objects such as a piece of paper, a pencil tin or a table.

- **Square millimetre (mm^2)**: used to measure very small items such as an eraser, a stamp or a bus ticket.

Task: Units of measurement

Which unit of measurement would be most useful to measure the following objects? Choose from:

km^2 ha m^2 cm^2 mm^2

a laptop computer		
a cricket pitch		
a USB plug		
a paddock		
a sheet of A4 paper		
your classroom floor		
a pencil case		
the surface of your desk or table		

Working Together © Brent and Millgate-Smith 2008

⑤ Step 8: Test yourself

How well can you remember the new words and terms you have learned in this unit? Complete the gaps in the sentences below.

1 A **rectangle** is an o_____ shape. It has two 2 l_____ sides opposite each other and two shorter sides o_____ each other.

2 The **area** of a figure (shape) is the amount of flat s_____.

3 The **length** is the _____est side.

4 The **width** is the _____est side.

5 A **method** or **procedure** for working something out is called a f_____.

6 The p_____ is the **length of the outside edge**.

7 A qu_____l is a **four-sided** p_____ figure.

8 x and y are examples of pro_____. They are **symbols** which represent n_____.

Score

7–8 Excellent! You really know your stuff.

5–6 Pretty good. You will need a little revision of the terms before you move on.

3–4 Getting there. Go back to the definitions chart at the beginning of the unit and try again.

0–2 Revision is needed before you move on. Go back to the definitions grid at the beginning of the unit and try again.

Notes to teachers and support staff

Key skills for mathematics in this unit

By completing this unit, students will learn how to apply a mathematical formula to calculate the area of a rectangle. The skills focused on include:

- recognition of shape
- learning a formula
- applying a formula
- converting units of measurement
- consolidating operational mathematical vocabulary.

Vocabulary in this unit includes:

- concrete words to do with shape
- specialist mathematical terminology, such as 'perimeter'
- instructional words, such as 'calculate'.

Retaining and reinforcing learning must continue on a regular basis after the unit is completed. Students really need to revisit the unit of study regularly throughout the year so that the concepts and the processes are not lost. Subsequent lesson planning should allow for opportunities to practise perimeter and area problems and vocabulary recall in repeated cycles throughout the year.

Connections to Section 1

- Anxiety: Chapter 2
- Vocabulary reinforcement: Chapter 4
- Memory: Chapter 7

ⓣ Step 1: Essential vocabulary

- Maths can be very difficult for LLD students because of the vast range of highly specific vocabulary. Many LLD students can complete the computations but struggle with the language. Without a solid understanding of the meanings of crucial words, students are unlikely to be able to complete the mathematical operations. Even apparently obvious instructional terms that we might assume have been learned in primary school need to be checked and reinforced. They may well have been taught, but not necessarily learned. A vocabulary grid or glossary should be provided at the start of every new topic.

- The grid should be reproduced and pasted into the students' workbooks. It could also be enlarged and displayed on the classroom wall.

- Provide opportunities for students to write key vocabulary. Model pronouncing the words and breaking them into syllables. When students are able to say and write words correctly, there is a greater likelihood of retention. This can be addressed in support classes as well.

- The crossword is designed to embed the definitions of these key words in the memory. By completing it, students are required to process and apply the definitions.

- Spend ample time on this step. LLD students need time to learn, absorb and process new vocabulary.

- Allow time for regular revision of vocabulary/terminology.

- See Appendix 8 for the crossword solution.

🅣 Step 2: Identifying rectangles

- The necessity of ensuring that students have a firm grasp of the basic vocabulary cannot be overstated. A concept such as 'rectangle' may seem simple, but LLD students may not be confident about its definition.

- This step exemplifies the importance of connecting to students' existing knowledge by simply asking what they already know about a rectangle.

- This step also directs students toward recognising the shape as one common in their environment. This will move it on from the status of abstract word to everyday shape, and provide a concrete way for students to visualise the meaning of the word and remember it.

- A similar approach can be employed with most shapes.

- Leave plenty of space even for short answers to be recorded. The cramping of information exacerbates processing difficulties.

ANXIETY FLASHPOINT
The simple, practical activity of measuring will aid students who are already beginning to perceive maths as a difficult, abstract subject.

🅣 Step 3: Area squared

- The grid provides concrete examples of a difficult abstract concept.

- Students will need to refer back to the definitions in the grid.

- The squared paper activity should reinforce understanding by providing concrete evidence and by helping students to visualise what is actually meant by the term 'squared'. It can be extended by further examples.

- An even more tangible extension could be devised in which students draw around the outline of a rectangular object and cover the area with 1 cm squares of coloured paper.

🅣 Step 4: Investigating the area of a rectangle

- Again, the emphasis is on concrete visualisation.

- Readily available objects can be used to calculate the area. This provides a concrete basis for the research.

- Students may need help to use the squared paper.

- Providing a worked example is vital. Remind students to return to it whenever they need to.

- The formula A= lw is introduced here. An understanding of it should begin to emerge from the students' investigation.

- Asking students to complete gaps in a sentence provides essential scaffolding: they do not need to concern themselves about the wording or syntax of the sentence, and so can focus on the mathematical operations.

ANXIETY FLASHPOINT
Some students will be intimidated by the abbreviations used in the formula. Encourage them to continue to use the words.

🅣 Step 5: Using the formula A = lw

- All formulae, such as A = lw, should be reinforced frequently to aid memory.

- Copies of the formula could be written on post-it notes and stuck on folders, exercise books, etc.

- The formula should be displayed on the classroom walls and/or written on the whiteboard.

- An increasing amount of mathematical jargon is being used in this step (calculate, substitute, result). It will need to be revised. Students should be referred back to the vocabulary work at Step 1.

🅣 Step 6: Having a go

- LLD students need to be encouraged to visualise as much as possible. The simple illustrations provide a vital step.

- The diagrams help to keep the task reasonably concrete. Students can more easily visualise the shapes.

- The subsequent task moves them straight on to providing their own visualisations. It is important not to leave a gap between these two activities or the connections will be lost. If there is insufficient time in the lesson, recap the more concrete examples before moving on.

🅣 Step 7: Units of measurement

- Plenty of pictures are included in this step to encourage visualisation. This makes the task more concrete and 'real', and forms a solid basis for retention of both concepts and terminology.

- When completing the task, students should be referred back to the definitions and pictures.

- This task is partially one of judgment and estimation. There is no theoretical reason why a paddock cannot be measured in millimetres so we need to encourage practical thinking. Providing measuring tapes and rulers will aid this.

Working Together © Brent and Millgate-Smith 2008

Ⓣ Step 8: Test yourself

- Whatever form it takes, it is important to conclude the topic by further consolidating and reinforcing learned vocabulary.

- Note the highlighting of key words, which will help students to know what to look for. Encourage them to do the same when reading maths problems.

- Students could be asked to design a quiz, crossword or board game for their peers. Such an activity will consolidate their knowledge of the newly acquired vocabulary.

- The feedback is simple but designed to reward any degree of success, while also reminding students of the need for revision.

CHAPTER 11

Animal farm: challenging texts in the mixed-ability English classroom

About this unit

The novel *Animal farm* was written by George Orwell in 1945. *Animal farm* parodies (copies in a funny way) the events leading up to and following the Russian Revolution of 1917. Orwell uses animals to represent the Russian leaders and people. They live on a farm (which represents Russia) owned by humans (who mirror the wealthy and cruel **Tsars** who ruled the **Russian Empire** before the Revolution). See the table below to check your understanding.

In the Russian Empire	In *Animal farm*
the Russian state	Manor Farm
the **Tsars**, or rulers of the empire	humans
the Russian **citizens**	the farm animals

We are going to look closely at a section of the book where the downtrodden farm animals gather together in a barn, to be addressed by Old Major, an elderly and respected pig. He delivers a speech aimed at persuading the animals to rise up against their human owners and improve their lives.

Ⓢ Step 1: Vocabulary

Complete this task as you read the speech. It will help you to understand the speech.

Using a dictionary or thesaurus to help you, insert arrows to connect the correct definition to each word.

158   *Working Together* © Brent and Millgate-Smith 2008

1	porkers	a buyer of old or useless horses for slaughter
2	stall	wealth
3	laborious	a sleeping compartment for a farm animal
4	prosperity	successful
5	abolished	firmness of purpose, determination
6	consumes	got rid of
7	confinement	organised resistance to authority
8	resolution	involving hard work
9	knacker	eats or uses
10	dignity	plenty
11	rebellion	a workmate, friend or fellow soldier
12	victorious	a composed and serious manner
13	comrade	the time of a female's giving birth
14	abundance	young pigs

Ⓢ Step 2: Reading for meaning

You will be given a copy of the speech reprinted out of sequence (in the wrong order). Your task is to work out the correct sequence and then to analyse the persuasive techniques the speech uses. Follow these steps:

1 Read each section (paragraph) of the speech to get an idea of what it is about.

2 After you have read each paragraph, complete the vocabulary exercise above. Make sure that you have the correct meaning by reading the word in context.

3 In groups, try to order the speech into the correct sequence.

4 Make a note of any clues you use to help you.

Ⓢ Step 3: Identifying the arguments

1 When your group is happy with the sequence of the speech, read it carefully in the right order. (Check this with your teacher.)

2 Take each section in turn and compile a brief list of the **ideas** and **arguments** presented by Old Major.

3 Group the ideas together to identify the main issues.

4 Agree on the contention: what is Old Major aiming to persuade his audience to do or believe?

Ⓢ Step 4: Identifying emotive language

Old Major uses many words which are intended to persuade his audience to agree with his perceptions. These emotive words and images carry either positive or negative connotations (ideas). Look at the following example:

Negative	**Neutral**	**Positive**
skinny scraggy paltry	*thin*	*slim lean slender*

Task: Finding emotive language

Using two different coloured highlighters, go through the speech. Use one colour to highlight all the emotive words that have **positive** connotations. Use the second colour to highlight all the emotive words that have **negative** connotations.

1 Copy out a chart like the one below. (You will need about 10 more rows.) Use it to record the emotive words you have found. You have been given an example to start you off.

Paragraph	Word	+ or –	Connotations	To what does it apply?
2	laborious	–	gruelling hard work	the animals' lives now

2 Now arrange the words you have extracted (found) into groups under the following headings:

Lives of the animals now	Life as it could be in the future

3 In your group, discuss what the group of words in each column has in common.

Task: Emotive images

Old Major also uses **emotive images**. These are word pictures that are designed to produce an emotional response in the reader. For example, 'You young porkers … will scream your lives out at the block'.

It is hardly an image designed to reassure the young pigs that death will be peaceful, is it?

Find another example of an emotive image. Produce a picture of it. This is the image that Old Major wants to implant in the minds of his audience.

Ⓢ Step 5: Understanding the structure

Design a simple diagram or graph to show when the various **ideas** and **arguments** are introduced and developed in the speech.

Here is one way you could do this.

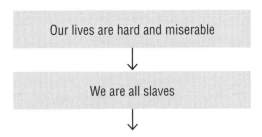

... and so on. Or you could use a bar chart or graph, or any kind of diagram that will help you to see how the speech is structured.

Are any ideas repeated or extended? Which ideas are carried through from beginning to end?

⑤ Step 6: Recognising audience and purpose

When your diagram is complete, discuss the following questions and make notes. Underlining will help again.

- What was Old Major's main purpose in delivering this speech?

- What effect would the speech have on the audience of animals listening to it?

Task: For writing

Imagine that you are one of the farm animals in the audience. Write for 10 minutes on your reactions to Old Major's speech.

For example, you could begin:

> *It's funny, but I've never really thought about the lives we lead here on the farm.*
> *I guess it never occurred to me to question the way we live ...*

Task: Role play

For this role play, work in groups of about six.

Imagine you have got together for a chat about last night's speech before beginning your day's work.

Allocate each member of the group the role of one of the animals that has listened to Old Major's speech. Try to include animals that will give you a wide range of opinion, from the gullible sheep who believe everything, to the cynical old donkey who doesn't believe that things can change for the better.

You might like to use the following lines of dialogue to start you off, then improvise the rest of the conversation:

> *Animal 1:*   *What did you make of Old Major's words last night, mate?*
> *D'you reckon he's a crackpot, or is there something in it?*
>
> *Animal 2:*   *Well, I must say, I've never stopped to think about our lives*
> *in that way before, have you?*

⑤ Step 7: Analysing rhetorical devices

You will have noticed that Old Major uses a range of rhetorical devices in his speech, including the emotive words and images we looked at earlier. Rhetorical devices are tricks used in public speaking in order to persuade the audience to agree with the speaker's contention, or point of view.

Copy out the chart on the next page and complete it. This will help you to identify some of the rhetorical devices and to analyse their intended effects on the audience.

Rhetorical device	Example from the speech	Effect on the audience
inclusive language	'comrades' used repeatedly	encourages a sense of unity
attention-catching anecdote or story		
slogan		finishes with a memorable catchphrase
repetition		
powerful images	'you will scream your lives out at the block'	
rhetorical questions		positions us to agree that there can be no answer except 'yes'
establishing speaker's authority and wisdom		
demonising opposition (the farmers, in this case)		rouses our anger and determination
emotive words	'miserable', 'cruel', 'slavery'	connotations of ...

Can you find any further examples of persuasive devices?

Task: Group work

Prepare a dramatised reading of part of Old Major's speech. Allocate a paragraph to each member of your group.

Annotate a copy of your paragraph with notes on how it should be delivered. Think about:

- pace (try to vary it, speeding up or slowing down as required)
- volume
- which words need to be emphasised
- pauses
- the tone or emotions behind the words.

⑤ Step 8: Individual writing task

Farmer Jones has, of course, been put in a difficult position, just as Old Major intended. He must now forestall (prevent) the rebellion Old Major has called for. How might he do this? By making an equally powerful speech to the animals, persuading them that they are actually quite well off!

Task: You as speech writer

Imagine that you have been given the job of drafting Farmer Jones' speech. Plan your speech carefully, perhaps modelling it on Old Major's speech. Look again at the structure and devices George Orwell has used.

Use the checklist below to guide your planning. Your speech must:

- have an attention-catching opening
- rebut (show to be wrong) Old Major's arguments by coming up with arguments that suit your purpose
- reassure the animals that they are treated fairly
- finish with a snappy slogan.

Each paragraph should conclude with a linking sentence that will link back to your main argument (the contention). Think about using conjunctions such as:

however   but   furthermore   additionally   therefore

Practise reading your speech aloud, preferably to an audience.

Task: Evaluation

Write an evaluation of your speech, using the guidelines below.

> The main purpose of my speech is …
> In order to get the attention of the animals I …
> To support my contention that …
> My main arguments are …
> I emphasise these arguments with rhetorical devices such as …
> My speech concludes with …
> Because …
> The most effective device I used is …
> By the end of my speech, the animals …

Notice that the evaluation is written in the **present tense**. This is the convention that is used when writing about texts. If you find it difficult to maintain the present tense, try completing the exercise below as practice.

Task: Writing in the present tense

The following paragraphs are taken from a student's evaluation of Old Major's speech. It is written in the **past tense**. Change it to the **present tense** by underlining the words (verbs) that need to be changed and replacing them with words in the present tense. The first two have been underlined for you.

> *The main purpose of Old Major's speech <u>was</u> to convince his fellow animals that change <u>is</u> possible in their lives. He wanted them to rebel against the farmer and take over the farm.*

In order to get the attention of the animals Old Major told them about his dream of a fair way of life. Then he reminded them of his age so that his wisdom was clear to them. These strategies helped him to get the animals to listen.

Old Major developed his argument by using many emotive words that were designed to shock them with the reality of their situation. These words included 'laborious' and 'miserable', which emphasised the mistreatment of the farm animals by the farmer. He used graphic images of the cruel deaths of the animals to implant pictures in their minds.

Glossary

anecdote	a brief account of an interesting incident
argument	a reason given to support the contention
audience	the listeners at whom the piece is aimed
contention	the speaker's opinion
inclusive language	language that is designed to draw the audience in ('We all agree …', 'we know that …' and so on)
purpose	main aim of the speaker
rhetorical question	a question to which the answer is obvious; it does not require an answer
structure	the organisation of a piece

Notes to teachers and support staff

Key skills for English and literacy in this unit

By completing this unit, students will develop their ability to work closely with an extract from a literary text. The skills focused on include:

- literal comprehension
- broadening of vocabulary
- interpretation of ideas
- understanding of authorial purpose
- analysis of literary techniques
- creative responses that employ the techniques identified
- individual and collaborative oral skills.

The step-by-step approach is designed to securely support students through various levels of challenge. They move from concrete to abstract tasks, engaging in higher order reading, thinking and creative skills in a highly structured framework.

There is considerable emphasis on the teaching of vocabulary. As previously mentioned, research shows this is a difficult area to develop. The intention here is to show how vocabulary teaching can be integrated into a unit of work. Explicit teaching is essential: students cannot successfully read for meaning if they do not fully understand the connotations of key vocabulary. There is also an emphasis on expanding students' working vocabulary and fostering more precise use of language.

Vocabulary tasks in this unit include:

- a step-by-step approach to identifying and defining key words
- emphasis on words the students will come across in a variety of settings
- work on connotations and visualisations
- grouping activities.

Connections to Section 1

- Anxiety: Chapter 2
- Decoding more complex vocabulary: Chapter 3
- Vocabulary and comprehension: Chapter 4
- Oral and written language skills: Chapter 5

The study of this unit does not require a detailed knowledge of the novel *Animal farm*.

Preteaching: ways into the text

This is an essential step for LLD students.

- Introduce the animal fable as a popular method of delivering a moral. Have students read a selection of Aesop's fables in small groups. They identify the moral and share it with the class.
- The fable is a quick way to reinforce narrative structure as well, providing a very clear-cut illustration of exposition, conflict and resolution.
- The children's picture book *Farmer Duck* by Martin Waddell works as a simple, condensed version of *Animal farm* and is useful to introduce the concept of the fable. It offers a straightforward illustration of the narrative structure model.
- Show Old Major's speech on a film version of *Animal farm*. It is important for students to hear texts read well to enable them to discern tone, inflection, emphases, etc. Audio books provide invaluable reading support and their use should be encouraged, either in class or individually.

- You may wish to provide more detailed background to the Russian Revolution and suggest that Old Major is modelled on Karl Marx. It is possible that the history department would be interested in working with you, especially if this historical period is to be taught as part of their program.

- Ensure that students have a broad understanding of the key terms **Tsar**, **citizens** and **Russian Empire**.

ANXIETY FLASHPOINT

For less able students, preteaching is particularly important as a way of introducing key concepts and engendering confidence. They can then begin study with their peers without the panic that often attends the introduction of new materials and concepts. Teachers and support staff should work closely together to decide when each stage of the topic should be introduced.

Ⓣ Step 1: Vocabulary

A completed chart is available as a photocopiable resource: see Appendix 9.

- Not all students will complete the task in the time given. Go over the answers as a class, so that students can add to their notes as they go.

- The completed chart (Appendix 9) can be used as a glossary for reference.

- Focus on comprehension and decoding. Look for any word patterns, such as base words, word endings, roots, etc. Identify a selection of nouns and verbs. Use them in sentences.

- Reinforce by returning to the words at the beginning and end of each lesson and explicitly discussing them as they arise in the context of the extract.

Ⓣ Step 2: Reading for meaning

- To prepare the sequencing exercise, photocopy the six paragraphs of Old Major's speech, from 'Comrades, you have heard already about the strange dream …' to 'All animals are comrades'.

- Organise the class into small groups, ensuring that each includes a strong reader who might be asked to read each section aloud for the group.

ANXIETY FLASHPOINT

Make it clear that not all students will be made to read aloud. Students who really dread doing so should not be embarrassed because it will serve no purpose—they will not comprehend meaning if their focus is on their performance.

- Support staff, or the teacher, may choose to read each section aloud. See original text for the speech in the correct sequence.

- A taped reading of each section in random order could be prepared to help students with severe decoding difficulties.

- The text clues will include syntactical signifiers, such as 'comrades', 'and', and 'now', but will largely focus on meaning. Understanding of the structural development of the speech will focus on clues in the text that one paragraph looks like an introduction, others follow and develop the argument, a slogan is used as a decisive ending and so on. This does not require detailed knowledge of rhetorical devices.

- LLD students can benefit twice from this if it is subsequently used for rereading for fluency practice.

ANXIETY FLASHPOINT
Disengage anxiety by assuring students that at this stage they need only to get the gist of each paragraph, not the finer detail.

Step 3: Identifying the arguments

- At this point, students need to hear the entire speech read aloud well: by the teacher, by listening to it on audio tape or by watching it on film.

- Define the key words for this task: **argument**, **issue** and **contention**. Reinforce memory by returning to the words at the beginning and end of each lesson and explicitly discussing them as they arise in the context of the extract.

- You could choose to complete the first paragraph together to model the task, either with the class or with individual groups.

- Consider allocating roles within the group, so that each member has responsibility for working on one paragraph and then sharing their findings with the group.

- Encourage students to annotate the text using highlighters to identify the arguments, and a numbering system to group similar ideas.

- Some students, if not all, will need guidance on setting up lists. Show them how to use separate headings for each part of the task.

- Once the task is completed, check that students have understood this by comparing findings as a class.

Note that sequencing is an area of difficulty for many LLD students. This task provides good practice by bringing sequencing to a conscious level. It also enforces the need for careful reading of each segment.

Step 4: Identifying emotive language

- This section emphasises the importance of synonyms and is particularly useful for expanding the vocabulary of less able students.

- Visualisation helps students to assess the intentions of imagery. Further work on connotations and visual images could include the study and design of cartoons, comic strips or posters.

- Close attention to diction and word choice will aid the teasing out of connotation, and will also help to develop vocabulary.

- Highlighting is a really useful device to help students to focus on the finer detail of text, as well as to isolate key points, examples and so on.

- Encourage the use of a computer thesaurus to extend this exercise.

- Students should be provided with frequent opportunities for repetition to reinforce memory. Key points and words (**emotive** and **connotation**, as well as the words identified by students in their charts) should be revised at staged intervals (several times during the lesson), at the conclusion of the lesson, at the beginning of the next class, and even in the longer term. Students should say the words and write them down.

ⓣ Step 5: Understanding the structure

- Draw on the annotations and highlighting completed at Step 3 to develop an awareness of structure.

- Students will notice that the first paragraph is designed to 'hook' the reader and establish the authority of the speaker. The arguments are not introduced until the second paragraph, and are gradually developed until the climax in paragraph 6. The last paragraph concludes with rallying slogans.

ⓣ Step 6: Recognising audience and purpose

- Both the short writing task and the role play activity will help students to empathise with Old Major's audience. Some students find it difficult to see more than one point of view.

- Discuss Old Major's intended effects and draw this into the context of the devices used to achieve them.

- Spend time discussing the differences between audience and purpose. For example, it needs to be understood that Old Major's audience is generally naïve and subservient. The intended shock value of his graphic imagery is therefore likely to be more pronounced. At the same time, he has to offer a plausible alternative.

ANXIETY FLASHPOINT
The short writing task should focus on ideas and intended response. These may flow with more ease if you assure students that technical accuracy is not the concern here. Perhaps they could share their responses orally instead of submitting them in writing.

🅣 Step 7: Analysing rhetorical devices

- This exercise presents an example of scaffolding, in which much of the deconstruction is completed and the students' task is simplified.
- Revisit the terminology used in Step 4, and make use of the glossary.
- The matching game/exercise in Appendix 10 can be used to further familiarise students with the specialised terminology. It draws on more familiar, everyday uses of rhetorical devices with the intention of demystifying the terms and enabling students to recognise them in everyday life.
- This step culminates in a dramatised reading of part of the speech. The intention here is to put the theory into action. Students should be encouraged to take cues about pace, expression and volume from the rhetorical devices they have studied.

ANXIETY FLASHPOINT
Make sure that anxious students are given plenty of time to practise. Try to ensure that they are placed within supportive groups.

- Providing a real audience can lend authenticity to the task of reading aloud. Ask students to record their readings for you to use with another class.

🅣 Step 8: Individual writing task

- Old Major's speech can be used as a model here, with students structuring their own speech in the same way. An example of a student's response to the task is included on the following page and can be used for class analysis and discussion, or as a model for students who need to see a concrete example of what they are expected to produce.
- The use of conjunctions should be encouraged to promote fluency. Providing students with a limited number of conjunctions to choose from encourages them to make informed choices with some variation.

ANXIETY FLASHPOINT
The scaffolded outline is designed to provide a supportive starting point to help students to organise their writing.

- Peer editing, in which each student works with a partner to offer constructive critical advice, provides immediate feedback. Research has shown immediate feedback maximises learning.
- The evaluation requires students to think explicitly about the writing process they have undertaken. It should be placed in the context of the learning experience, allowing them to identify and build on their achievements.

Student writing example

Farmer Jones' speech to the animals

by Sarah, Year 10

My great grandfather ran this farm, and his grandfather before him. The knowledge I possess has been passed down through all of these generations. I have been looking after you with this sound knowledge. I have feed you and I call a vet when you need one. I make sure you have the best care I can possibly give to you.

Your produce and work has given me the money to do this. The harder you work, the more you produce, the more I can give back to you. Have I refused any care you might need? You are valuable to me, and I would not be able to have such a prosperous farm with out you. I am sure other farms have it much worse, because their animals and farmers don't work as hard as we all do.

Just imagine if I was not here to pay the vet bills, who knows what would happen to you. Just imagine, Mrs Hen, all of your precious little chicks could be stolen during the night if I was not here to look after them.

You all work hard, myself included, but are we not all healthy? We can carry out our work can't we?

I take only so I can give back to you.

I also have an understanding of the world beyond this farm you animals could never have. You would not understand it purely because you have never had any interaction with it. Humans can be tricky, but only because they are trying to do the best by their animals. I understand this, so can get the best for you, while you animals would quickly become lost and confused.

All I ever try to do is the best by you, and you should follow Farmer Jones.

CHAPTER 12

Starting with the language of science: a science unit for the mixed-ability classroom

About this unit

This unit introduces the study of elements.

S Step 1: Essential vocabulary

Key words	Definition	Example
element	a pure substance; it contains only one type of atom. It cannot be split into simpler substances	Oxygen and nitrogen, which make up most of the air we breathe, are elements. Gold and silver, which we use to make jewellery, are elements.
atom	the smallest part of a substance you can find anywhere	
iron	an element that is a metal	A nail can be made of iron.
pure	unmixed; a pure substance contains only one type of atom	An ingot of gold contains only gold atoms—that is why it is so valuable.
reaction	the process that happens when chemicals are mixed	When a car rusts, there is a reaction between the air and the iron. The iron is made into iron oxide, which we call 'rust'.
oxygen	a gas which is an element; it supports breathing and burning	Oxygen is the part of the air that we use when we breathe.
compound	two or more elements that have been joined together and cannot be separated easily	Iron oxide is a compound. Remember the reaction that causes rust on a car? Oxygen combines with iron to make a compound–iron oxide. Once rust starts it is very difficult to reverse.

Working Together © Brent and Millgate-Smith 2008

Ⓢ Step 2: Identifying pure substances

With a partner, discuss what you understand by the word 'pure'. Make a list of items at home or at school that might be described as pure.

Was water on your list? It is probably one of the first things to come to mind as a pure substance. But is it really pure in a chemical sense?

Follow the experiment below to find out.

Task: Hoffman's voltameter experiment

Aim

To discover whether or not water is a pure substance.

You will need

- a Hoffman's voltameter
- water
- matches
- a wooden splint (taper)
- collecting test tubes.

Hypothesis

Predict what will happen.

Method

1 Fill the Hoffman's voltameter with water.

2 Pass an electric current through the water.

3 Release gases into the collecting test tube.

4 Test the hydrogen with a lighted taper. Note what happens.

5 Test the oxygen with a glowing taper. Note what happens.

Result

Describe what happens to the water.

- Are the quantities of water the same as they were before?
- Are the quantities of gas the same in each tube?

Discussion

You will have observed that bubbles formed in the water. These bubbles indicate that a gas has been formed. We tested the gases and found that they were different. We found that there was hydrogen and oxygen, so water contains hydrogen and oxygen elements.

Conclusion

You have discovered that water contains both hydrogen and oxygen elements. It is not, therefore, a pure substance.

- There are two atoms of hydrogen to every one atom of oxygen. In other words, there is twice as much hydrogen as oxygen.
- We started with water.
- Water is a compound of hydrogen and oxygen.
- The compound (water) has now separated into two pure elements—hydrogen and oxygen.

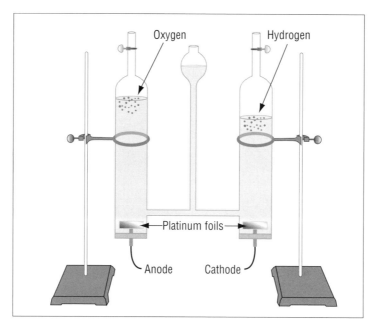

If you continue to watch the water that still remains in the Hoffman's voltameter, you will observe that the level in each tube is different. In fact, there will be a double quantity of hydrogen, which is how the symbol H_2O was devised.

So what *is* pure?

Task: Pure substances

Elements (as we have already discovered) are pure substances. They contain only one type of atom. They cannot be split into simpler substances.

Magnesium is an example of an element.

1 Look at a piece of magnesium ribbon. Choose some of these words to describe it in a sentence:

> *flexible   silver   bendy   shiny   reflective   glossy   polished*

2 Now watch your teacher burn some magnesium.

Choose some of these words and use them in a sentence to describe its appearance after burning:

> *white   powder   ashen   pale   particles   dust*

- **Question**: What has happened to the pure substance that started out as magnesium ribbon?
- **Answer**: It is no longer pure. The process of burning it has caused it to combine with oxygen in the air so that it has become a compound of magnesium and oxygen.

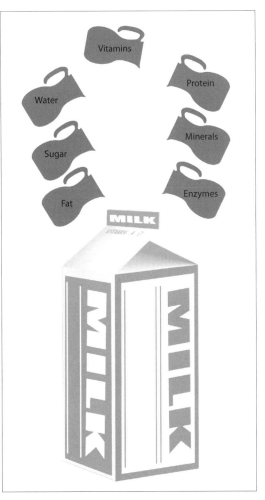

Look back at the beginning of Step 2, to the list of substances you thought could possibly be pure.

Was milk on your list? The label might say 'pure', but milk is actually a compound consisting of seven main components: water, fat, protein, sugar, minerals, vitamins and enzymes.

Orange juice is another drink that is often described as 'pure', but is it? Find out by searching for 'ingredients of orange juice' on the Internet.

So, you can see that scientists use the term 'pure' in a much more precise (exact) way than we use it in everyday life.

⑤ Step 3: Revision: what is an element?

Elements are **pure** substances that are made up of only one type of particle or atom.

Oxygen, which is a gas, is an **element**. The precious metal **gold** is an **element**. The liquid metal **mercury** is an **element**.

Most of these elements are found in nature: in the air, water and the ground.

In nature there are only 92 **elements** to be found. There are 19 more that can be manufactured in laboratories.

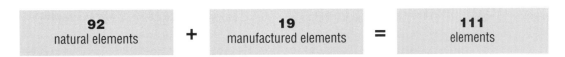

Elements cannot be broken down or split up by a chemical reaction.

There are two groups of **elements**: metals and non-metals.

Non-metals

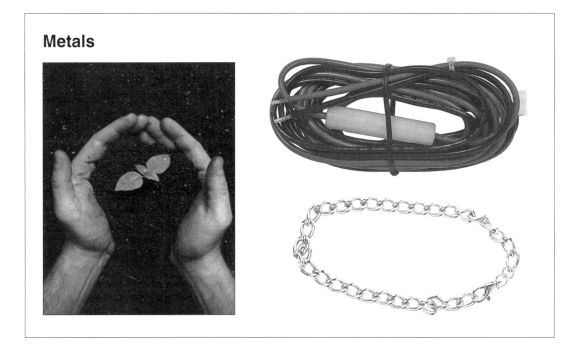

Metals

Look at the illustrations above. Here is some information about these elements:

Element	Definition	Example
helium	a non-metallic element	It is used in party balloons.
nitrogen	a non-metallic element	It is found in the air we breathe.
copper	a metal element	It is used in electrical wires.
silver	a metal element	It is found inside the earth's crust and is used for making jewellery.
potassium	a metallic element	It is found in the soil and is an important element for plant growth.

Working Together © Brent and Millgate-Smith 2008

Ⓢ Step 4: Test your knowledge of elements

Use the information you have learned so far in this unit to complete the sentences below.

1 An element is a _____ substance.

2 Gold and _____ are both metallic elements.

3 _____ is an example of a non-metallic element.

4 Elements can be divided into _____ groups.

5 There are 111 _____ known to scientists. Most of them are found in _____.

6 When the iron in a car reacts with air, a chemical _____ takes place and causes rust to form.

7 The smallest piece of anything is called an _____.

Notes to teachers and support staff

Key skills for science in this unit

By completing this unit, students will be introduced to the study of elements. The skills focused on include:

- identifying elements
- grouping and categorising
- developing subsections of data
- recognising scientific characteristics
- structuring descriptive sentences.

  Vocabulary in this unit includes:

- concrete words to do with elements
- specialist scientific terminology, such as 'pure' and 'gases'
- adjectives used to describe elements.

Connections to Section 1

- Teaching the sounds and syllables in new words so that LLD students can more accurately say, read and retrieve these new words from memory: Chapter 3
- Structuring descriptive sentences and extending the use of adjectives: Chapter 5
- Anxiety: Chapter 2
- Vocabulary: Chapter 4

🅣 Step 1: Essential vocabulary

- This initial step provides the core words and their definitions.

- Definitions should be read aloud by the teacher and their meanings discussed to ensure effective processing of the information. Students should be given as many opportunities as possible to link vocabulary with a visual image to aid comprehension and retention.

- Encourage students to say and write new science vocabulary to assist in retention. Model how to divide words into syllables if appropriate.

- The vocabulary chart should be kept for reference as the unit progresses. It could also be enlarged and posted on the classroom wall.

🅣 Step 2: Identifying pure substances

- The meaning of 'pure' in this context should be illustrated and established. Start at a point where previous knowledge can be drawn on. For instance, you might bring to class a carton of ice-cream labelled 'pure' and read the list of ingredients. This will establish that the product is not pure because it contains water, sugar, cream, etc. Similarly, after the experiment, looking at and discussing a jug of water will lead to the conclusion that it contains two atoms—hydrogen and oxygen—and is therefore not pure. It also makes explicit the very different meanings of the word 'pure': its general or marketing sense, compared to its very specific, measurable meaning in science.

- Use a gold ring to illustrate that in this form gold is not pure but includes copper to make it durable (explain the meaning of 'durable'). Discuss what would happen if a ring was produced without copper. Tap into their possible knowledge about the carat purity ratings.

- Use an H_2O water bottle (brand name) as a visual reminder of the compound ingredients of water.

- This line of investigation could be continued as group research or as homework. Students could locate further items that might be considered 'pure' and challenge the perception.

Voltameter experiment

- Practical experiments ground the students' comprehension and provide a basis for visualisation and retention of terminology.

- Note that the water needs to be slightly acidified.

- The hydrogen test should produce a popping sound and the oxygen test should result in the taper reigniting.

- Discuss what elements they are and point out that '$_2$' means 'twice as much hydrogen as oxygen'. Ensure that students can say element names, correctly segment them for syllables, and spell them.

- The experiment will take about half an hour to produce the required quantity of water/gases. Use the waiting time to discuss terms used in a science experiment and hypothesise. For instance, go over the significance of the ratio of hydrogen to oxygen. Use the Internet to research the ingredients of apparently pure substances.

- When enough water has been processed, use a ruler to measure the quantities.

- Remember to keep returning to the vocabulary list to reinforce understanding and retention.

🅣 Step 3: Revision: what is an element?

- This is an information-heavy section but it is essential to the progress of learning.

- Note the highlighting of key words that will help students to know what to look for.

ANXIETY FLASHPOINT
Emphasise that this section can be used throughout as a reference section. Immediate learning of the information is not essential at this stage.

🅣 Step 4: Test your knowledge of elements

- This step requires the application of newly learned vocabulary and is an essential consolidation exercise. Look at how the student spells a word as this will give a clue into possible future difficulties with recall. Check that the student can break a word into syllables as they say it.

- The provision of the core words helps students to narrow their search while still necessitating the careful reading and processing of information.

- The construction of cloze exercises requires care. Make sure that enough information is provided before the gap to establish meaning.

ANXIETY FLASHPOINT
It is a small point, but the wording of the heading is deliberately chosen to minimise stress. By putting the emphasis on the words 'test yourself', we are subtly urging students to take responsibility for their own learning.

CHAPTER 13

From page to stage: Shakespeare in the mixed-ability classroom

About this unit

This unit presents a taste of plays of William Shakespeare. You will learn some strategies to read and perform extracts from some of the many plays he wrote, including *A midsummer night's dream*, *Julius Caesar*, *Romeo and Juliet* and *Macbeth*.

S Step 1: Understanding the plot—*A midsummer night's dream*

Whichever play you are working on, the first step is to familiarise yourself with its plot. Don't worry about all the details—get the gist (main ideas) of the story. You can do this in a number of ways:

- view a film version

- watch a live theatre production

- read a story version of the play, such as *Lamb's tales from Shakespeare*

- read a synopsis (summary) like the one below—most editions of the play script include a synopsis.

As an example, let's consider *A midsummer night's dream*.

A midsummer night's dream is a **comedy** set in ancient Athens. In folklore, midsummer night is associated with fairy celebrations. While many obstacles (problems) threaten the safety and happiness of the characters, all is resolved at the end: hence the play is categorised as **comedy**.

The plot of this play is complicated, full of twists and turns, mistaken identities and changes in appearance. That's part of its comic appeal—to some extent the confusion is deliberate.

Read the synopsis of *A midsummer night's dream*.

Working Together © Brent and Millgate-Smith 2008

In Athens

- Hermia and Lysander are in love.
- Helena is in love with Demetrius, but he loves Hermia.
- Hermia's father wants her to marry Demetrius. If she refuses, she will either be put to death or sent to live the rest of her life as a nun.
- So Hermia and Lysander run away through the woods, but Helena and Demetrius follow them.

In the woods

- Some workmen are rehearsing a play that they hope to perform for the Duke of Athens on his wedding day.
- The King and Queen of the fairies, Oberon and Titania, are fighting.
- King Oberon acquires a magic potion that is designed to make its victim fall in love with whatever they see first upon waking up.
- A mischievous fairy, Puck, changes one of the workmen, Bottom, into a donkey.
- When Titania wakes with the magic potion in her eyes, she falls madly in love with the donkey-headed Bottom.
- Meanwhile, both Demetrius and Lysander have received the magic potion, and both fall in love with Helena.
- Hermia and Helena fight.
- King Oberon uses magic to restore harmony (good relationships).
- Demetrius now loves Helena and Lysander is again in love with Hermia.
- Titania and Oberon resolve their quarrel.

Back in Athens

- The two couples are married, along with the Duke, and as part of the celebrations the workmen perform their play.

A number of key scenes are depicted in the following frames.

1 Using the synopsis, sequence the frames into the correct order.

2 In the space below each frame, write a sentence to identify which characters are depicted and what is happening.

Sequence number

Sequence number

Sequence number

Sequence number

Working Together © Brent and Millgate-Smith 2008

Sequence number

Sequence number

Sequence number

Ⓢ Step 2: Reading the text—*Julius Caesar*

Julius Caesar is set in ancient Rome and is a **tragedy**. It recounts the assassination of Julius Caesar, a leader of the Roman Empire, and the civil war that follows his death. This play tracks the downfall of a tragic hero who is undone (destroyed) by a weakness in his character. This is why it is categorised as a **tragedy** play.

Task: Speech

In this speech from *Julius Caesar*, Mark Antony stands over the dead body of his friend and comrade, Julius Caesar. He thinks aloud, addressing his thoughts to Caesar.

Work in groups and follow the steps below.

1 Read the speech aloud as a group.

The first person reads up to the first slash. Allow a pause. Then the second person reads to the second slash. Allow a pause. Continue in this way, each person reading to a slash until you have read the speech.

Read slowly. Take in the words.

> O pardon me,/thou bleeding piece of earth,/
> That I am meek and gentle with these butchers!/
> Thou art the ruins of the noblest man
> That ever lived in the tide of times./
> Woe to the hand that shed this costly blood!/
> Over thy wounds,/now do I prophesy,/
> Which like dumb mouths do ope their ruby lips,/
> To beg the voice and utterance of my tongue,/
> A curse shall light upon the limbs of men./
> Domestic fury,/and fierce civil strife,/
> Shall cumber all the parts of Italy./
> Blood and destruction shall be so in use,/
> And dreadful objects so familiar,/
> That mothers shall but smile when they behold
> Their infants quartered with the hands of war./
> All pity choked with custom of fell deeds,/
> And Caesar's spirit, ranging for revenge,/
> With Ate by his side,/come hot from hell,/
> Shall in these confines,/with a monarch's voice,/
> Cry havoc,/and let slip the dogs of war,/
> That this foul deed shall smell above the earth
> With carrion men/groaning for burial.

You might have noticed that the speech is written in **blank verse**. This is a pattern (metre) that uses 10 syllables per line. Usually the stress is on the even syllables, so it creates a certain rhythm that you might have heard when listening to your group reading. However, actors always try to make the meaning clear by speaking as naturally as possible. The regular metre helps them to learn their lines.

2 Test out the metre for yourself by splitting a few lines into syllables, like this:

Blood/ and/ des/truc/tion/ shall/ be/ so/ in/ use
And/ dread/ful/ ob/jects/ so/ fam/i/li/ar.

However, when reading any form of blank verse, it is vital to read in sentences, observing the punctuation marks. If you simply read as a collection of separate lines, stopping at the end of each one, it will make little sense.

3 In your group, read the speech again. This time, read an entire sentence each.

Reader 1: *O pardon me, thou bleeding piece of earth,*
       That I am meek and gentle with these butchers!

Reader 2: *Thou art the ruins of the noblest man*
       That ever lived in the tide of times.

Reader 3: *Woe to the hand that shed this costly blood!*

... and so on.

4 Discuss what you have learned from this speech about the feelings of Mark Antony towards Julius Caesar and towards the conspirators who have just assassinated him.

Then read the statements below and select one or two you agree with most strongly.

Mark Antony is:
- grief-stricken
- set on revenge
- sad about his friend's death, but forgiving of the conspirators (plotters)
- worried about the Roman citizens
- ashamed of his gentleness
- bloodthirsty
- enraged and passionate.

Find some evidence to support your choices and then compare your group's conclusion with those of the others.

Task: Writing

How would you describe the thoughts and feelings that Mark Antony expresses in this speech? You will shortly be asked to explain what he is thinking and feeling at this point. You will be able to do this more precisely if you can choose a variety of verbs to describe how he speaks. Do not use the verb 'says'.

As an example, compare the two phrases below and think about which is the most accurate and precise:

- Mark Antony says to the dead Caesar, 'O pardon me'.
- Mark Antony pleads with the dead Caesar, 'O pardon me'.

The verb 'says' does not give as many clues about his underlying feelings. 'Pleads' makes it clear that he feels guilty for associating with Caesar's killers and that he hopes for forgiveness.

1 Copy out the list of verbs in the box below. Using a thesaurus, write down their meanings.

pleads	
cries	
beseeches	
threatens	
laments	
whispers	
shouts	
rants	
spits	
praises	
complains	
argues	
protests	

2 Use a highlighter to colour-code the verbs which suggest the strongest feelings.

3 Now write a paragraph on the thoughts and feelings Mark Antony expresses in this speech. Use some of the verbs in the box above to make your description as precise as possible. This will give your writing a more adult and literate sound.

⑤ Step 3: Word attack—*Macbeth*

Macbeth is set in Scotland in the Middle Ages and is a tragedy. It recounts the downfall (ruin) of Macbeth, a brave and highly regarded soldier, who kills the king. This leads to many more murders and enormous guilt for Macbeth himself. Macbeth is a tragic hero who is undone (destroyed) by a weakness in his character, hence it is categorised as a tragedy play.

Shakespearean English

While much of Shakespeare's language is quite recognisable, there are quite a lot of differences from modern English. How could it be otherwise? Shakespeare was writing about 400 years ago and language use has changed considerably over that time.

Here are some of the ways in which Shakespearean English differs from modern English.

- Some words are identical to their modern English counterparts: for example, 'where' 'had' and 'about'.

- Some words look and sound very similar to their modern English counterparts, for example, 'art' instead of 'are'.

- Some words are unfamiliar because they are rarely used now, such as 'cumber' (*Julius Caesar*). We can often guess at an approximate meaning by getting the gist of the sentence. Use the notes in your script to find the precise meaning.

- Some words might remind you of modern English words but actually mean something different, for example, 'wherefore', which means 'why'. (When Juliet calls, 'Wherefore art thou Romeo?' she is frustrated that he has the name of her enemy: she is not wondering where he is.)

- Words such as 'hither' and 'thither' will sound familiar. You can probably work out from the context that they mean 'here' and 'there'.

- Words are often contractions of two words, such as 'th'art' or 'thou'rt' for 'thou art'. The 'ed' ending was usually pronounced, so if this is not the intention the 'e' will be omitted, for example, 'lived' has two syllables and 'liv'd' has one.

- Some of the words seem to be in a rather strange order, for example, 'but in a sieve I'll thither sail'. Remember, this is poetry and rhythm is important.

- Try to find more examples of the features described in the play you are studying.

Task: Test your word knowledge

In the extract below from *Macbeth*, three witches meet on the heath (open land covered with low scrub) in a thunderstorm. In groups of three, read the parts aloud. Then work out the likely meaning of the highlighted words.

First Witch	Where hast thou been, sister?
Second Witch	Killing swine.
Third Witch	Sister, where thou?
First Witch	A sailor's wife had chestnuts in her lap, 5
	And munch'd, and munch'd, and munch'd:
	'Give me,' quoth I:
	'**Aroint thee**, witch!' the **rump-fed ronyon** cries.
	Her husband's to Aleppo gone, master **o' the Tiger**:
	But in a sieve I'll thither sail, 10
	And, like a rat without a tail,
	I'll do, I'll do, and I'll do.
Second Witch	I'll give thee a wind.
First Witch	Thou'rt kind.

You will probably have learned that it is possible to get a good idea of the meaning of a word by reading it within the context of the sentence in which it appears. Don't forget to do this as you read and listen to the play.

Using the script of the play you are studying, see how many of the words in the chart below you can find and work out. Add to the chart as you come across more words.

thy	
thine	
wither	
hither	
thither	
doth	
wherefore	
art	
methinks	
methought	
ay	
wooed	
o'er	
beguile	
fell	

>>

 Working Together © Brent and Millgate-Smith 2008

>>

Add more words:	

Remember that Shakespeare would often contract two words into one to make it scan (fit) within the verse, therefore 'over' becomes 'o'er', and 'thou art' becomes 'thou'rt'.

Task: Syllable revision

Break down the following words into separate syllables. Complete the right-hand column to show how many syllables are in each word or phrase.

Contraction	Full version	Number of syllables in full version
I'll	I will	2
o'er		
ne'er		
munch'd		
thou'rt		
ope		

S Step 4: The witches in film: analysing a film text

Numerous film versions of *Macbeth* have been made. With the benefits of cinematography (the use of film), the witches' scenes can be presented in many ways depending on the interpretation of the director. Some directors have used female actors and some have used male. They can be young, old or a mixture.

View the scene we have considered above on film (in a couple of different versions if you can).

Film technique prompt sheet

This sheet is designed to be used alongside a blank version. Its purpose is to remind you about the terminology (vocabulary) you have learned in class and to provide clues about what you should be looking for in your selected scenes.

After you have viewed the scene once, watch it again. Make notes in the boxes that follow the prompts. Use the examples given to guide your thinking.

Film technique prompt sheet

Dialogue

What do the characters say, and how do they say it? Consider:
- the words they choose
- their accent and dialect
- how much their feelings are revealed by words (and how much by other means, such as facial expression, gesture, etc.)
- their tone of voice: does the character speak angrily, sadly, reluctantly, sympathetically, softly, gently, dismissively, hopefully, brightly, dully, with irritation, etc.?

Soundtrack

What sounds other than dialogue are heard, and why were they chosen?
Consider the effect of each sound effect on the audience. For instance:
- birdsong may be used to suggest morning or natural beauty
- a screeching violin might warn of danger and so heighten tension
- a song can reflect a character's state of mind
- a heartbeat could build suspense and help us to identify with a character
- a telephone might link two scenes or characters
- music can set the tone of a place or mood.

Framing and camera angles

Look carefully at what the camera focuses on in each frame. Think about the following:
- From whose point of view do we follow the action or conversation?
- What objects or symbols are included, and why are they important to our understanding of the scene? For example, is there evidence of wealth or poverty? Does a vast open landscape suggest freedom or danger?
- Are we being invited to focus on a detail or the whole picture?
- What is left out of the frame? Is action taking place elsewhere?
- **High-angle camera shots** are often used to look down on a subject. The effect can be to make the subject appear small, insignificant or threatened.
- **Low-angle camera shots** give an impression of looking up at a subject, which can suggest a position of power.
- **Close-ups** are used to focus our attention on a particular character. What emotions are revealed?
- **Long shots and wide angles** provide information about setting and often lead us into a situation. What information are we given?

Lighting and colour

Think about the visual appeal of the scene and the mood created by lighting and colour.
Think about the effects of:
- a harsh, glaring light
- darkness and gloom
- soft sunlight streaming through a window
- dazzling sunshine?

What is suggested by the predominant (main) colour in a landscape or room? Think about the effects of:
- rolling, green hills
- craggy, blackened hills
- a smoky, brown interior
- sunlight filtering through trees.

Setting

Setting refers to the time, place and weather. An audience responds to it with particular expectations of what the story will be and how the characters will behave. Think about:
- how a sense of period is established
- what the setting reveals about the way of life of those who live there
- how well the characters fit into their setting
- how the weather adds to the atmosphere.

Blank film techniques prompt sheet

Dialogue

What do the characters say, and how do they say it?

Soundtrack

What sounds other than dialogue are heard, and why were they chosen?
Consider the effect of each sound effect on the audience.

Framing and camera angles

Look carefully at what the camera focuses on in each frame.

Lighting and colour

Think about the visual appeal of the scene, and the mood created by lighting and colour.

Setting

Think about the time, place and weather in the scene.

Task: Interpreting the scene

- How are you intended to interpret the witches in the film version you viewed? Are they to be seen as real or figments of Macbeth's imagination? Are they malevolent (evil) or well intentioned?

- In groups, discuss how you would present the witches in a stage play.

Ⓢ Step 5: Bringing imagery alive— *Romeo and Juliet*

Romeo and Juliet is set in Italy and is a tragedy. It recounts the story of two teenagers from feuding (fighting) families who fall in love and marry in secret. This leads to the death of both of them.

An **image** is a word picture. The purpose of **images** is to help us to see things as the writer wants us to: to plant certain pictures in our heads.

Images can be simple and direct: we instantly picture the object being described. They can also be more complex, often comparing one object to another, sometimes building on these to make what is almost a little cartoon in our mind's eye.

When you encounter an image in a Shakespeare play (and you will encounter many), work at visualising it first. Think about the connotations (meanings) afterwards. Try to actually draw some of the images used so that you can see them in concrete form.

Look at these examples.

There'll be fireworks

He's really cool

At the end of the day

Feeling stuck

Task: Exploring word pictures

Let's work on some examples.

1 Below is the speech Romeo makes when he first sets eyes on Juliet. A number of key words are missing. Read the speech through first and then work out what the missing words might be.

> O, she doth teach the torches to burn _____!
> It seems she hangs upon the _____ of night
> Like a rich jewel in an Ethiop's ear.
> Beauty too _____ for use, for earth too dear!
> So shows a _____ dove trooping with crows
> As yonder lady o'er her fellows shows.
> The measure done, I'll watch her place of stand,
> And, touching hers, make blessed my rude _____
> Did my heart _____ till now? Forswear it, sight!
> For I ne'er saw true _____ till this night.

Notes
- Ethiop: an Ethiopian, therefore very black-skinned
- measure: dance
- rude: rough
- forswear: deny

Now check the original speech (provided in Appendix 11).

2 Illustrate the speech by drawing the four main images used by Romeo to describe Juliet. These are listed below.

Note that many of the various images are linked to forms of light. What insights does this give us into the effect that Juliet's appearance has on Romeo?

Romeo's images
- she doth teach the torches to burn _____
- she hangs upon the _____ of night
- like a rich jewel in an Ethiop's ear
- a _____ dove trooping with crows

Ⓢ Step 6: Understanding the characters— *Romeo and Juliet*

Act 4 Scene 3: 'What if it be …'

In the speech that follows, Juliet has to decide whether to risk drinking a mysterious potion given to her by Friar Laurence. He has told her that it will make her appear to be dead so that she cannot be forced to marry a man she doesn't love. She will then wake later to be reunited with her secret husband, Romeo and the two will escape together.

However, she has to weigh up the consequences:

- The potion might not work.

- The potion might **actually** kill her, instead of just appearing to do so.

- If it works, she will awake in a dark tomb alongside the rotting corpse of her recently dead cousin and the bones of her ancestors.

Task: Understanding character

1 Read the speech carefully.

2 Separate it into Juliet's main trains of thought. Make a note of these.

3 Look for the points at which her thinking changes, taking her in another direction.

> What if this be a poison which the friar
> Subtly hath minist'red to have me dead,
> Lest in this marriage he should be dishonour'd
> Because he married me before to Romeo?
> 5   I fear it is; and yet, methinks, it should not,
> For he hath still been tried a holy man.
> How if, when I am laid into the tomb,
> I wake before the time that Romeo
> Come to redeem me? There's a fearful point!
> 10   Shall I not then be stifled in the vault,
> To whose foul mouth no healthsome air breathes in,
> And there die strangled ere my Romeo comes?
> Or, if I live, is it not very like
> The horrible conceit of death and night,
> 15   Together with the terror of the place,—
> As in a vault, an ancient receptacle,
> Where, for this many hundred years, the bones
> Of all my buried ancestors are pack'd;
> Where bloody Tybalt, yet but green in earth,

Lies fest'ring in his shroud; where, as they say,

At some hours in the night spirits resort;—

Alack, alack, is it not like that I,

So early waking,— what with loathsome smells,

And shrieks like mandrakes' torn out of the earth,

25 That living mortals, hearing them run mad;—

Or, if I wake, shall I not be distraught,

Environed with all these hideous fears,

And madly play with my forefathers' joints,

And pluck the mangled Tybalt from his shroud,

30 And, in this rage, with some great kinsman's bone

As with a club, dash out my desperate brains?

O, look! Methinks I see my cousin's ghost

Seeking out Romeo, that did spit his body

Upon a rapier's point. Stay, Tybalt, stay!

35 Romeo, I come! This do I drink to thee.

4 Copy out a graph like the one below. Use it to record Juliet's emotional journey in the course of her speech.

Label each point you plot to indicate your textual evidence. You can do this either with a brief quotation on the graph, or, if you prefer, use a key.

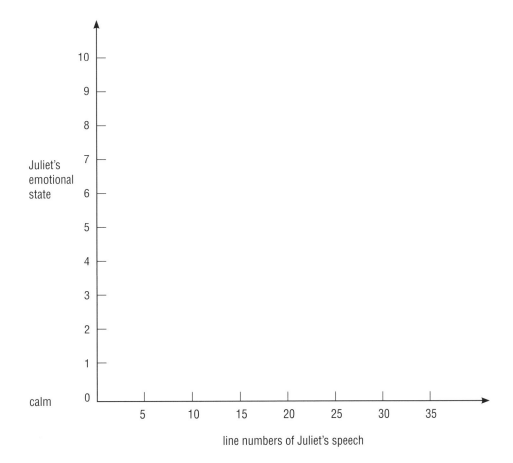

line numbers of Juliet's speech

5 What can you conclude about the structure of the speech? Complete the following statements based on your findings, by selecting the most appropriate word from those offered.

- At the beginning of the speech, Juliet is:

  concerned   terrified   calm   anxious   afraid

- By the end of her speech, Juliet is:

  concerned   terrified   calm   anxious   afraid

- In the end, what scares Juliet the most?

⑤ Step 7: Getting the words off the page

The purpose of the activities we have completed so far in this unit is to help you to understand the characters and the language. Now it is time to put that understanding into action as Shakespeare intended—on the stage.

As a class, perform a condensed version of the play you are studying. You will work in groups. Each group will be allocated a scene or part of a scene, and some time to rehearse it. Eventually, you will all be ready to show your scene to the rest of the class in sequence.

Work out how many people you will need in your group. If there are a number of small speaking parts, it is often possible for someone to play more than one part.

1 Agree with your teacher on the section from the play that you wish to perform. Allocate parts.

2 It can be effective to open and close your scene with a tableau, or freeze-frame. Try to capture a pose that reveals your character's reactions at that stage in the play.

3 Decide whether you want to use any of the following.
- *Costume.* You might like to choose one symbolic item for each character, for instance, a hat, apron, cape or scarf.
- *Props.* Again, a single item can suggest an important element of your character—it could be a sword, spectacles, a hammer, a book, etc.
- *Soundtrack and/or music.* You would probably want to prerecord this unless you have a musician in your group who could perform live.
- *Setting*: If time allows, you might want to create a painted backdrop. Alternatively, the grounds of your school could provide a suitable backdrop for an outdoor performance. Remember, Shakespeare's stage sets were very simple.

Now work on your script.

Make sure you fully understand the words you have to say. It can help to 'translate' your lines into modern English.

You may prefer to present a modernised version of your scene. Why not try a rap version, or use a modern local accent? Think about what is suited to the scene you are preparing.

4 Practise saying the lines clearly, varying your expression to get the meaning across. Work on movement and gesture. The more you rehearse, the better your performance will be.

Have fun!

Notes to teachers and support staff
Key skills for literature and drama study in this unit

This is an introduction to the plays of Shakespeare. It suggests approaches to a number of the more accessible plays, namely *A midsummer night's dream*, *Julius Caesar*, *Romeo and Juliet*, and *Macbeth*. It can be used as a freestanding unit to give students their first taste of the plays. Alternatively, teachers may choose to focus on a single play and adapt some of the activities to suit.

There are many excellent teaching aids available to support the study of the most popular Shakespeare plays. This unit is not intended to replace those but to offer suggestions that can be adapted and modified to suit any play (and many challenging literary texts, including poetry).

We sometimes need to remind ourselves that Shakespeare wrote his plays for live performance rather than as implements of torture to be sweated through as examination preparation. In terms of his audiences, his challenge was very similar to ours as teachers in the mixed-ability classroom. This unit, therefore, culminates in a performance activity rather than a written one. If students can get an idea of the fun of drama and gain some confidence in their ability to study it, in say, Years 8 or 9, then we are preparing the ground for further study in subsequent years.

By completing this unit, students will be given an introduction to the study and dramatisation of various Shakespeare plays. The skills focused on include:

- interpretation of ideas
- interpretation of character
- analysis of imagery
- individual and collaborative oral skills.

  Vocabulary tasks in this unit include:
- strategies to work out unfamiliar words
- emphasis on the changes in language over time
- work on connotations and visualisations
- hints on how to read blank verse.

Connections to Section 1

- Anxiety: Chapter 2
- Vocabulary and comprehension (including visualisation): Chapter 4
- Oral and written language skills: Chapter 5

Preteaching: ways into the text

- Set a mini-research task on the life of Shakespeare, or a task to recount some of the more entertaining aspects of his life. This will demystify a name which students often anticipate with apprehension. The discovery that Shakespeare left school at 13, was caught poaching and left his second-best bed to his wife makes him seem more human.

- Don't feel that it's cheating to give the students a plot outline first. They will find it difficult enough to follow the action and dialogue without having to work out the plot as well. Additionally, the plots are selling points that will often capture the students' interest.

- Be sure to use an edition of the script that has good, clear annotations. The 'parallel text' versions can be helpful as they provide a modern English 'translation' as well as the original.

ANXIETY FLASHPOINT

Shakespeare's reputation precedes him—and not only for his wit and wisdom. From the start, offer reassurance that detailed study and knowledge will not be required. Put the emphasis on fun. Point out that Shakespeare wrote his plays to entertain the masses, who were mainly uneducated, and that they were intended for live performance rather than close study.

Ⓣ Step 1: Understanding the plot

- Make use of performance opportunities, whether live theatre or film. The *Animated tales from Shakespeare*, available on DVD or video, are a terrific introduction to certain plays, as they condense the action into 30 minutes. They are also a useful source of important quotations.

- *Lamb's tales from Shakespeare* retells the plays in prose form, which is much more familiar and accessible to most students. They are helpful as an introduction in place of, or as well as, the viewing of a performance of some kind.

- All student editions of the plays contain synopses. These can be photocopied and cut up, so that the students have to sequence them.

- The sequencing frame activity on pages 181–83 should be retained as an aide-mémoire. Refer also to the cartoon and notes presented in *One in eleven* (Brent, Gough & Robinson 2001, p. 42).

ⓣ Step 2: Reading the text

- At some point, have the class listen to a good reading of the speech, perhaps on film or on an audio recording. Play it several times.

- This is a group-work activity that requires all members to participate in some reading aloud but does not require lengthy reading. It should therefore be possible to involve readers of most levels of ability.

- In verbal instructions, emphasise that it is an exploratory task designed to help them to analyse how blank verse should be read. It is expected that they will help each other and play around with pronunciation and pacing.

- It is important that readers recognise that the language will often not make sense unless it is read in sentences. Pausing at the end of every line might seem natural because of the shape of the verse, but can impede the meaning.

- The follow-up task asks students to articulate their responses to the speech in the form of a judgment about character and tone. The prompt statements make the task more accessible and provide scaffolding, yet require the student to read closely for evidence. Such an activity can readily be adapted to other speeches.

- The process of selecting descriptive statements from a series of choices provided is an opportunity for teacher modelling: the reasoning process of both teacher and students should be explicitly discussed. The LLD student who has difficulty distinguishing and isolating emotional nuance needs to hear clearly articulated examples of such thinking.

- As an extension, students can be asked to work in groups and provide a list of prompt descriptors for other groups, based on a range of speeches. In this way, the insecure student is engaging closely with the linguistic and literary devices in a supported manner.

- The short writing task is designed to encourage the use of a wider range of mental and linguistic verbs. Students with more limited writing skills can be taught to increase the precision of their expression by focusing on the verbs they use. (The natural response for many would be to include in this paragraph a list of sentences beginning with, 'He says …') This task specifically targets verb choices. Similar activities can be devised to focus on adverbs, adjectives, etc.

ⓣ Step 3: Word attack

- The aim of this section is to develop an awareness that the meaning of unfamiliar words can often be guessed by reading them in context. Such an approach is effective in any textual study, whether it be a literary or a factual text.

- The information gathered here should be developed into a personal word list to be used throughout the unit. Further use can be made of this in individual sessions, where the words may be used for further syllabification work, spelling practice, etc.

- A certain amount of time should be allowed for the students to complete the chart in pairs or small groups. If this is followed up with a class sharing, most meanings should be identified.

🅣 Step 4: The witches in film: analysing a film text

- The use of selected scenes from films is invaluable in many ways. The task provided is structured to allow students to focus on individual film techniques, drawing them together gradually. It assumes that students have been taught the vocabulary of film production. This is an essential step which must precede analysis of a film text.

- Showing the selected scene without sound first helps students to concentrate closely on visual effects. Show it several times, focusing on each technique in turn. Then show it with sound, focusing on dialogue and then on sound effects separately.

- The film technique prompt sheet is designed to work with any film.

🅣 Step 5: Bringing imagery alive

- It is critical to ensure students are familiar with the vocabulary underlying this activity—'image', 'imply', 'connotation', etc. It should also form part of the support program.

- The cloze procedure operates as a strategy to encourage close and careful reading. It is not possible to 'fill the gaps' without some understanding of the content. Students should be instructed to read the entire speech through once or twice before attempting to supply missing words so that they get some feel for the ideas and imagery patterns.

- The cloze exercise will help students to identify the rhyme scheme. This can be developed, depending on the needs of the class, into an introduction to the role of the couplet in iambic pentameter.

ANXIETY FLASHPOINT

Reassure students who are anxious about 'getting it wrong' by pointing out that there are many alternatives for most words and theirs may be different from the original but equally valid. Tell them that writers redraft many times. They may even come up with a 'better' word.

- LLD students need to be encouraged to visualise as much as possible to establish comprehension. The illustration activity is a vital step in the learning of all literature students.

- Visualisation tasks can be extended to many areas of study of the Shakespeare play. Try getting students to produce a collage, a cartoon strip, a 3D model, paintings and drawings. These can focus on a character (appearance or the psychological landscape), a scene or incident, imagery patterns, the setting, and so on.

ⓣ Step 6: Understanding the characters

- This task is a challenging one in that it requires close and careful reading, interpretation of thought and feeling, and awareness of the nuances of figurative language.

- Most students will be used to thinking in terms of a scale of 1 to 10. For example, we might ask, 'On a scale of 1 to 10, how much do you want this?', or 'How excited are you about this excursion?' Similar questions can be posed to elicit understanding of the emotional shades of feeling of a character.

- The selection of adjectives to describe a character's feelings provides an opportunity for teacher modelling: the reasoning process of both teacher and students should be explicitly discussed, as suggested in Step 2. The LLD student who has difficulty distinguishing and isolating emotional nuance needs to hear clearly articulated examples of such thinking.

- A basic outline of Juliet's concerns is provided. With this understanding of the basics, readers will be able to explore the subtleties of meaning more easily.

- The speech is approached methodically, and findings recorded on a simple graph to aid visual understanding of tonal shifts and structure.

- Show the speech on film, or play an audio recording of it.

ANXIETY FLASHPOINT

For students whose anxiety impedes their ability to commence tasks, a starting point can be introduced by asking students to identify the point at which Juliet seems most afraid, and plotting this point first.

ⓣ Step 7: Getting the words off the page

- Get each group to spend time working on the meaning of the dialogue. Emphasise that the words won't make sense to an audience if they don't themselves understand them.

- This task can be amended to fit the time available. A couple of lessons should be enough for a 'book in hand' performance without elaborate costume. It can, however, be expanded to a longer period of time with students required to learn their lines.

- The emphasis should be on originality of interpretation. The most successful scene performances are often the more imaginative adaptations which update the language, adapt the text into a rap song, etc.

- LLD students will often revel in the chance to use their oral talents. However, they will need time to work on it. Allow plenty of time to practise. Liaison with support staff may be advisable.

- Provide a film or recording of the scene to act as a model and help with pronunciation.

ANXIETY FLASHPOINT

The organisation of students into groups can be crucial here. It may be better to discreetly separate LLD students from each other so that they can integrate and gain support from students with stronger reading skills. On the other hand, if extra help is available outside the classroom it can be beneficial for them to work together. The crucial thing is to be sensitive to their perceptions of being singled out in any way.

SECTION 3

Backing up the curriculum

CHAPTER 14

Monitoring comprehension: tracking learning in the classroom

In secondary school, most units of work lead to formally assessed outcomes. These might take the form of essays, tests, reports or summaries. However, much of the assessment that we conduct in the classroom is formative—that is, part of ongoing learning—and it is this assessment that reveals the depth of our students' comprehension of the new materials and concepts we present. Properly implemented, such formative assessment should ensure, at least, that students are equipped to embark on the summative assessment task. Just as importantly, it will progressively provide information that can be used to adjust future teaching plans in the light of students' understanding of the work so far.

All of the units of work in this book are designed to incorporate frequent and regular learning checks. It is through these that we are able to make formative assessments, and to identify points at which we need to reteach, explain again, or explain in a different way that might be more effective. To a large extent, the learning checks are designed to help individual students test their own understanding, and to be explicitly aware of their progress as learners. The underlying principle is to teach a bit at a time and to consolidate, ensuring that students are ready to move on to the next part of their learning journey.

Often we can predict stumbling blocks and, with some forethought, avoid them. A significant barrier to learning for LLD students (and many others) is the requirement to grapple with unfamiliar vocabulary. If vocabulary is not grasped, or is only partially understood, it is often impossible for students to make sense of information or complete an operation. If, for instance, a mathematical operation directs the learner to 'find the difference' and the learner has forgotten precisely what that means, a correct answer is unattainable, regardless of mathematical ability.

Opportunities for students to test and express their understanding should be built into any sequence of teaching. This will initiate the process of formative assessment that aids learning. These checks need to be consciously designed and structured into the work, since students often will not instinctively grasp what it is they need help with and when to seek assistance. A student is much better equipped to ask for help—and a teacher to give it—if both can identify the particular difficulty rather than trying to work through the 'I don't get it' scenario, which arises when students feel that they have lost the plot of the activity altogether.

Real and effective teamwork between teachers and support staff is the key to the successful deployment of mechanisms for educational and learning support. The importance of these agencies working together to monitor comprehension and follow through work for struggling and anxious students cannot be overstated. It is vital that teachers supply support staff with units of work in advance. Support staff can then access materials to preteach, agree on task modification, check comprehension and support students to achieve their highest potential. Final assessment tasks need to be published at an early stage so that both students and support staff know what they are working towards. Such planning is demanding on teachers but is unavoidable if a genuine teaching and learning partnership is to operate.

Our goal should be for every student to have a good working awareness of his or her own areas of strength and difficulty. Where significant and widespread difficulties exist, we need to make remedies or improvements attainable by prioritising and working methodically through selected individual targets. Achieving this productive level of awareness requires us to put in place a clear and manageable method. The section on recording student progress at the end of this chapter aims to assist in this. Once again, it is all about clear, attainable short-term goals.

Strategies to check ongoing comprehension

Vocabulary

- Start every unit of work with direct teaching of essential vocabulary. Never assume that students understand these key words. Provide vocabulary lists or glossaries. Test learning and the ability to apply learning of vocabulary with word games, cloze procedures, writing the words in sentences and so on. It is necessary to build in quick, direct reminders of the meanings of the key words and terms at the beginning of the next lesson and repeatedly throughout each class.

Time limits

- Build in time limits and expectations so that students are aware of the goal they are working toward. This can reduce prevarication. It also provides the teacher with completion checkpoints for subsections of the work. By stopping regularly to check comprehension, teachers can ensure that each step is understood. Asking students to see how much they can do in 10 minutes enables teachers to monitor their use of time.

- On the other hand, time limits can exacerbate panic and anxiety in some students. For these students, the level of structure and instruction needs to be extremely detailed. Modifying the task to become more manageable can often reduce anxiety. For instance, a student could be permitted to write in bullet points rather than in sentences, or might be asked to write only key words or use highlighters to identify key parts of the text. If the act of writing is a barrier, allow the use of a computer or scribe. It is important that something is achieved in these circumstances, and it should act as a stepping stone to the next part of the task.

- Students who process ideas and writing tasks very slowly will also benefit from some of these strategies, but should be allowed additional time to consolidate this stage rather than pushing on to the next task.

- When new information or concepts are to be delivered, consider following the 10-2 system devised by Rowe (1986), in which the teacher stops after each 10-minute block to allow two minutes of reflection/processing time. For more details, refer to Chapter 7.

Clear instructions

- Of course, it is essential that written task sheets and questions be expressed in a way that is very clear and unambiguous, and in language that is readily accessible to all students. This minimises the scope for misunderstanding or confusion. Sentences can often be simplified: aim for no more than one instruction to each sentence.

- Verbal instructions are particularly difficult for many students to follow and should be supported by written instructions. Dictation of any kind is fraught with the dangers of misunderstanding and inaccurate transcription. It is advisable always to check that students have recorded such information correctly. This includes the recording of homework tasks in the student diary.

Questions, discussion and thinking time

- Probably the main device used by teachers to check understanding is the use of questions and class discussion. While this is an entirely valid method, and indeed the lifeblood of many classes, steps need to be taken to ensure that all members of the class are involved, not just the vociferous ones who feel confident that they 'know the answers'.

- In this kind of culture, many students never get the opportunity to express their understanding, perhaps because they lack confidence in their ideas and so feel that they risk possible humiliation, or because they don't think as quickly as others. Building in thinking time is one way to tackle this: give warning that you are going to ask for comments and feedback in a designated length of time, and then insist on thinking time. This may only be a minute, but even a minute can give time to those who need it to organise their responses. In the mixed-ability classroom, enforced thinking time often enriches the quality of debate and discussion by allowing all participants to refine and articulate their contributions.

- Extend this by setting up thinking partnerships or small groups, where each member is asked to contribute an idea. The video *How difficult can this be?* (1989) proposes a private arrangement between the highly anxious student and the teacher, whereby the student is forewarned that they will be called on to respond only after a mutually agreed private signal. This could certainly be an excellent method of increasing participation in discussion, although it must be handled sensitively: the student who spends the first half of a lesson in trembling dread of the forthcoming spotlight will not be attending to anything much beside that dread.

Note taking

- Don't assume that students know how to take notes efficiently. Many senior students still attempt to write notes in full sentences, spelling out every word carefully. Model note taking on the board or projector. Point out the importance of intended audience: if the notes are intended only as an aide-mémoire for the note taker, then only the note taker needs to be able to read them. Why not use the language of today's young SMS users? Make it clear, of course, that such abbreviations would be inappropriate in a formal written task intended for a third party. A little time spent on this skill can provide invaluable assistance for students—in all curriculum areas and for years to come.

- Provide frameworks for note taking, so that material has to be processed, summarised and reworded. A simple chart is an effective way to do this. Give careful thought to headings so that students are directed and supported in their research. This is of particular importance when using the Internet for research, where information is often densely packed, detailed and bewildering, and the temptation to simply 'cut and paste' is strong.

- The difficulties presented by active listening tasks, in which students can quickly become bewildered and lose the sense of what they should be listening for, can be alleviated by the provision of the suggested note taking structures. See Chapter 7 for further discussion of this.

Chunking

- Chunk learning activities into stepped tasks which allow for frequent checking of comprehension. This does not mean that we have to keep the bigger picture hidden—by all means, inform the class of the assessment task that you are leading to—but allow them to take it a step at a time. In this way, learning can be more securely established and consolidated, and tasks seem less intimidating.

Reading

- Teach directed reading activities using highlighting, underlining and annotating techniques. When close reading of a relatively small section of text is required, provide photocopies so that these techniques can be applied.

- Wherever possible, new text should be read aloud. The experienced reader will employ intonation, expression and pacing that will aid the students' comprehension of content, meaning and tone. Less accomplished readers will be better able to take in meaning when they do not simultaneously have to struggle to decode the words.

Individual consultation

- Allow time for individual consultations. To make this possible, reduce whole-class teaching, increase collaborative group work and use response/thinking partners. Encourage independent resource-based learning so that you can spend time with individuals. Set up an individual consultation area in the classroom. Develop thoughtful, reflective dialogue between teacher and student, designed to elicit and explore understanding.

Testing for learning

- Tests of ongoing learning should be frequent and short. They should be paced to occur immediately so that newly learned material is cemented. Allow students to test each other, and to mark each other's answers or even their own. The point here is not to trick them into getting the answers wrong but to allow them opportunities to examine their own understanding. Give opportunities for them to revise and relearn where necessary. Promote the self-assessment and self-awareness that this process requires.

Using technology

- Encourage the use of information technology as a self-supporting resource. Use of the computer spellchecker should be taught: direct instruction needs to accompany the choices that users are required to make between homonyms, for example. If a word is not recognised, it is probably because the attempted spelling is far from the correct one, so teach strategies that can be employed to self-correct. Teach discrimination in the use of the computer thesaurus, perhaps showing how it can be accompanied by a dictionary to ensure synonyms are used appropriately.

Feedback

- Check the effectiveness of your written feedback on students' work. Examine a sample and consider how clear its meaning is to the students. For example, will they understand what is meant by 'explain in more depth' and, if so, how they could do so? Try to replace general warnings such as 'watch spelling' with a more specific focus, such as setting up a personal spelling list or checking homonyms. Instructions to 'show working out' may need to be modelled, and so on.

- Students need to be taught how to give and receive feedback, including negative feedback. Model presenting feedback in a constructive way, pointing out the importance of encouragement by identifying strengths. Set up partnerships between students so that they can provide support and feedback to each other. Teach the importance of providing reasons for criticisms: for example, 'I really like this point here but I think you could choose a word that would make it even clearer'. It is worth pointing out that perfect mastery of tasks we set is something that students should work towards, and is not expected at the beginning of the learning process.

Homework

- Homework tasks should reinforce and consolidate learning, not introduce new concepts or skills. If a research task is set, ensure that questions are specific and clear and that a structured framework is provided for the recording of information. Aim for LLD students to complete as much as possible in class. Set time limits on homework tasks, for example, 'Answer as many questions as you can in 30 minutes', or 'Spend one hour drafting your essay'. Encourage them to use a timer so that time is measured accurately: when we say half an hour we mean half an hour, not 10 minutes that feels like an hour!

Encouragement through feedback

- The question of what to write on an unsuccessful piece of work is one that vexes teachers. This is the work of a student who has tried hard but not got it. The usual resort is 'Good effort', which we hope will be perceived as complimentary in some way. It won't. Talk to students about what this comment means to them and they will tell you it means, 'You tried but you failed'. A few alternatives, to which many more could be added, include the following.
  - 'I can see that you have worked hard on this. You have begun to understand the requirements.'
  - 'This was a challenging task and you have made some progress towards mastering it.'
  - 'I really appreciate the work that has gone into this.'
  - 'With your hard working approach, you will ...'
  - 'What a lot of thought you have put into this! I can see that you are thinking along the right lines. Next time ...'
  - 'This is a promising start to the process of learning about how ...'
  - 'While you still need to work on ..., you have made terrific progress with ...'
  - 'Look at all the parts I have ticked—these are really good points, and you should build on these.'

Recording student progress

Every teacher knows the importance of giving students clear feedback on their work. We aim to reinforce progress by commending successes, and to encourage further improvement by indicating what should be done to achieve this.

We might spend many hours marking a set of essays or reports to fulfil these aims. But how effective is our feedback if it is not read or processed? We are all familiar with the catchcry, 'What did you get?' as students compare the grades on those essays. Many of them, in fact, look no further and we realise that we might as well have simply slapped a grade on.

We must find ways to get students to read, comprehend, process and act on our advice. The student progress record (p. 211) is designed to encourage this. It requires students to read the teacher feedback carefully, seek clarification if necessary and then record the advice *in their own words*. Furthermore, it nurtures a classroom culture of 'personal best' rather than competition: students are urged to compare their performance in essay 2 against essay 1 and not against their peers' results.

The headings of the chart should be self-explanatory. From your feedback, students should be able to:

- elicit positive feedback, so that the identified strengths can be repeated and consolidated
- understand where they need to improve, so that they are aware of this the next time such work is completed
- set a small, manageable number of targets for improvement
- revisit their progress record before each new task to identify patterns and thus focus on improving problem areas.

The student progress record:

- should be negotiated between teacher and student
- should set agreed targets
- can be developed to include specific review dates
- can involve parents, so that they have a clearly designated role in aiding their child's progress
- can be used across the curriculum and even with cross-curricular accord, so that teachers set common targets for some students and work together to help them.

This cross-curricular accord might mean that the history, English and geography teachers all agree to focus on a particular student's use of paragraphs, or that the student is encouraged to focus on the orderly presentation of information in maths and science.

The information should feed into formal and informal reporting systems. Most parents are very keen to receive detailed and precise advice about what their child needs to do to improve.

The system is an effective learning tool for all students, as the sophistication of the targets can be adapted significantly.

Student progress record

Name:				
Subject:				
Task	**Topic**	**What I did well**	**What I could have done better**	**Target**

Student progress record exemplar

Name:				
Subject: English				
Task	**Topic**	**What I did well**	**What I could have done better**	**Target**
Personal writing	'My grandma'	1 paragraphs 2 described my feelings	1 described Grandma's appearance more vividly 2 sentence punctuation	1 use a thesaurus to find better words 2 check full stops and capital letters
Essay	*Lord of the flies*	1 clear topic sentences 2 good ideas about characters	1 used quotations 2 made sure that everything was relevant 3 sentence punctuation	1 use more quotations 2 check full stops and capital letters
Group discussion	*Lord of the flies*	1 spoke clearly 2 used cue cards	1 a little quiet 2 more eye contact needed	1 practise speaking loudly

CHAPTER 15

Something's got to give: planning and people changes

It is becoming increasingly clear that there are ways in which existing school structures would benefit from change. The curriculum is too crowded, time is at a premium for core skills, and there is limited flexibility to meet the diverse needs of individual students. Without change, we run the risk of underdeveloping the intelligence and talent of a large proportion of students with LLD. Many LLD adolescents can develop their language skills, and be taught to read, write and spell to a much higher level than they are currently achieving, if they are given appropriately targeted and long-term instruction. This chapter will focus on three specific areas that will improve learning for LLD students:

- changing school organisation and structure to improve LLD students' access to teachers
- continuing language and literacy instruction
- maintaining a positive outlook and supporting emotional maturation.

Order within change: using teacher time effectively

It is important to identify a core curriculum and increase the time teachers have to interact with LLD students. The core curriculum should be juxtaposed with an individualised learning program and wider community contact. Appropriate software should be more extensively used to support the language and literacy development of LLD students and this should be integrated into the core curriculum.

Core curriculum puts boundaries on the amount of material schools are expected to cover in a day. While exciting learning environments are admirable, without careful structure there can be too much squeezed into the curriculum, resulting in a feeling of chaos. Overly busy environments complicate learning for LLD students who struggle to make connections and hold sequences in their minds. This leads to confusion, anxiety and poor skill development. Planned curriculum can help maintain an interesting learning environment, especially if it is available in advance and online, and includes clear instructions for students, parents and specialist staff. This does not imply a sense of rigidity in the curriculum.

Rather, greater access in advance provides a road map where there is room for variation in how the destination is reached. Considering the many people involved in the life and learning of LLD students, this flexibility will offer a better chance of incorporating the necessary work on comprehension, recall and repetition, and arriving at the same destination—even if slightly different paths are taken.

This narrower curriculum means that some of the traditional areas (such as second language classes and outdoor education) would no longer be in the core, but would be provided using a district rather than an individual school model. Agencies outside the school could have a role in assisting a student's acquisition of competencies. A less crowded curriculum gives more time and choice for LLD students to accommodate their individual differences and needs. Support staff can then use the time to develop a more individualised program for LLD students and make the necessary additions to the core curriculum to improve the comprehension and participation of LLD students.

Handy (1994) envisages all students building a portfolio of competencies across all subject areas. While this has been done for LLD students in options like first aid, it would be beneficial if it was extended to language and literacy tasks throughout secondary school, and across year levels and subject areas not traditionally identified with language and literacy development. Individual target records can be used by support staff to identify common cross-curricular language and literacy goals at a level of detail not usually documented by subject teachers (see examples from Chapter 4 for steps in teaching comprehension, and Chapter 3 on decoding and fluency). If support staff document skill development in language and literacy using individual target records, LLD students will not be overwhelmed with different targets for different subjects.

The focus away from year levels to discrete, identifiable steps in skill development is needed to track the learning of students. Given the lifelong nature of LLD and the length of time needed to develop skills, greater awareness and monitoring of individual learning is possible when a portfolio approach is utilised. If this approach were to include only LLD students, it could be coordinated by special education staff. However, it is likely to be more effective if used for all students in a school and managed by a changed role and skill set for form/pastoral teachers, along with input from other staff. A 'student manager' monitors skill development and makes sure the portfolio is developing a range of competencies for the student. Generally, a teacher would fulfil this role but it could be fulfilled by other educational professionals. A 'student administrator' (who could be a trained teacher, but would not necessarily have to be one) organises the timetable to achieve the skill development at the school, district and community level.

For a student like Tom (Chapter 3), with severe language and associated literacy difficulties, a program such as this would give him three days (full or half days) on core work (with curriculum structured as in Section 2), leaving two days for a more individualised program, giving additional instruction in areas as needed, as well as time for mentoring, sport and community activities. A longer school day would be necessary to accommodate this type of program, with the option of a free afternoon. In this way, LLD students could complete most of the activities, including homework and revision, during the longer school day and this would be very helpful for those students who, for a range of reasons, find it hard to complete work at home.

It is not difficult to see that these changes would add to the already demanding level of coordination of services for LLD students. Support staff need the time to consult and coordinate the range of people who provide services to LLD students: speech pathologists, occupational therapists and psychologists, as well as parents. To move to this higher level of coordination, schools need greater administrative support, so that when professionals come to the school, their time is used efficiently. The head of learning support needs to be a senior position within a school because of the level of coordination across faculties, the need to participate in curriculum development, the heavy administrative load and the amount of contact with external agencies.

Teachers of the core curriculum need more time available for individual and small-group instruction in addition to full-class instruction. LLD students need opportunities for regular individual feedback so that they avoid progressing too far down the wrong track or becoming discouraged. To give teachers this time, they need to be relieved of a significant amount of administration and supervision tasks like assemblies, yard and bus duty. New schools need large spaces and more interview spaces to cater for a wider range of large-group, individual and small-group instruction. It is hard to give the necessary level of private feedback to LLD students when there is nowhere private to go in the school.

In the presentation of the curriculum, LLD students benefit from more small-group and individual instruction, and less large, undifferentiated group instruction. This allows for better comprehension and, where there is a significant weakness in literacy, allows a level of confidence and skill to be obtained before moving into larger groups. This is especially useful for those students who feel very anxious and humiliated by their learning difficulty.

Language and literacy can be further supported by appropriate software integrated into the LLD student's individualised program. While it can be very difficult to effectively integrate the appropriate computer software into the daily program of individual students, it is essential to recognise that computers play an important part in improving the language and literacy of LLD students. They make the training and repetition of core decoding and fluency tasks more interesting and keep motivation higher. They have enormous advantages when teaching writing, enable structure and editing to be less frustrating, and provide independence to students who want to read more complex text. But they *do not* take the place of the teacher, as their success is highly dependent on selecting the correct software and targeting the work for the individual student. Enormous effort is still required on the part of teaching staff, aides and support personnel if language and literacy skills are to reach a usable, independent level.

Learning environments outside school assist in the development of practical skills, and also help LLD students to realistically assess their strengths and work options. The cases of Dan and Helen (Chapter 6) illustrate how LLD students need both time and experience to make good choices based on their strengths, rather than pursuing careers which highlight their weaknesses. These developments take place over years, but eventually, an LLD student can realise a dream or reach a goal that builds on their strengths. It is very important that LLD students feel 'I can do this' and select achievable goals, otherwise some will continue with their well-established avoidance, while others will persist in working in areas which accentuate their language learning difficulties. Lack of success and lack of confidence can quickly become entrenched. When this occurs, LLD students find it hard to develop in a way that allows them to mature and assume adult roles.

A summary of the organisational changes needed

The structure outlined above would allow LLD students to follow a different learning path to adulthood. They would undertake core learning with their peers but, along with all students, would take different non-core subjects and learning activities at other times. Often LLD students need considerable change to their learning paths in Years 9 and 10 but may be reluctant to leave their peer group. An individual, district and community model of education would enable change while allowing students to keep their peer groups. This way, time with peers and greater time with adults in a range of environments could become the norm and give LLD students a greater opportunity to build on their strengths.

To achieve this, schools need:

- highly coordinated, organised and interesting environments
- a narrower core curriculum to allow more space for change
- skilled staff with time to coordinate the curriculum and the individual learning needs of LLD students
- restructuring of the role of head of learning support to allow for the significant amount of coordination across faculties and heavy administrative load required in the role
- more individualised programs for LLD students, and a portfolio approach
- curriculum that is available in advance and online, with clear instructions for students, parents and specialist staff
- increased time to achieve skills identified in the core curriculum, and a broader range of settings in which to do so
- learning environments outside school to assist LLD students to develop practical skills, and to help them be realistic about their strengths and work options

- greater use of computers and software to improve language and literacy skills of LLD students
- the opportunity to complete homework and revision during a longer school day
- greater administrative support to allow for the high level of coordination needed
- a change in how teachers work so that they are available for individual and small-group instruction, as well as full-class instruction
- more opportunities for staff development and training
- both large spaces and more spaces for small group and individual work.

Ongoing reading and writing instruction: language learning for life

Being as literate as possible is the best way for LLD students to support their language and STAM difficulties, and to give them the resilience and confidence they need as adults to continue their lifelong learning. Furthermore, increasing the amount of attention given to concise, structured and well-sequenced oral and written language instruction helps with comprehension.

There are great benefits to developing a curriculum at schools that is detailed in the way outlined in Section 2. Existing or new curriculum can be expanded to include more detailed language and literacy planning within core subjects. Vocabulary, grammar, and the structure of oral and written language should all be considered, and decisions should be made regarding the methods by which students will be taught to comprehend, remember and use the critical language of their subjects. In addition, texts and websites that utilise different levels of language and literacy need to be identified, to provide access to students whose skill levels vary. Those students who are still struggling with the curriculum will need the option to participate in individual or small-group instruction on language and literacy.

In addition to content, planned curriculum should also include effective strategies and suggestions from experienced teachers who have taught a particular unit. A DVD that shows them teaching a class can be very helpful, especially as a teaching model for good oral language instruction. The staffing required to prepare such material would probably best be provided at a district level, and should include input from experienced teachers, librarians and other support staff. As large numbers of experienced teachers are due to retire in the next five years, curriculum development and specification, as well as the modelling and mentoring of teaching strategies, will also need to take into account a less experienced and more mobile pool of teachers.

Literacy needs regular checking and instruction. While it is important to check decoding and comprehension using normed tests, it is not sufficient to stop at this. Equally important is checking the decoding of classroom and media materials, including newspapers and texts from the Internet. Students' decoding and comprehension of these materials are often much poorer than formal test results might lead one to expect, even for those students who fall within the average range—these skills are frequently at the lower levels of the average range. This is because of both vocabulary, which is more likely to be unfamiliar for both decoding and meaning, and for comprehension, which requires greater connection to knowledge base built up over time.

Biancarosa and Snow (2006) suggest, therefore, that adolescents need 2–4 hours per day of literacy-connected learning instruction. For those whose reading is so low that they cannot readily access the curriculum, a specific program of two hours per day for a minimum of 80 hours is needed. Only then will they have the language and literacy skills to cope with the curriculum. Even then, they need follow-up instruction to make the transition into curriculum materials, and into reading text, newspaper articles and Internet sites. Such instruction requires changes to the curriculum and the structure of the school day. It also challenges the belief that instruction for LLD students should emphasise the use of visual modes of learning—which, while helpful, should not be used to the exclusion of oral or written language skill development. Oral and written language skills underlie all learning, including practical, 'hands-on' work.

LLD students need curriculum that is skills-oriented, that allows the time (often years) to build up base skills, and that provides ample opportunity for *repetition*, *revision* and *recall*. There should be clear guidelines regarding core curriculum and skills so that all teachers, professionals, volunteers and parents working with students know what is expected and can plan accordingly. With new technology, curriculum can be easily accessed online. It is increasingly possible to present material at different levels of complexity, to regularly and randomly check important skill retention, and to assist LLD students with their memory, comprehension and literacy difficulties. For example, it is much more effective to teach vocabulary and comprehension strategies to secondary students using material to be presented in upcoming classes. With curriculum available in advance and online, this is much quicker and easier to do. Likewise, LLD students with decoding difficulties could select to have the material read to them, or, if comprehension is an issue, select simpler material on the same topic as well as a summary.

Given more space in the curriculum for building skills and for practising them, LLD students' mastery increases. This is the 'doing' that accompanies the acquisition and building of more sophisticated language and literacy skills. For example, 6–8 practices are required to become familiar with the structure and language of report or essay writing. These practices need to take place over several years. With appropriate time, instruction and the use of new technologies, the language and literacy of many LLD students can improve—and, over the coming years, we can expect to see even more improvements in our skill and knowledge of how to help them.

Supporting emotional maturity: more adults, please

LLD students enjoy learning with their peers and are motivated by it. However, an equally strong case must be made for the importance of adults in the lives of LLD students, and the benefits to them of increased adult contact both individually and in small groups. Greater adult contact is important for the development of resilience, for dealing with anxiety and for combating a sense of isolation. It provides grounding and a friendly reality check for students. A significant adult in the lives of LLD students is so important for their learning and their emotional development. There are periods in a student's life and learning when support is particularly needed, especially those periods when they are coming to terms with some of the implications of LLD and some of the limitations it places on their life choices.

Handy (1994) describes the advantages for students whose parents are 'strategic analysts'. These parents have careers that deal with 'numbers and ideas, problems and words' (p. 200). According to Handy, about 20 per cent of people in the workforce are strategic analysts, and the advantages they give their children are enormous as they mentor and coach the intellectual skills of 'conceptualising, coordinating and consolidating' (p. 207). The advantages of mentoring and coaching are what we want to give LLD students, especially those whose parents do not belong in this category. According to Handy, 'What small groups and close mentoring and learning from life can do, and which larger classes rarely do, is give a child self-confidence' (p. 209). Adults also provide important support for those LLD students who have weak social skills, since adults adjust their behaviour in a way that peers often do not. This can make LLD students feel hopeful at critical and vulnerable times in their learning.

Adult mentoring extends to the expansion and modelling of vocabulary and language beyond the abbreviated teen language of peers. It is interaction, rather than watching films or television, that best provides the language expansion and experience that LLD students need. Not everyone has strategic parents like Dan's (Chapter 6). Emotional and practical engagement with adults is critical in adolescence. Without it, LLD students struggle unnecessarily to get over the line into adulthood.

Many LLD students are expected to function at a greater level of emotional maturity than they are ready for. Reflection, monitoring, perseverance and self-analysis take time to develop. Many LLD students get stuck on emotional rather than curriculum content issues. They focus on questions like 'Do I like this person?' rather than the more empowering 'What can I learn from this person/situation?' Anxiety can more easily be diffused through input from mature adults who can place experiences in a broader life context. Increasingly, studies are finding that the brains of many young people are not fully mature until 25 to 30 years of age, and that we are stopping this work on learning and emotional maturity too early for LLD students (Jensen 2005). Mentoring from adults is critical, both for emotional development and content.

Teachers and other professionals currently at the coalface of working with LLD students are making a significant difference to their lives, even within a busy and crowded curriculum. To make the improvements needed in skill acquisition for all students (and for LLD students in particular) there needs to be an increase in the time teachers and support staff have to work with students and give them feedback. This does not mean that teachers should take the place of parents, nor that they should become social workers. Their focus should remain on the teaching of skills and in providing stimulating, respectful and secure environments in which to learn.

It is a hopeful time for LLD students, as our knowledge of how and what to teach them improves. Strategically used, technology is enhancing their options and can be harnessed to improve their skills. The possibility of real change to the organisational structure of schools and the school day is increasingly likely. Within curriculum, it is acknowledged that language and literacy are real issues that must be addressed at the secondary level, and that currently the curriculum is too crowded. There seems to be an acceptance that not everything is achievable for every student within a large classroom with a single teacher, and a realisation that it is necessary to consider individual and small-group options for instruction. There are teachers and specialist staff excited by the challenge of taking adolescent students with language learning disabilities through to their full potential. Outcomes for LLD students should improve significantly over future years with these things in place—for them, the best is yet to come.

And, finally, a story ...

Despite excellent teaching at primary school, Jenny's language and literacy were still developing when she started secondary school. A well-liked girl with a dreamy smile, she never seemed to get around to starting anything she was asked to do in class. Despite her overall normal IQ, she had difficulty following instructions in both maths and English. Her spelling and reading were below her peers. With support and preteaching, however, she began to participate better in class and to understand and complete work. Individual spelling and reading instruction continued weekly throughout Years 7 and 8, with an emphasis on syllable division and suffixes.

This logical and systematic work suited her. So that she could approximate spontaneous writing in sentences and paragraphs, she gave oral answers to questions from assignments, which were analysed for syllables and sounds and then dictated to her. This had the double advantage of working on subject-specific vocabulary and spelling while completing curriculum-based work. Her maths continued to develop slowly, with careful explanation and additional time to complete assessments—time was of the utmost value. Improvement in her ability to segment longer words into syllables became apparent in Year 9, so her individual sessions increased to twice a week for six months to capitalise on this gain. Significant improvement took place in decoding and spelling, and she found herself independently able to write short paragraphs.

Holding audience and purpose in mind, even at the paragraph level, took time to master, but once spelling became more automatic, further improvement took place and Jenny was able to write paragraphs that were largely on topic. With her full involvement, spelling and writing instruction continued throughout Year 10 and the first half of Year 11. Meanwhile, with her increased self-assurance and determination, she recognised her strengths in logical thinking and analysis. Maths and computing subjects developed as real strengths. She completed all Year 12 subjects without assistance and, following school, began a TAFE course. She transferred to a degree course after her successful first year.

Today, Jenny is an independent (although not perfect) reader, writer and speller. She asks questions when she is not sure, and has a good circle of friends and a supportive family. She has a language learning disability but is not defined by it. She has the skills to continue studying and training to reach her potential. There is joy in knowing that she has choices, and the freedom to be the best she can be.

Appendices

Appendix 1

The presentation of racism in the film *The long walk home*

Evidence of racial discrimination and prejudice is seen very early in *The long walk home*, but what techniques does the director use to show the audience what it was like to live in that society?

Use the chart below to record evidence of racism from the film. Beside it, make a note of the film technique used to expose the racism. You have been given an example.

Scene	Evidence of racism	Film technique(s)
2	People are segregated on buses	Camera shot of Odessa standing, then camera pans to empty seats

Working Together © Brent and Millgate-Smith 2008

Appendix 2

The long walk home: character development

Character: Miriam Thompson

How, and in what ways, does Miriam Thompson change her attitudes, ideas and views about black people during the course of the film?

Read each of the statements below. Indicate whether each one is true of Miriam at:

- the beginning of the film (B)
- the middle of the film (M)
- the end of the film (E)
- not at all.

In the space underneath **each of the statements you agree with**, write brief notes on the textual evidence you can draw from the film to support this view of Miriam.

Miriam Thompson is ...
• prepared to rethink her attitudes
• unaware of the effects of racism
• a woman of principle who is prepared to act on her convictions

>>

>>

- a vicious racist

- brave and courageous in the defence of the black cause

- an unthinking racist

- willing to stand up to prejudice in others

- deliberately cruel and insensitive

Appendix 3

The long walk home: character development

Character: Odessa Carter

How, and in what ways, does Odessa Carter change her attitudes, ideas and views during the course of the film?

Read each of the statements below. Indicate whether each one is true of Odessa at:

- the beginning of the film (B)
- the middle of the film (M)
- the end of the film (E)
- not at all.

In the space underneath **each of the statements you agree with**, write brief notes on the textual evidence you can draw from the film to support this view of Odessa.

Odessa Carter is …
• prepared to rethink her attitudes
• unaware of the causes of racism
• a woman of principle who is prepared to act on her convictions

>>

>>

- an unthinking person

- resentful of white people

- brave and courageous in the promotion of the black cause

- willing to stand up to prejudiced people

- caring and sensitive to the needs of others

Appendix 4

Structuring a film text response essay

1. Analyse the question carefully, underlining the key words and phrases that indicate what you are being asked to write about.

2. Define the key words in the question. Use a dictionary and a thesaurus to help you.

3. Rewrite the question in your own words.

4. Decide what your main hypothesis (contention or argument) will be and note this in the introduction box.

5. Identify between three and six main points that will be used to structure your essay. Each paragraph will deal with a different point.

6. Each paragraph will begin with a topic sentence that identifies that point.

7. Select a scene, event, conversation, image, quotation, etc. from the text to support each of the points you intend to make. This is your textual evidence.

8. Now think about how you will analyse the techniques used to convey that point to the audience. You will need to discuss the ways in which your sympathies and responses are shaped in the examples that you describe.

9. Each paragraph should conclude with a linking sentence that will link back to the hypothesis.

10. Use TEEL to help you remember this method. Memorise what the letters TEEL stand for and you will be able to use the same structure every time you write an essay:
    - T = topic sentence
    - E = explanation
    - E = evidence
    - L = link

    (See Chapter 5 for further information.)

11. To develop your argument by leading on to the next point, use conjunctions such as:

    similarly   furthermore   additionally   therefore   because   although

12. Use quotations to illustrate your argument. Use the quotations to show that you can analyse the effects of language closely.

13. In the conclusion, briefly restate your thesis or contention. Comment on the effectiveness of the text in conveying its message. Comment on the way in which it ends, and the thoughts and feelings it leaves you with.

Planning outline

Use the boxes below to help you to plan your essay. Complete the topic sentence and linking sentence of each paragraph in full. Make brief notes (in bullet-point form) on the main arguments you intend to use in each paragraph. Also, decide which textual evidence you will use.

Write the topic question here:
Define the key terms:
Re-write the topic question in your own words:
My hypothesis (answer) is:
The arguments (reasons) I will use are:
Evidence that backs up my arguments:
Structure each **paragraph** using the TEEL structure: • **T**opic sentence • **E**xplanation • **E**vidence • **L**ink

Introduction checklist

The introduction should include:	Done?
• the full title of the film/text, underlined	
• the full name of the writer/director	
• a definition of the terms used in the topic question	
• your hypothesis (your position in response to the topic question)	
• a brief indication of the evidence you will use to support your hypothesis	
• an outline of the writer's overall intentions in writing the text (e.g. to warn us against something, to entertain, to make us think about the ways in which we live and treat others, etc.)	

Outline of your response

INTRODUCTION

PARAGRAPH 1

Topic sentence:

Arguments:

Evidence (include quotations):

PARAGRAPH 2

Topic sentence:

Arguments:

Evidence (include quotations):

>>

PARAGRAPH 3

≫ Topic sentence:

Arguments:

Evidence (include quotations):

PARAGRAPH 4

Topic sentence:

Arguments:

Evidence (include quotations):

Now write a sample paragraph. Ask your teacher or another student to read it and check that you have fulfilled all of the criteria set out above. You will then be ready to draft the response.

When you have finished the first draft, use highlighters to mark:

- topic sentence
- evidence
- analysis
- linking sentence.

This way you will see at a glance if there are important elements missing, or if there is not enough quotation and analysis.

Then:

- **revise**
- **redraft**
- **refine**

  and, finally:

- **proofread**.

Appendix 5

PowerPoint presentations

Writing PowerPoint presentations: harder than it looks!

Writing for PowerPoint is an advanced language skill. It is easy to assume that because PowerPoint presentations involve fewer words than conventional prose, LLD students will find writing a PowerPoint presentation less demanding than other forms of written work. In fact, the following specific skills have to be taken into account.

Summarising

To write a concise presentation, the student must be able to analyse the key issues and select only the most meaningful data. Other less critical information needs to be omitted, or presented in a different format or as a subcategory. This involves a clear understanding of the relative weight of the information, and how to organise it for clarity.

Note taking

As with summarising, note taking involves sorting and selecting data. It also requires that the student can process input (either spoken or written) and simultaneously sort, discard and write notes. Any errors made in this complex procedure will affect the quality of the notes that the student will then work from to complete the PowerPoint presentation.

Sequencing

Once information has been selected for slides, it must be organised into an order that represents the key focus of the presentation. Students with language difficulties often present a problem with the sequencing of information. This can be observed in poor narrative formulation, trouble with procedural writing, and so on. PowerPoint provides another forum for this difficulty to become apparent.

Questions

Students will need to formulate questions for themselves, for example:

- 'What should I put in first?'
- 'What will my audience already know?'
- 'Should I include this here or later?'
- 'Is this relevant?'

  It will also be necessary to formulate content questions, for example:

- 'What happened first?'
- 'Why did these events happen?'
- 'What were the consequences?'
- 'How could the outcome have been changed?'

Problems here will relate not only to the student's difficulty with aspects such as sequencing, but also the ability to formulate and answer questions.

Subject-specific vocabulary

The highly focused nature of a PowerPoint presentation means that subject-specific vocabulary will be needed to preserve the concise nature of the content. LLD students will need support to understand, retrieve and use this vocabulary accurately.

Key words

Any subject area will have key words that provide the necessary specificity and concision to a PowerPoint presentation. For LLD students to use these key words effectively, clearly the words will have to be learned and understood. LLD students often find the acquisition of new vocabulary a challenge.

Audience awareness

Understanding and accommodating the needs of the reader or listener is a sophisticated metalinguistic skill. It involves judging the level of knowledge the audience members bring to the presentation, their need for context or background information, and the level at which new information should be pitched—in short, an understanding of someone else's point of view, and someone else's needs. Students with language difficulties may find this level of analysis difficult. If the student has any pragmatic language difficulties, this area will need support.

Rebecca Brown

Hyperlinking in PowerPoint

A hyperlink is a quick and easy way to jump to another place in a PowerPoint presentation. There are two sorts of hyperlinks.

- A text hyperlink uses the text you have typed to make a link to another place.

- An action button hyperlink creates a button you press to make the link to another place you choose to go.

Text hyperlinks

1 Open PowerPoint.

2 Type your text.

3 Highlight your text.

4 Right-click on the text and select 'Hyperlink'.

5 Select the 'Place in This Document' icon in the Hyperlink menu.

6 Select the slide you wish to hyperlink to. The selected text will change colour.

7 During your presentation, click on the hyperlinked text to jump to the desired slide.

8 To return to the original slide, either insert another hyperlink, or right-click and select 'Last Viewed'.

Action button hyperlinks

1 Click on the AutoShapes button on the Drawing taskbar.

2 Select Action Buttons on the menu. Select the action button you want (e.g. Next, Previous, Home).

3 Drag the button onto your slide.

4 Right-click on the button and select Hyperlink.

5 Select the slide you wish to hyperlink to.

6 During your presentation, click on the button to jump to the desired slide.

7 To return to your original slide, either insert a 'Return' action button hyperlink, or right-click and select 'Last Viewed'.

Robin Brown

Appendix 6

Glossary of useful words and terms

The glossary below corresponds to the vocabulary-matching exercise in Chapter 9, Step 1. It is provided to support students who are unable to fully complete the exercise, and can also be used to check the accuracy of the completed task. However it is achieved, a glossary should be readily accessible to reinforce vocabulary knowledge throughout the unit.

Word	Definition
anecdote	a little story based on a personal experience
appeal	the attraction or interest for the reader
article	a type of story in a newspaper or magazine
caption	text which describes or explains a photograph
colloquial language	everyday, informal spoken language
column	a part of a magazine regularly devoted to a particular interest or theme, e.g. gossip column
connotation	the significance and meanings implied by a certain choice of word
contention	the main point argued, or contended, by the writer
editorial	an article written or approved by the editor
graphic	a cartoon, graph, diagram, etc.
headline	the main title of an article, set in large, bold font
imply	to suggest or hint at something without directly stating it
infer	to draw a conclusion from an implication
journalist	a writer employed by the publication
juxtaposition	the effect created by placing specific and often contrasting words, images, phrases, actions etc. side by side
layout	the arrangement of text, graphics, headlines, etc. on the page
subheading	a heading in the body of the text which highlights the content of that section of the text
tone	this might be described as the 'speaking voice' of the piece
vernacular	the everyday language of a particular group in society

Appendix 7

Maintaining tenses

Journalists generally use the present tense when writing articles. This helps the content to sound up-to-date and relevant. We don't buy magazines to learn about something that happened in the past (even if that was only last week!).

1 Read each of the contention statements below.

2 Highlight the verb tenses.

3 Change them from the **past tense** to the **present tense** and rewrite each statement in the space below.

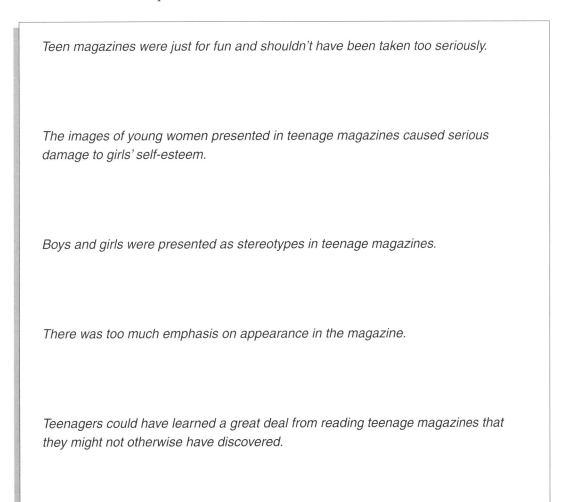

Teen magazines were just for fun and shouldn't have been taken too seriously.

The images of young women presented in teenage magazines caused serious damage to girls' self-esteem.

Boys and girls were presented as stereotypes in teenage magazines.

There was too much emphasis on appearance in the magazine.

Teenagers could have learned a great deal from reading teenage magazines that they might not otherwise have discovered.

When you write your letter to the editor (Chapter 9, Step 6), use the present tense. Here are some sentence openings you could use:

• Your magazine is ...

• Like many of my friends, I buy your magazine regularly because ...

• Who cares what the oldies think ...

• While I usually enjoy your magazine, it does concern me that ...

4 Reread the comments (from Step 13) below. Work out which of the highlighted verb tenses is in the **past tense** and which is in the **present tense**.

With a partner, read it aloud in the past tense. Then read it in the present tense. Which sounds best?

> *Teen mags **are/were** okay to flick through as long as you **don't/didn't/won't** take them too seriously. The problem **is/was** you can end up feeling that **you're/you were** the only 14-year-old with pimples, homework and no boyfriend. The image of girls **is/was** not realistic.*
>
> (Kate, 14)

Because the teenagers are talking about magazines that exist now and about how they feel at this time, it makes more sense to use the present tense.

5 Fill in the gaps with words that keep the comment below in the **present** tense.

> *What worries me most about guys' magazines _____ that they _____ us feel we should all be primitive man, treating girls as sex objects and pumping iron. Most of my mates _____ much more rounded than that.*
>
> (Josh, 16)

6 The comment below is rewritten in the **past tense**. Underline the words that make it clear that the speaker is talking about something that she thought in times gone by.

> *Where were the articles about the sport we played, the footy teams we followed, the problems of juggling homework and part-time jobs? This was the stuff that took up most of our time. Yeah, relationships were important but I liked to think of myself as an independent girl with a brain, not an ornament to dangle off some guy's arm.*
>
> (Alex, 15)

It has a different feel, doesn't it? There is a sense that Alex is looking back from a later stage in life, rather than reflecting on her feelings at this time.

For further practice, find an article in your magazine. Work out which tense it is written in. Rewrite a section of it in a different tense.

Appendix 8

Crossword solution

From Chapter 10, p. 144

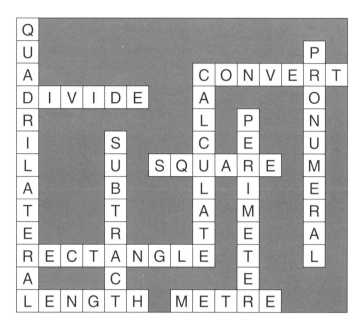

Appendix 9

Animal farm: completed vocabulary chart

1	porkers	young pigs
2	stall	a sleeping compartment for a farm animal
3	laborious	involving hard work
4	prosperity	wealth
5	abolished	got rid of
6	consumes	eats or uses
7	confinement	the time of a female's giving birth
8	resolution	firmness of purpose, determination
9	knacker	a buyer of old or useless horses for slaughter
10	dignity	a composed and serious manner
11	rebellion	organised resistance to authority
12	victorious	successful
13	comrade	a workmate, friend, or fellow soldier
14	abundance	plenty

This glossary is provided for students who, for whatever reason, are unable to complete the word matching exercise in Chapter 11, Step 1. It may also be used to check the accurate completion of this task and to accompany the reading of the text of Old Major's speech to elucidate meaning.

Working Together © Brent and Millgate-Smith 2008

Appendix 10

Animal farm: rhetorical devices

The examples of rhetorical devices used in this activity are not drawn from the text because the intention is to reinforce understanding by drawing from real life. This activity could be followed up by asking the groups to skim and scan through a newspaper to find further examples of rhetorical devices.

1 Photocopy and cut out the cells.

2 Organise the class into groups.

3 Instruct each group to match the device to an example.

4 The groups might then be asked to produce a second example which can be passed on to the next group for further matching.

Rhetorical device	Example
inclusive language	Mate, we need to work together.
attention-catching anecdote or story	You'll never believe what happened to me yesterday ...
slogan	Slip, slop, slap
repetition	I've said it before, I'll say it now and I'll say it again ...
powerful images	The moon was a pirate ship in full sail.
rhetorical questions	Do you want me to take your allowance away?
establishing speaker's authority and wisdom	In my many years as a zookeeper I have discovered much about the habits of the echidna.
demonising opposition	His words are sweet but he's lying in wait to trick the unsuspecting voter.
emotive words	• helpless • squalid • savage

5 Photocopy and cut out the cells below. Give a set to each group, with the instruction to produce an additional set of examples of the different rhetorical devices. These examples can then be passed on to the next group to match with the appropriate rhetorical device.

inclusive language	
attention-catching anecdote or story	
slogan	
repetition	
powerful images	
rhetorical questions	
establishing speaker's authority and wisdom	
demonising opposition	
emotive words	

Working Together © Brent and Millgate-Smith 2008

Appendix 11

Task: Exploring language

(Chapter 9, Step 3)

1 The verb: find synonyms for the word **appeal** as a verb.

pl**ea**d   re**qu**es**t**   be**g**   entr**ea**t

bes**ee**ch   imp**lor**e

2 The noun: find synonyms for the word **appeal** as a noun.

att**rac**tion   pl**ea**   all**ur**e   int**eres**t   entr**ea**ty

....

Task: Exploring word pictures

Romeo's speech

(Chapter 13, Step 5)

O, she doth teach the torches to burn bright!
It seems she hangs upon the cheek of night
Like a rich jewel in an Ethiop's ear.
Beauty too rich for use, for earth too dear!
So shows a snowy dove trooping with crows,
As yonder lady o'er her fellows shows.
The measure done, I'll watch her place of stand
And, touching hers, make blessed my rude hand.
Did my heart love till now? Forswear it, sight!
For I ne'er saw true beauty till this night.

(*Romeo and Juliet*, Act 1, Scene 5)

References

Chapter 1: Setting out the basics

Brent, M, Gough, F, & Robinson, S 2001, *One in eleven: practical strategies for adolescents with a language learning disability*, ACER Press, Melbourne.

Catts, H, Adlof, SM, Hogan, TP, & Weismer, SE 2005, 'Are specific language impairment and dyslexia distinct disorders?' *Journal of Speech, Language and Hearing Research*, vol. 48, no. 6, pp. 1378–96.

Shaywitz, S 1996, 'Dyslexia', *Scientific American*, November, pp. 78–84.

Chapter 2: Reducing anxiety and increasing motivation

Brent, M, Gough, F, & Robinson, S 2001, *One in eleven: practical strategies for adolescents with a language learning disability*, ACER Press, Melbourne.

Catalyst 2006, 'Choice', television program, Australian Broadcasting Corporation, Sydney, 13 April, viewed 9 July 2008, <http://www.abc.net.au/catalyst/stories/s1615006.htm>.

Jensen, E 1998, *Teaching with the brain in mind*, Association for Supervision and Curriculum Development, Alexandria, VA.

—— 2005, *Teaching with the brain in mind*, 2nd edn, Association for Supervision and Curriculum Development, Alexandria, VA.

—— & Dabney, M 2000, *Learning smarter: the new science of teaching*, The Brain Store Inc., San Diego.

Martin, AJ 2003, *How to motivate your child for school and beyond*, Bantam, Sydney.

—— 2007, Lifelong Achievement Group, Lifelong Achievement Group, Sydney, viewed 9 July 2008, <http://www.lifelongachievement.com>.

McGrath, H, & Edwards, H 2000, *Difficult personalities: a practical guide to managing the hurtful behaviour of others (and maybe your own!)*, Choice Books, Sydney.

Milburn, C 2006, 'Program perks up listless learners', *Education Age*, 20 February, p. 3.

Pipher, M 1996, *Reviving Ophelia: saving the selves of adolescent girls*, Doubleday, New York.

Rowe, MB 1986, 'Wait time: slowing down may be a way of speeding up!', *Journal of Teacher Education*, January–February, pp. 43–9.

Stober, J, & Borkovec, TD 2002, 'Reduced concreteness of worry in generalized Anxiety Disorder: findings from a therapy study', *Cognitive Therapy and Research*, vol. 26, no. 1, pp. 89–96.

Wilson, RR, 2007, Anxiety workshop descriptions, Anxieties.com, Durham, NC, viewed 9 July 2008, <http://www.anxieties.com/wsall.php>.

Chapter 3: Enhancing decoding and reading fluency

Biancarosa, G, & Snow, CE 2006, *Reading next—a vision for action and research in middle and high school literacy: a report to Carnegie Corporation of New York*, 2nd edn, Alliance for Excellent Education, Washington DC.

Brent, M, Gough, F, & Robinson, S 2001, *One in eleven: practical strategies for adolescents with a language learning disability*, ACER Press, Melbourne.

Davidson, G 2002, *Learners companion to English vocabulary*, Learners Publishing, Singapore.

Hasbrouck, J, & Tindal, G 2005, *Oral reading fluency: 90 years of measurement*, technical report no. 33, College of Education, University of Oregon, Eugene, OR, viewed 9 July 2008, <http://www.brtprojects.org/techreports/ORF_90Yrs_Intro_TechRpt33.pdf >.

Merriam-Webster 2008, Merriam-Webster Online dictionary, Merriam-Webster, Springfield, MA, viewed 9 July 2008, <http://www.m-w.com>.

Nuance Communications 2008, Dragon NaturallySpeaking, Nuance Communications, Burlington, MA, viewed 9 July 2008, <http://www.nuance.com/naturallyspeaking>.

Paul, R 2006, *Language disorders from infancy through adolescence: assessment and intervention*, Mosby-Year Books, St Louis.

Shaywitz, S 2003, *Overcoming dyslexia: a new and complete science-based program for reading problems at any level*, AA Knopf, New York.

Stahl, SA 2004, 'What do we know about fluency? Findings of the National Reading Panel'. In P McCardle & V Chhabra (eds), *The voice of evidence in reading research*, PH Brookes Pub., Baltimore, MD, pp. 187–211.

Chapter 4: Enhancing comprehension and word power for LLD students

Bell, N 1986, *Visualizing and verbalizing for language comprehension and thinking*, Reading Academy, California.

—— & Lindamood, P 1993, *Vanilla vocabulary: a visualized/verbalized vocabulary book*, Academy of Reading Publications, California.

Bishop, DVM 1997, *Uncommon understanding: development and disorders of language comprehension in children*, Psychology Press, Hove, East Sussex.

Brent, M, Gough, F, & Robinson, S 2001, *One in eleven: practical strategies for adolescents with a language learning disability*, ACER Press, Melbourne.

Bush, CS 1979, *Language remediation and expansion: one hundred skill building reference lists*, Communication Skill Builders, Tucson.

Davidson, G 2002, *Learners companion to English vocabulary*, Learners Publishing, Singapore.

Disher, G 1998, *The divine wind*, Hodder, Sydney.

Jensen, E 1998, *Teaching with the brain in mind*, Association for Supervision and Curriculum Development, Alexandria, VA.

—— 2005, *Teaching with the brain in mind*, 2nd edn, Association for Supervision and Curriculum Development, Alexandria, VA.

Jones, S, Resource Room & Team Prairie 2006, The Resource Room, Resource Room, Urbana, IL, viewed 9 July 2008, <http://www.resourceroom.net>.

Jordan, M, Jensen, R, & Greenleaf, C 2001, 'Amidst familial gatherings: reading apprenticeship in a middle school classroom', *Voices from the middle*, vol. 8, no. 4, pp. 15–24, viewed 9 July 2008, <http://www.wested.org/cs/sli/query/q/1351>.

Langrehr, J 1993, *Better questions, better thinking*, Longman, Melbourne.

Parkin, C, Parkin, C, & Pool, B 2002a, *PROBE: key into evaluation*, Triune Initiatives, Upper Hutt, NZ.

—— 2002b, *PROBE: key into inference*, Triune Initiatives, Upper Hutt, NZ.

—— 2002c, *PROBE : key into reorganization*, Triune Initiatives, Upper Hutt, NZ.

—— 2002d, *PROBE: reading assessment with an emphasis on high-level comprehension*, Triune Initiatives, Upper Hutt, NZ.

Rowe, MB 1986, 'Wait time: slowing down may be a way of speeding up!' *Journal of Teacher Education*, January–February, pp. 43–9.

Wordweb Software 2008, Crossword Compiler, Wordweb Software, Cambridge, UK, viewed 9 July 2008, <http://www.crossword-compiler.com>.

Chapter 5: Connecting oral and written language skills

Apel, K, & Masterton, J 2001, 'Theory-guided spelling assessment and intervention: a case study', *Language, Speech and Hearing Services in Schools*, vol. 32, pp. 182–94.

Ashton, M, & Beardwood, R 2006, *English for Year 11*, Insight Publications, Melbourne.

Bolt, A 2000, 'Oh that nasty Naomi. Well we knew she wasn't little Bo Peep', *Herald Sun*, 10 February, p. 20.

Brent, M, Gough, F, & Robinson, S 2001, *One in eleven: practical strategies for adolescents with a language learning disability*, ACER Press, Melbourne.

British Broadcasting Corporation (BBC) 2008, Skillswise: words: grammar, BBC, London, viewed 9 July 2008, <http://www.bbc.co.uk/skillswise/words/grammar>.

Jones, S, Resource Room & Team Prairie 2006, The Resource Room, Resource Room, Urbana, IL, viewed 9 July 2008, <http://www.resourceroom.net>.

Marsden, J 1995, *The third day, the frost*, Pan Macmillan, Sydney.

Noll, P, & Noll, B 2008, List of adjectives in American English, Paul Noll, Pleasant Hill, OR, viewed 10 July 2008, <http://www.paulnoll.com/Books/Clear-English/English-adjectives-1.html>.

Paul, R 2006, *Language disorders from infancy through adolescence: assessment and intervention*, 3rd edn, Mosby, St Louis.

University of Ottawa 2008a, HyperGrammar, University of Ottawa, Ottawa, viewed 10 July 2008, <http://www.arts.uottawa.ca/writcent/hypergrammar>.

—— 2008b, Using verb tenses in sequence, University of Ottawa, Ottawa, viewed 10 July 2008, <http://www.arts.uottawa.ca/writcent/hypergrammar/vbseq.html>.

UsingEnglish.com 2008, List of English irregular verbs, UsingEnglish.com, London, viewed 10 July 2008, <http://www.usingenglish.com/reference/irregular-verbs/>.

Westby, C 1989, 'Assessing and remediating text comprehension problems'. In A Kamhi & H Catts (eds), *Reading disabilities: a developmental language perspective*, Allyn & Bacon, Boston.

Chapter 6: Nurturing self-awareness, empathy and resilience

Baines, R (ed.) 2000, *Paper families: an anthology of short, short stories*, Cambridge University Press, Melbourne.

—— 2001, *Paper windows: an anthology of short, short stories*, Cambridge University Press, Melbourne.

Bloom, B 1984, *Taxonomy of educational objectives*, Allyn & Bacon, Boston.

British Broadcasting Corporation (BBC) 2008, Religion & ethics: ethical issues, BBC, London, viewed 10 July 2008, <http://www.bbc.co.uk/religion/ethics>.

Collins Cobuild English dictionary for advanced learners 2001, 3rd edn, Collins, Glasgow.

Dalton, J, & Smith, D 1986, *Extending children's special abilities: strategies for primary classrooms*, Department of School Education Victoria, Melbourne. Material available at Aussie

SchoolHouse 2008, Teachers on the web, Aussie SchoolHouse, Belconnen, viewed 10 July 2008, <http://www.teachers.ash.org.au/researchskills/dalton.htm>.

De Bono, E 1992, *Teach your child how to think*, Viking, New York. Material available at Edward de Bono's Web, viewed 16 July 2008, <http://www.edwdebono.com>.

Gardner, H 1983, *Frames of mind: the theory of multiple intelligences*, Basic Books, New York.

Lee, H 1960, *To kill a mockingbird*, Heinemann, London.

Ryan, T 1990, *Thinker's keys for kids*, South Coast Education Region, n.p. (Qld), viewed 16 July 2008, <http://www.thinkerskeys.com/cms/files/PDF's/Thinkers_Keys_all.pdf>.

Someone had to be Benny 1997, video recording, Marcom Projects, Eight Mile Plains, Qld.

Chapter 7: Memory: helping LLD students remember what you teach them

Alloway, TP 2007, *Automated Working Memory Assessment (AWMA)*, Harcourt Assessment, Oxford.

—— & Gathercole, SE 2005, 'The role of sentence recall in reading and language skills of children with learning difficulties', *Learning and Individual Differences*, vol. 15, pp. 271–82.

Baddeley, AD 2006, 'Working memory: an overview'. In SJ Pickering (ed.), *Working memory and education*, Elsevier, London.

Brent, M, Gough, F, & Robinson, S 2001, *One in eleven: practical strategies for adolescents with a language learning disability*, ACER Press, Melbourne.

British Broadcasting Corporation (BBC) 2008, Religion & ethics: ethical issues, BBC, London, viewed 10 July 2008, <http://www.bbc.co.uk/religion/ethics>.

Centre for Working Memory and Learning 2006, Articles on working memory, University of York, York, viewed 11 July 2008, <http://www.york.ac.uk/res/wml/ArticlesTeachers.htm>

—— 2008, Centre for Working Memory and Learning, University of York, York, viewed 11 July 2008, <http://www.york.ac.uk/res/wml>.

Collins Cobuild English dictionary for advanced learners 2001, 3rd edn, Collins, Glasgow.

Crowe, S 2006, 'Memory: a user's guide', presentation at Continuing Education for Health Professionals seminar, Melbourne, February.

Gathercole, SE, & Alloway, TP 2006, 'Practitioner review: short-term and working memory impairments in neurodevelopmental disorders: diagnosis and remedial support', *Journal of Child Psychology and Psychiatry*, vol. 47, pp. 4–15.

Gathercole, SE, Lamont, E, & Alloway, TP 2006, 'Working memory in the classroom'. In SJ Pickering (ed.) *Working memory and education*, Elsevier, London.

Hein, P 1968, *More grooks*, Hodder, London.

Jensen, E 1998, *Teaching with the brain in mind*, Association for Supervision and Curriculum Development, Alexandria, VA.

—— 2005, *Teaching with the brain in mind*, 2nd edn, Association for Supervision and Curriculum Development, Alexandria, VA.

Landsberger, J 2008, Using memory effectively, Study Guides and Strategies, St Paul, MN, viewed 11 July 2008, <www.studygs.net/memory>.

Macmillan Publishers Australia 2008, Macquarie study guides, Macmillan, Melbourne, viewed 11 July 2008, <http://www.macmillan.com.au/Secondary>.

Nelson, A 2005, *The Harvard Medical School guide to achieving optimal memory*, McGraw-Hill, New York.

Pickering, SJ (ed.) 2006, *Working memory and education*, Elsevier, London.

Rowe, MB 1986, 'Wait time: slowing down may be a way of speeding up!' *Journal of Teacher Education*, January–February, pp. 43–9.

Sousa, D 1995, *How the brain learns*, National Association of Secondary School Principals, Reston, VA.

SparkNotes 2006, Memory, SparkNotes, New York, viewed 26 July 2008, <www.sparknotes.com/psychology/cognitive/memory>.

Chapter 14: Monitoring comprehension: tracking learning in the classroom

How difficult can this be? The F.A.T. City Workshop 1989, video recording, PBS Video, Arlington, VA.

Rowe, MB 1986, 'Wait time: slowing down may be a way of speeding up!' *Journal of Teacher Education*, January–February, pp. 43–9.

Chapter 15: Something's got to give: planning and people changes

Biancarosa, G, & Snow, CE 2006, *Reading next—a vision for action and research in middle and high school literacy: a report to Carnegie Corporation of New York*, 2nd edn, Alliance for Excellent Education, Washington DC.

Handy, C 1994, *The age of paradox*, Harvard Business School Press, Boston.

Jensen, E 2005, *Teaching with the brain in mind*, 2nd edn, Association for Supervision and Curriculum Development, Alexandria, VA.

Index

WITHDRAWN

MAY 0 2 2024

DAVID O. McKAY LIBRARY
BYU-IDAHO